# Forbidden Fruit and Fig Leaves

# Forbidden Fruit and Fig Leaves

*Reading the Bible with the Shamed*

Judith Rossall

scm press

© Judith Rossall 2020

Published in 2020 by SCM Press
Editorial office
3rd Floor, Invicta House,
108–114 Golden Lane,
London EC1Y 0TG, UK
www.scmpress.co.uk

SCM Press is an imprint of Hymns Ancient & Modern Ltd (a registered charity)

Hymns Ancient & Modern® is a registered trademark of
Hymns Ancient & Modern Ltd
13A Hellesdon Park Road, Norwich,
Norfolk NR6 5DR, UK

All rights reserved. No part of this publication may be
reproduced, stored in a retrieval system, or transmitted,
in any form or by any means, electronic, mechanical,
photocopying or otherwise, without the prior permission of
the publisher, SCM Press.

The author has asserted her right under the Copyright, Designs and Patents Act 1988
to be identified as the Author of this Work

Scripture quotations are from New Revised Standard Version Bible: Anglicized
Edition, copyright © 1989, 1995 National Council of the Churches of Christ in the
United States of America. Used by permission. All rights reserved worldwide.

British Library Cataloguing in Publication data

A catalogue record for this book is available
from the British Library

978-0-334-05920-2

# Contents

| | |
|---|---|
| *Introduction* | vii |
| 1 Two Exits | 1 |
| 2 Exodus and Exile | 21 |
| 3 Recovering Abel and Learning from Cain | 45 |
| 4 We Need to Talk about David | 76 |
| 5 Job: The Truth but Not the Whole Truth | 92 |
| 6 The Welcoming Messiah | 109 |
| 7 The Demanding Messiah | 136 |
| 8 The Shamed Messiah | 163 |
| 9 Looking at Jesus, Jesus Looking at Us | 190 |
| *References and Bibliography* | 207 |
| *Index of Bible References* | 213 |
| *Index of Names and Subjects* | 215 |

# Introduction

> Shame is an incredibly inarticulate emotion. It's something you bathe in, it's not something you wax eloquent about. It's such a deep, dark, ugly thing there are very few words for it. (Ronson, 2016, p. 236)

So, who wants to talk about shame? It's a cold, hard pain around the heart, a lurch in the guts, a hot rush in the cheek (insert your own physical reaction here), it's something we feel, but who wants to talk about it? It makes us want to curl up and disappear, leaves us stammering and wishing we were somewhere else, so who wants to talk about it? It is, as the quotation above puts it, 'a deep, dark, ugly thing', and even admitting that we struggle with shame can make us even more ashamed, so, really, why would we want to talk about it?

Who wants to talk about shame with Christians and look at shame in the Bible? Don't Christians only want to talk about guilt? The classic distinction between shame and guilt is becoming known more and more widely; we feel guilty about what we do, but we feel shame about who we are. For many people the heart of the message of Christianity is forgiveness for our actions. In fact, it can seem that Christianity invites us not simply to admit that we have done wrong but also to label ourselves as sinners – doesn't that lead to more shame? On the cross, Jesus bore our sins and ensured that those sins could be forgiven. So, what does that have to do with shame?

Here is my overall argument for this book. Read the Bible carefully and it says as much about shame as it does about guilt; there is a clear understanding that sin, guilt and shame *all* distort human living and prevent us from flourishing. Sin, guilt and shame can work together to produce a toxic mix that leaves us sighing with Paul: 'I do not understand my own actions. For I do not do what I want, but I do the very thing I hate' (Rom. 7.15). It is not that ideas of Christianity that revolve around forgiveness are wrong, more that they have not noticed everything that the Bible has to say. We are complicated creatures and

God is ultimately beyond our understanding; theology must therefore perform a balancing act that holds equally important truths in tension. If we fail to take the broader message into account we can leave people struggling with a toxic shame. What is more, we are likely to become more and more irrelevant to a world that is very concerned with issues such as self-esteem and self-worth.

In the next few chapters, therefore, I am going to attempt to read Scripture (that is, the overall story of Scripture along with some concentration on particular passages) with a focus on what is said about shame. How does shame distort our living and prevent our flourishing and what does Scripture have to say to those who struggle with a shame so deep-seated that it seems to shape all of their living? In looking at shame I will raise key questions that every Christian needs to take seriously, including what the gospel has to say about what shames us and what brings us honour and esteem. Since some (but not all) who struggle with shame have been injured by the actions of others, I will also give some attention to those injured by sin and what is needed for their healing – and this will include the issue of what forgiveness looks like in the context of the gospel.

Since that makes for a quick sweep through a lot of material, let's start with a summary of where we are going.

Chapters 1 and 2 give an overview of some of what the Bible says about shame and how that is born from sin, and can lead also to sin. The basic thesis is that theologians are right to argue that the story of Adam and Eve in Genesis 3 has dominated Christian thinking about sin too much, but this does not mean that we should abandon it altogether. Rather, I want to propose that we should read further into the story and include what happens in the next generation and that we should balance the story of the Garden of Eden with two other iconic stories of how sin distorts human flourishing – namely, the Exodus and the Exile. If we read these stories together, we can begin to see that shame is insidious, it damages us and the people around us in ways we do not always recognize, and that God is equally concerned for both the offender and the injured.

Chapter 3 asks some questions about what it means to recover Abel, or read the Bible with the shamed. If we want to talk about shame, however, we also need to be able to describe its opposite. Describing the opposite of shame is surprisingly difficult. One way is to talk about what

## INTRODUCTION

we call self-esteem or pride (a proper pride that comes from knowing that you are wanted and valued). The problem is that the Bible never talks about self-esteem; it talks about honour, but honour is subtly but importantly different. So, having swept fairly rapidly through the First Testament, we will pause to try to understand what honour meant in the biblical world and how we can (or cannot) talk about honour today. I want to argue that doing this work matters – if we can grasp some of the cultural differences between our world and that of the biblical writers, not only will we read the Bible differently, we will also grasp some of the weaknesses in the ways we currently try to help people who are struggling with shame.

In Chapters 4 and 5 we return to the First Testament to read two stories that I believe are all about the relationship between sin and shame, but that traditionally have been read very differently. The story of David and Bathsheba is about privilege, power and distorted honour. It has a lot to teach us about sin because it illustrates the fatal ways in which a focus purely on our own honour can make us shameless and blind to any perspective except our own. Equally, the story of Job, so often read as being about suffering, is also about what happens when an unbalanced theology seeks to unfairly label someone as a sinner. Reading it carefully will introduce us to Job's fight for his own sense of worth and integrity.

We will then take a pause between Testaments to do some more background work. Having already raised the question of the relationship between shame and being injured by another person's sin, we cannot escape the issue of forgiveness, but again there is work to do. We need to grasp just how being sinned against damages us, why it sometimes provokes deep shame and why a struggle with shame can make forgiveness particularly difficult. Overall, I will argue that grasping the relationship between sin and shame can give us a deeper understanding of what forgiveness involves, and that can lead us to a theological model that can begin to address the cost and process of forgiving more fully.

It is not possible to understand the New Testament without a good background in the First Testament, so only after we have laid this foundation will it be possible to turn to the story of Jesus. It is common to discuss Jesus and shame by pointing to some of the ways in which he gave people back their sense of self-worth, and we will cover some fairly similar themes. We will also pay attention to Paul's use of adoption as an image for discipleship but will read it against the Roman background in which adoption implied taking on the honour status of your adopted family and an obligation to uphold that honour in the way that you lived.

However, the New Testament has more to say, so we also have to grapple with what it means to believe in a God who was shamed in the crucifixion and who turns upside down everything that we understand about what is shameful and what is glorious. Only if we grasp this (or at least begin to grasp it) can we really begin to understand both what the gospel says to those struggling with shame and also why this subject is vital for all Christians, including those who do not see themselves as personally affected by the issue.

This is why we will look at just how shaming the cross was in Jesus' context, and also follow some of Paul's struggles as he attempted to understand how he was supposed to preach about a God who was seen in a Messiah who had been shamed. We will try to grasp why it mattered to proclaim that the resurrection was a vindication of Jesus and how believing in a shamed Messiah should change our very sense of the nature of God.

Then, finally, we will look at how faith might be experienced by a person struggling with shame. Using the example of Peter when he met the resurrected Jesus for breakfast on the beach, we will see how Jesus trusted Peter when he was at his lowest. This will lead us to what I increasingly see as a key verse for those who struggle with shame – one that encourages us to look to the Christ who has experienced shame at its worst and who leads us on an exodus out of a life dominated by shame's distortions towards a life lived in the full knowledge of God's love and grace:

> Let us also lay aside every weight and the sin that clings so closely, and let us run with perseverance the race that is set before us, looking to Jesus, the first to live out this life of faith and the one who will finally bring it to completion, who for the sake of the joy that was set before him endured the cross, disregarding its shame, and has taken his seat at the right hand of the throne of God. (Heb. 12.1–2 (mainly NRSV but expanded in an attempt to bring out the meaning))

And finally, for those who find it helpful, I've included an explanation of some choices I have made in writing this book.

INTRODUCTION

# A Word about Words

## *How to Describe Long-term Shame*

The last time I moved to a new house I put my arm down the back of some furniture to unplug something. I remember holding my arm at an awkward angle and having to wriggle the plug to get it out. I think that is when I did it, although I will never know for sure. A few months later I went to the doctor because twisting anything caused a flare of pain in my wrist. It was something of a surprise to be told that the cause was tennis elbow and that I needed physiotherapy.

I am fortunate that this was my first experience of living for several months with a part of my body that ached permanently and could flare up into acute pain quite unexpectedly. It probably says something about my priorities in life that what now sticks in my mind is that I was unable to lift a full mug of coffee. More importantly, I accurately predicted what very nearly happened. My wonderful physiotherapist tried very hard to explain that I probably had some degeneration in the joint without actually using the phrase 'at your age' (in the end I used it for her). It did not take very much medical knowledge to know that both my elbows are the same age, and to realize that what was true of one elbow was likely also to be true of the other. I spent the months of recovery with a small but niggling worry that, in protecting the injured elbow, I would damage the other one. I count myself extremely fortunate that the other elbow only began to hurt just as the first was nearly better and so I avoided any real problems. However, I do now assume that both my arms are vulnerable to a flare-up of tennis elbow.

While all this was happening, I was reading about shame as a long-term experience and the way in which the coping mechanisms we adopt to cover up the pain of shame can become the cause of more hurt, either to ourselves or others. There are many ways to describe the difference between the brief flare-up of shame that is a normal part of life and the chronic, long-term experience that afflicts some, but the struggle with tennis elbow may explain why I found John Bradshaw's phrase 'shame-ache' most helpful.

## How to Talk about God

I was brought up with the idea that the word 'man' could at times include women and that God could be called 'he' even though God has no gender. I have, therefore, lived through the growing realization that non-inclusive language contributes to hiding women and our experiences. Like all writers, I have struggled over the years with how to write in a way that is genuinely inclusive but also vaguely grammatical, and speaking of God has proved particularly difficult. For some time, I tried avoiding personal pronouns altogether and always said 'God', but this makes God seem much less personal, which is not helpful when you are trying to convey the importance of grasping and trusting God's overwhelming love. Over the years, I have noticed that the form of inclusive language that I find most helpful is to simply alternate the personal pronoun, so I have learned to do the same for God and change pronoun each paragraph. This is not an exact science, not least because if, for example, I am describing God interacting with a man, it is simpler to call God 'she' so that it is abundantly clear who I am talking about. This is the option I have chosen for this book.

## How to Talk about the Bible

There is some discussion among scholars today about how to refer to what we normally call the Old Testament. It is important to recognize that for the Jewish people the 'Old' Testament is actually their entire Bible and the use of 'old' appears to imply that there should be a 'new'. I also suspect that the word 'old' means something very different now to when it was first used. Old can (and did) imply wisdom and something that should be revered; but we live today in a world where my tablet computer is old (and therefore obsolete) almost as soon as I have begun to use it. Scholars will often refer to the Hebrew Bible instead, but this has its own problems. First, it ignores the fact that there are subtle but important differences between the Bible of the Jews and the Christian Old Testament. Second, the term is not helpful in church life, where we need constantly to be reminded that we cannot understand the New Testament without a good background in the Old. To call the first books of the Bible 'The Hebrew Bible' risks people assuming it has little to do

## INTRODUCTION

with Christianity. I have therefore gone for the more neutral term 'First Testament', which I think was coined by James Sanders.

All quotations come from the NRSV, unless I have indicated otherwise. Where I refer to the original meaning of a Greek or Hebrew word I have worked either with the books indicated, or with *Strong's Concordance,* which is now generally available on the Bible Hub website, https://biblehub.com/interlinear/genesis/1-1.htm.

# 1

# Two Exits

I was terrified that I would no longer be able to tell the narrative of my life ... that every time I performed on stage his judgement of me would echo forever, deciding who and what I was. (Ronson, 2016, p. 154)

How we tell the story of our lives matters to us – quite rightly. When it comes to fundamental questions of who we are, we care deeply about how others perceive us, and that caring about how we are seen is part of being in relationships and what it means to live as a community. Shaming can, therefore, be a powerful weapon and being publicly shamed can be destructive. Part of our self-worth comes from being able to tell our stories so that we are known and valued and loved, and telling them to people who know us and value us and love us.

How we tell the story of Scripture matters as well. The Christian claim is that to read the story of our ancestors in the faith is, in one sense, to read our own story; the scriptural stories help us to understand something fundamental about who we are. In the next few chapters we are going to read the biblical stories so that they might shape the way in which we tell our own story. However, the stories of the Bible also help us to understand something fundamental about who God is – which is why it matters to realize from the beginning that (from a Christian perspective) the scriptural story reaches one crucial pinnacle in the public shaming of God Incarnate.

On the cross, *God* was held up for ridicule, contempt and the judgement of others, and reflecting on what this might mean for our understanding of both shame and God will lie at the heart of this book, but it will take us some time to get to that part of the story. We are going to start back in Genesis and see that shame is introduced into the scriptural story very early, and from the beginning we will need to grapple with the relationship between what feels like the most individual and personal of experiences (which we struggle even to put into words): our relationship with others and the results of our actions for others. Our society tempts us to believe that self-worth is a purely individual matter and that shame is only about personal feelings. The scriptural story reminds us from the beginning that this is not true; shame *is* personal (deeply so) but it is not *only* personal. We cannot talk about shame without eventually talking about how we treat one another, which is why I want to argue that ultimately we cannot deal with shame unless we are prepared to re-examine what we have to say about sin.

The Bible has a lot to say about shame, but we cannot pick out a few verses to give us a nice, neat 'Christian answer'; rather, we need to read again the story that gives a context to our story, starting with Genesis. This is not simply because Genesis happens to be the first book, it is also because in telling stories of creation and fall Genesis begins to examine fundamental questions about who we are and how we are valued. Scripture addresses shame from the beginning, and from the beginning it is closely tied to issues of sin and how sin affects both offender and injured.

So in this chapter we are going to look at the story of Adam and Eve and their sons, looking particularly for issues of shame, but we are going to begin at the very beginning and argue that how Scripture tells the story of our creation provides a foundation for understanding ourselves and why shame is so deeply painful. It also gives us a context – before Adam and Eve get themselves thrown out of the garden, we need to understand why they were there in the first place.

## Genesis and Creation

There are two creation stories in Genesis and they tell us slightly different things. Let's start with the first where God creates the world and all that is in it in six days and then takes a well-deserved day off. This is the story in Genesis 1. The 'days' quickly develop a rhythm – God says; it happens; there is evening and there is morning; and that is another day done. However, on the third day the rhythm gets interrupted – God decides to start admiring her own handiwork and we are told that 'God looked and saw that it was good'. Apparently, this inspires her so much that she decides to create a little more, so on the third day God manages all of the following. She creates dry land and sea (and stops to see that they were good) and then also fits in all of vegetation, plants, trees and fruit. Then she has another look – and yes, sure enough, it was good. From this point on, every time God creates something we get the same assurance, 'God saw that it was good'.

The rhythm changes again on the fifth day when God manages to create all the animals and the birds, and even the great sea monsters. This time, not only does he see that it is good, he also blesses them and orders them to be fruitful and multiply. So, we are ready for day six when God creates cattle, wild animals and 'everything that creeps upon the ground'. And, guess what, 'God saw that it was good'; by now, God is clearly getting into this creation thing because that is only half of what he achieves on day six. Finally, on this last day of work, God creates humankind and blesses them and then we are told that 'God saw everything that he had made, and indeed, it was very good' (Gen. 1.31).

Just let that sink in for a moment – 'God saw everything that [she] had made, and indeed, it was very good.' We need to focus in particular on the looking – she looked, she saw, and what she saw was good. Shame, it seems, is intimately linked to how we think others *see* us. We can feel intense shame when our errors or intimate secrets are made public, but we can also experience shame about something that only we know about; all shame needs is the fear that we would be held in contempt if it were known. Genesis tells us that seeing ourselves reflected in the gaze of others is an intrinsic part of being human – we were created to be seen by God, by the loving, welcoming gaze of God who looks and sees that we are good.

One of the most common responses to shame is to argue that we should not worry how others see us and what others think – and there is something in that advice, but it is not the whole truth. Like it or not, we are social animals and can be injured or built up by the way that others see us (or at least by how we think they see us). Humans are wonderfully varied and there may be some who are entirely untouched by others' opinions, but for most of us the reality is that we do care, at least about how those we love see us. So here is my very first suggestion – a biblical response to shame starts with a biblical understanding of who God is and how he sees us. God looked at creation (including human beings) and what he saw was so very good that he took the next day off to celebrate. We are going to get to sin and shame and the miserable bit soon enough, but we need to pause here, with the warm, loving gaze of God.

And on to story number two. God has to work a little harder in this version; she does not get to just say it and it happens. This time God takes the dust of the ground (Hebrew word: *adamah*) and uses it to form a human being (Hebrew word: *adam*). When God creates a second human being from out of the first, *adam* will become the name of the male, but for now the point is that God has formed a creature from the ground, so closely related that ground/dust and human share a name. The creature only becomes a living being when God breathes life into him/her.

Why does all of this matter? For the last 2,000 years or so, Christians have struggled to remember something fundamental about who we are – Genesis says that we are bodies into which God breathed life, not spirits for which God had to find a body. If we are to really understand how to live with or even be healed from shame we need to get this right. In general, we find mental and emotional difficulties more shaming than physical ones (and physical ones can be difficult enough). Why is that? Could it be because we see ourselves as souls implanted in a body and therefore believe that it is the internal stuff that is really 'us'. Therefore, if something goes wrong with our bodies, it is easier for us to believe that is not our fault. But if something goes wrong with our minds or our emotions, we take that as a personal failure. So, I will say it again – Genesis says that we are bodies into which God breathed life. It is worth noting that, increasingly, modern science is emphasizing that our bodies and our inner life are more intimately connected than we realize. For one example, see www.medicalnewstoday.com/articles/324362.php for an article on how mental health might be affected by our guts.

Let's push that point a little further. Some people have a real struggle with the negative voice in their head, one that constantly criticizes. We can criticize ourselves far more viciously than we would think of speaking about someone else. If that is you, then perhaps you allow the voice to carry on because it feels as if it is somehow 'you'; perhaps you even think that it is a sign of being more spiritual to constantly notice and exaggerate your own faults. However, what if that constant self-criticism is the result of a complex mixture of your previous experience and your physical make-up? If we admit that we are bodies into which life was breathed, then we also need to be careful about assuming that our inner lives and inner voices represent the authentic 'us'.

What is more, this story tells us something else very important about who we are – God created women and men in his image. This seems to be an echo of the earlier story when the climax to each day is that God looked and saw that it was good. If we are created to reflect God's image, then we are reminded again that our self-image should come (at least in part) from seeing ourselves in God's gaze. This means that how we experience that gaze is a vital theological issue and we will come back to it.

One final point from this creation story; God makes a second human being out of *adam* and when the chapter ends we are left with a picture of two people who are at home with each other and with God. They 'were both naked, and were not ashamed' (Gen. 2.25). If shame is intimately linked with our sense of how others see us, then it is even more intimately linked with a fear of exposure. For many of us our greatest fear is that if our real naked self is seen, then we might be rejected. Genesis begins with the exact opposite. Both Adam and Eve are able to live comfortably together and with God while naked; there is no covering up and apparently not even the desire to hide, for shame does not rear its ugly head. What could possibly go wrong?

The answer, of course, is quite a lot, and understanding what the First Testament tells us about what goes wrong is key to grasping a biblical view of shame. To put things as generally as possible, we need to get away from our sense that sin is simply about the wrong things that we do and to move towards seeing sin as a multi-faceted experience of the way in which both human beings and the world that we have shaped and formed are distorted and out of alignment with God. What is more, to really understand this and to grasp both the breadth of what the Bible has to say and to understand how sin and shame feed each other, we need to read more than one scriptural story.

Our view of sin and shame will be much more nuanced and realistic if we read all of the following stories and allow their different emphases to balance one another and to speak to different parts of our experience. We need to hold together:

- Two Exits (the story of Adam and Eve and also of Cain and Abel will introduce us to both sin and shame).
- The Exodus (the story of how God called the Israelites out of Egypt tells us of the first redemption from sin and shame).
- The Exile (the story of the captivity of the Israelites in Babylon tells us something of what it means to live in a world dominated by sin and shame when our hope for salvation is not yet fully realized).

Of course, this overview misses out entirely the story of Genesis after Cain and Abel, the entry into the Promised Land as well as the story of the Judges and the Monarchy. It does not claim to be a complete introduction to Scripture; rather, it claims to give us somewhere to start. To focus on three patterns of what sin is and does to us will give us a more rounded understanding, as well as help us to think more fully about what Christian salvation might look like.

## The First Exit (introducing sin and shame)

Here is our first problem with reading the story of Adam and Eve; it is so well known and has had such an influence on the development of Christianity that most of us come to it bringing a set understanding of what it says, or even what it should say. This can make reading it afresh quite a challenge. We need a bit of a clearing-out exercise before we start – a quick look at what it doesn't say before we can read it again. Let me give you some examples.

We can start with the well-known example that we all talk about eating the apple when in fact Genesis refers to the 'fruit of the tree' (Gen. 3.3) without ever specifying which fruit.

Equally, the common assumption used to be that this was a story about sex, even though sex is mentioned about as often as apples. Some have assumed that this is a story about how the wicked woman used sex to tempt the poor innocent man into a disastrous sin. What the text says is different. Genesis tells us why Eve ate the fruit, she saw that it looked nice, and she realized that the tree was desirable to make her wise (Gen. 3.6). None of these motives is bad in themselves. Genesis is silent on why Adam acted as he did; he simply took the fruit when it was offered.

Behind this version of the story lie all the old stereotypes. The couple are naked (gasp!) so sex must be involved. The woman talks too much when she should obviously allow her male companion to take the lead; put these together and she must be tempting him with sex – what else would a *woman* be doing? Read the story closely, however, and all these stereotypes collapse. Adam is present throughout the conversation, although since he just stands there (rather uselessly) we do not discover this vital fact until verse 6. He knows everything that Eve knows and has plenty of opportunities to speak up, but he just does not take them. In fact, we could argue that the difference between the two is Eve is the one who actually puts up a fight, quotes what God has said and has to be persuaded to eat the fruit. Adam says nothing and does nothing – and then caves in instantly when the fruit is handed to him.

Finally, we have also been told that this is a story about pride and that this tale demonstrates that pride is the worst sin and the root of all other sins. Guess what? Pride is mentioned in the text about as often as apples and sex. According to this interpretation, Adam and Eve were too proud to listen to God; they wanted to be like gods themselves and they were not content with the place that God assigned them. Again, we can only look at what the text actually says. The serpent does mention the possibility of being 'like God, knowing good and evil' (Gen. 3.5), but when the woman acts we are told that she had several motives (the tree was good for food, looked nice, and would make her wise). The man, on the other hand, simply conforms; his problem is not pride, it is passivity – a refusal to take responsibility and a willingness to do what he is told without question. There is nothing in the story about a single root for sin, and pride is not made a motive for the couple's actions.

We have been told so often 'what the story is about' that it can be difficult to read it with fresh eyes. However, it is worth the effort; I want to argue that Genesis 3 and 4 (read together) are a profoundly wise description of human nature and that they explore in story form some of the effects that sin and shame can have upon human beings and their relationships. What is more, these ancient stories include some truths that modern psychologists are pointing out today.

So how are we to read it? Let's start with the most obvious point of all – this is a story that is part of a bigger story; and, as with all well-told stories, some of what happens earlier has prepared the way for what happens in this part. There are deliberate moments of tension and dissonance, by which I mean times when the earlier part of the story encourages us to expect that the couple will do one thing, but they actually do something different. If we allow ourselves to be drawn in and to wonder about those moments, Genesis 3 will tell us something about ourselves. In this story, human behaviour is a complex and subtle affair with many factors influencing what we do.

The first dissonance is the existence of the tree of the knowledge of good and evil whose fruit they are banned from eating (Gen. 2.17). In the earlier part of the story God's generosity has been emphasized. She gave the couple everything they needed and more, and her creation was described as very good. In chapter 2 she laboured to produce a bountiful and beautiful garden in which just one limit was placed on what was given to the couple. Despite the plenitude that surrounds them, our attention is drawn to the one tree that has been declared off limits. It seems that the story invites us to ponder on what it is about human nature that makes it so difficult for us to be content with the plenty we have and leads us so often to keep reaching for what we do not have.

The second dissonance lies in the fact that the couple are tempted by a creature. In the earlier part of the story they were given 'dominion' over all other creatures (Gen. 1.28). We tend to interpret 'dominion' as an excuse to exploit but it is better read as the kind of leadership exercised by, for example, a shepherd who cares for, tends and feeds his sheep (Brueggemann, 1982, p. 32). This is the more constant biblical image of the proper way to be a king or have power while serving God in this world. So what is happening here is that despite having been appointed to a position of responsibility, they allow a creature to take control and to lead them astray. Again, we have to insist this is not pride; they are listening to another rather than acting and thinking for themselves. Adam, in particular, only speaks up when everything has gone wrong and there is blame to be assigned.

The third dissonance is in the couple's view of themselves. We have already seen that in the first creation story in Genesis 1: God rejoices over all of creation because it is good; we were also reminded that humankind is not just the climax of this good creation, but that we are made in the image of God. An image is a representation or a likeness – there is something here about both reflecting God and knowing ourselves in that reflection. Genesis invites us to recognize that we were formed to learn something about ourselves in the gaze of God – and in the first part of the story that gaze has been understood to be one of love and approval. That is why it is so important to start from the point where the couple were naked but not ashamed (Gen. 2.25). This is about their experience of the gaze of God as being warm and loving, which allows them to have a proper love of self and of each other. They can be comfortable while being totally exposed because they know to the depth of their beings that they are wanted and loved.

All of this changes the moment the fruit is eaten; both Eve and Adam have one immediate reaction (and note this is before God does anything at all). They realize that they are naked and they want to cover themselves. Shame has entered the picture and the very first result of the consumption of the forbidden fruit is that the couple can no longer bear to be exposed to each other, so they make some rudimentary clothing out of fig leaves. But the fig leaves do not work (and, presumably, were very uncomfortable). They cannot cover their sense of shame by themselves. By the next verse, they are hiding from God, because, as Adam explains, 'I was afraid, because I was naked; and I hid myself' (Gen. 3.10). We need to note that shame leads directly to fear of God. This is a classic description of the effects of shame and takes us directly to the next dissonance.

We can see the contrast between the relationship that the couple have in chapter 2 and the one that exists by the end of chapter 3. In chapter 2, the only thing about creation that was 'not good' was the fact that *adam* was alone. God created the woman as a 'partner' according to the NRSV. The original Hebrew word meant 'helper', which might sound as though this makes Eve the subservient half of the couple until we realize that the word is most often used for God as the 'helper' of Israel or an individual. When woman was created out of *adam* he recognized her as part of himself, as 'bone of my bones and flesh of my flesh' (Gen. 2.23). Creation was complete when there were two; they needed each other and were comfortable being naked around each other. If we are created to know ourselves in the gaze of God then there is also a hint here that we will also know ourselves in our relationship to others. Our sense of self is social, more social than our individualistic society admits.

After the fruit is eaten we see one more result of shame; they cover themselves, they hide from God, and they start blaming each other for what has gone wrong. The man blames the woman and even tries to blame God – the 'flesh of my flesh' has now become 'The woman whom you gave to be with me' (Gen. 3.12). (She's nothing to do with me, God, this was all your idea!) The woman, in turn, blames the serpent (Gen. 3.13). All God has done is ask a couple of questions; he certainly has not pronounced any judgement, and the harmonious relationship that used to exist has collapsed into shame and blame. Why does shame lead so quickly to blame? Could it be because blaming someone else is a quick way to direct that dreaded hostile gaze elsewhere? Don't look at me, it was her fault!

I suggest, therefore, that the story itself resists any sense that in dealing with sin we should be concerned only with the relationship with God and with God's judgement on our actions. In this story, the couple's judgement against themselves comes first; they are devastated by shame and their first reaction is to make fig leaves, and the second is to blame someone else. Their relationship with themselves is distorted, which soon distorts their relationship with each other. Having begun to judge themselves, they promptly assume that God will judge them – in other words, their expectation of the gaze of God alters before God does anything at all. Sin has profound implications for our relationship with ourselves and with each other as well as with God. Mike Higton, commenting on this passage, says that shame

> has something to do with seeing yourself as you imagine others see you – an internalized version of the external scrutiny you imagine yourself to be under. And so, it is indeed a form of knowledge, of self-knowledge ('this is what I look like') but it is knowledge without love. Shame involves a form of knowledge that sees accurately but judges harshly, and knowledge that consists in unforgiving scrutiny. Adam and Eve have their eyes opened, but apparently only to become aware for the first time of their naked precariousness – whether the emphasis is supposed to fall on the frailty that they discover in themselves, or whether it has more to do with their discovery of the uncontrollable nature of their desires. They see themselves accurately as finite, weak, needy or unreliable.
> 
> The fruit of the tree, we might say, makes them judges – and this is what, in this reading of the story, 'knowledge of good and evil' means. They do not gain information about what is right and wrong; they gain the stance of a judge who metes out sentences, condemning and accepting – the position that (as the story itself shows) belongs properly to God. Adam and Eve seek to stand in the place of God and then condemn themselves for not being gods. And in this, of course, they do see accurately (they are finite creatures, they are not gods) but they do not see truly: they do not see the proper dignity (rather than shame) of their position. (Higton, 2008, p. 267)

This, it seems to me, is a vital insight into how shame distorts our living – not only do we judge ourselves harshly, we also believe that others (including God) will do the same. *Shame fundamentally changes our perception of the gaze of God* – now we imagine that God sees only our faults and that his gaze will be one of pure judgement, it's no wonder we just want to hide. The problem, of course, is that hiding is self-defeating; we end up hiding from the very relationships we need in order to flourish. Genesis chapters 2 and 3 tell us that eating the forbidden fruit produces a cycle of shame and blame; the couple are trapped and changed as a result of their actions and the fact that God throws them out of the garden is only one result.

Shame also distorts their vision of themselves. In Higton's words, they see accurately but not truly. For some people, that distortion in the vision of themselves becomes the single, dominating issue in their lives. Here I want to borrow an image from John Bradshaw who compares experiencing shame to having toothache; asking us to remember how one small part of your body can dominate life when it hurts (Bradshaw, 1988, p. 195). We will look later at the way in which our experience of shame can be very varied – some of us are much more affected by it than others. At this point, we reflect on a story of the first couple when they seem, to me, to epitomize shame-ache. Their actions and perceptions are dominated by the shame that they feel. It has become the filter through which they see themselves and each other, and through which they expect that God will see them as well.

No wonder they reached for their fig leaves; exposed and fearful, they scramble to cover themselves and grab the first form of cover they can find. The problem is that their own attempt to hide their nakedness is hopelessly unsuccessful. Here I want to introduce a second image that we will use throughout the book. If shame-ache can be used to describe the experience of being dominated by shame, then 'fig leaves' represent our own attempts to deal with our shame. In modern language these are our coping mechanisms, our first instinctive reactions which may help in the short term, but can often prove to be counter-productive over the longer term. The problem with shame is that our fig leaves become so embedded that they begin to do more harm than good – the story of Cain and Abel will help us to explore this more fully. For now, let us note the nice touch of grace in this story – God replaces the fig leaves with garments of skin (Gen. 3.21); this is a beautiful description of God's gentleness with the couple's shame-ache. It is God who provides covering that works long term. Could there also be a challenge here? In order to receive God's covering we first need to give up our fig leaves, and that might not be as easy as we hope.

This is, of course, the point at which many tellings of the story finish, but it is not the real end. There is a second exit after Adam and Eve have left the garden when the story continues into the next generation and their son also leaves the presence of God (Gen. 4.16). This part of the story is less often told, but it develops for us the distortions that happen when sin and shame-ache and fig leaves dominate.

## The Second Exit (the growing effect of sin and shame)

Adam and Eve have two sons, who take up very different roles in life. The eldest, Cain, becomes an arable farmer while his younger brother, Abel, becomes a shepherd. In this, the second generation of the human race, we begin to see how shame distorts human flourishing and can lead to devastating results. Let's speculate a bit and assume that Adam and Eve continued to struggle with shame-ache; throw in such minor issues as God cursing them and being kicked out of the garden, and there was plenty of opportunity for them to continue blaming each other. In other words, I am assuming that they were far from perfect parents and what we see now is how the cycle of shame and blame works out in the next generation.

The details are given tersely and, to the modern mind, are not described sufficiently. Cain and Abel both bring sacrifices from their work and we are told that God 'had regard for' Abel's sacrifice but not for Cain's (Gen. 4.4–5). The Hebrew word translated as 'to have regard for' has the sense of directing one's gaze or paying attention to – in other words, we are back again to the issue of God's gaze. One of the ways in which the First Testament regularly describes being blessed by God (knowing you are wanted and valued) is with the idea that God turns his face towards us. The classic blessing that is still used goes like this:

The LORD bless you and keep you;
the LORD make his face to shine upon you, and be gracious to you;
the LORD lift up his countenance upon you, and give you peace.
(Num. 6.24–26)

Notice that this blessing refers twice to God looking at us and it is perceived as affirming and desirable. English translators try to make the blessing more interesting by using both 'face' and 'countenance' in the two verses. The Hebrew makes sure that we get the point by using 'face' (*panaw*) both times. The blessing is describing having God's attention and we are reminded again that being made in God's image is linked to a sense of flourishing under God's benevolent gaze.

In the story of Cain and Abel, however, there is a clear and stark division between the brothers – God turns her face to one and not the other. This is a primitive story and no reason is given for God's behaviour; rather, a situation that we can all recognize is described. Equally, hard work does not lead to an equal reward. What is more, these are brothers born to parents with shame-ache; to have one of them, but not the other, receive benevolent attention is almost bound to be incendiary.

The focus of the story is not on the unfairness of what happened but on the brothers' reaction. Let's start with the one who survives the story. Cain's reaction goes something like this – he becomes angry and he withdraws and looks away. We are told twice that 'his countenance fell' (Gen. 4.5–6). The English translation could be taken to imply that he frowned or pouted, but the Hebrew is using the idea of 'face' (*panaw*) again. Just as God turned her face towards Abel's sacrifice, now Cain turns his face away. This, I suggest, is his instinctive fig leaf. We could take it literally and imagine him looking at the ground rather than at those around him, but it is meant to describe turning away from companionship and withdrawing into himself. He no longer looks his brother in the eye. This is one classic reaction to shame-ache – exclude the outside world and fix your attention firmly within yourself. God's assurance that there is no permanent rejection is not heard (Gen. 4.7) and neither is the accompanying warning. Cain has pulled back inside his own head and, apparently, he is now only listening to his own anger while ignoring the world around him.

The assurance and the warning are worth noting. First, Cain is told that if he does well he will be accepted. The implication is that there is a problem with the sacrifice, but there is no permanent rejection of him as a person. The problem, of course, is that Cain does not see it that way. He clearly feels that *he* has been rejected, and not just his sacrifice. We remember that a basic way to distinguish between guilt and shame is that we feel guilt about our actions, but shame about who we are. When we feel shame it is as if our whole self is being judged and is not wanted. Guilt and shame are easy to distinguish in theory, but in the messiness of actual life they often merge into each other. Certainly, Cain does not respond to this assurance.

Second, Cain is warned that sin is lurking and wanting to master him. In this ancient story the problem with sin is not simply one of human actions, and human beings are not the sole source of sin. The serpent was there before Adam and Eve decided to go scrumping, and sin is a power at work in the world; it is part of the human situation into which Cain has been born and he faces a struggle to ensure that he masters sin rather than sin mastering him. The implication of what comes next is that he loses that struggle.

However, Cain has shown us only one possible response to shame. What about the other brother? Abel is remarkably silent throughout the story (he takes after his dad in this). We are not told if he did anything to contribute to Cain's anger, and we are not told if there had been earlier clashes between the brothers of which this is merely the climax. We are not told if Abel made an unsuccessful attempt to be reconciled with his brother. Instead, Abel is silent, acted upon, and the passive recipient of his brother's anger. Psychologists tell us that the fig leaves that we create to cope with our sense of shame can, paradoxically, drive us in at least two different directions. We will come back to this more fully at the end of the story, but here we note simply that some of us become Cain and others become Abel: driven into ourselves, not speaking perhaps because we have no expectation of being heard. Could it be that shame has also warped Abel's life and even set him up to become Cain's victim?

The story of Cain and Abel seems to suggest something very important for the way that we read Scripture. We need to pay attention to the ones who do not speak, those who are made the passive recipients of other people's actions. The moment one person in a biblical story disappears we need to be alert to the possibility that the one who dominates the story may have lost that basic love and respect that treats the other as a child of God, a person who is equally beloved and valued and who is not (or should not be) available simply to play a bit part in someone else's story.

And so the story proceeds to what now feels like the inevitable conclusion and the cycle of shame and blame takes another turn. Cain does not listen to God but instead prefers to blame his brother; in his mind, Abel is somehow his rival and responsible for what has happened. Therefore he lures his brother out into a field where he murders him. Sin now has a human victim and in this part of the story we are faced not simply with the issue of wrongdoing where Adam and Eve suffer the consequences of their own actions, but also with the issue of the balance of justice when there is both an offender and an innocent victim; how is God to respond when a shamed and imperfect Cain murders the apparently innocent and passive Abel?

Just as in the eating of the forbidden fruit, once the sin has been committed God appears and there is a question and answer session in which he seems, at first, to be ignorant. Cain uses the opportunity to deny all knowledge of, and responsibility for, Abel, but the story reaches a climax when God demonstrates that this is not the case. 'What have you done? Listen; your brother's blood is crying out to me from the ground!' (Gen. 4.10). In other words, Abel 'speaks' for the first time after his death and is able to deny his brother's version of events. In fact, the ground that has absorbed Abel's blood becomes the source of Cain's punishment; the arable farmer is told that he will find that this ground will no longer cooperate with him. Like his parents, he is sent away from God's presence, leading to a slightly mysterious second exit. Cain is to live with the results of both his parents' actions and his own. Both have, in some way, separated him from that first, open and trusting relationship with God.

Not surprisingly, Cain is most distressed at what has happened; he is to be driven away and hidden from God's face (Gen. 4.14); in other words, he is to lose the joy of God's presence and regard. He responds with a word play that only works in Hebrew: 'My *awon* is greater than I can *nasa*.' The word *awon* can mean either sin or punishment, depending on the context, while *nasa* means either to carry or to carry away (that is, to remove), again depending on the context. In later Hebrew, the form *nasa awon* comes to mean literally 'to carry away sin' or to forgive.

This has made Cain's comment quite difficult for the translators to convey. The phrase carries any number of implications that are virtually impossible to put across in English, as Gary Anderson argues. First, there is the fact that the sin and the punishment can both be described by the same word; this seems to imply that in Hebrew thinking sin carries its own consequences for the offender. Dealing with sin, therefore, means more than imposing or avoiding punishment. Second, the fact that sin has to be carried tells us that in Hebrew thinking sin is imagined as a weight or a burden upon the person who sinned. What is unique to Hebrew is the use of the same phrase to mean 'bear the burden of sin' apparently describing one who is not forgiven, and 'to bear away the burden of sin' describing when a person is forgiven. This appears confusing at first but also makes sense in helping us to recognize that, in Hebrew thought, sin has a reality of its own – it is seen as a 'thing' that creates a burden for the offender (Anderson, 2009, pp. 17–21).

Translators, therefore, usually rely on the context to help them put *nasa awon* into English. However, that does not work for this first sin that has a human victim, because the context does not give us enough clues. Commentators are divided between those who translate Cain's outcry as 'My punishment is too great to bear' and those who put it as 'My sin is too great to be forgiven'. Personally, I like Anderson's suggestion that we translate it as 'the weight of my sin is too great for me to bear'. By using this translation, Cain is neither arguing that his sin is beyond forgiveness nor complaining about the severity of his punishment; he is facing the reality of his actions and their consequences. He has moved from 'am I my brother's keeper?' to a recognition that what he has done is truly evil (Anderson, 2009, pp. 24–5). If this is the correct translation, then we might be able to argue that Cain's focus has finally moved from himself to Abel and to the recognition that his brother is dead; the tragedy is that he does this too late.

The Bible uses two stories to introduce sin and, in both, the issues are greater than just whether God can forgive wrong actions. A fuller understanding of sin recognizes that it brings its own consequences: it distorts our perception of ourselves, ruins our relationships and produces both offenders and injured parties – both of whom are damaged by what has happened. Sin in the First Testament is a weight and a burden, and shame can be both a consequence and cause of sin. The stories of Adam and Eve and Cain and Abel reflect what psychologists have also noted about the way in which shame influences human behaviour. It is such a primal, painful experience that we have developed a number of mechanisms to cope with shame or even to attempt to avoid its misery. In fact, Nathanson argues that almost any feeling is preferable to shame and has developed what he calls 'The Compass of Shame', describing four possible main defences:

- Withdrawal – which can mean quite literally walking away, or can be withdrawing internally, resulting in depression.
- Attacking yourself – for example, putting yourself down before others can, or self-harming.

- Avoidance – either by becoming a perfectionist or by addictions and other behaviours that allow the self to be forgotten.
- Attacking others – it is possible to feel better about ourselves by projecting the problem on to others, through anger, bullying and blame. (Nathanson, quoted in Jewett, 2011, p. 16)

Naturally, in our actual lives our defence mechanisms will be more complex than can be conveyed by an ancient story that focuses on just four people, and only describes their actions (rather than letting us inside their heads in the way a modern storyteller would). However, I believe that Nathanson's list helps to illustrate what Genesis describes; certainly, the first and the last points are very evident in our stories. Adam and Eve withdraw physically, and Abel withdraws into silence. Adam blames Eve, Eve blames the serpent, and Cain blames Abel. Cain responds with aggression against his brother, leading to murder, and this spiral from shame to aggression to murder matches what some have suggested is the major cause of violence:

> The emotion of shame is the primary cause of all violence, whether towards others or towards the self. Shame is a necessary but not a sufficient cause of violence ... The different forms of violence, whether towards individuals or entire populations, are motivated (caused) by feelings of shame. The purpose of violence is to diminish the intensity of shame and replace it as far as possible with its opposite, pride. (Gilligan, quoted in Jewett, 2011, p. 40)

What is more, the story of Cain and Abel also reminds us of the need for justice as well as forgiveness. Abel's blood speaks from the ground – in other words, the seemingly voiceless victim is not silenced before God. The idea that the voiceless is given the ability to speak (but only after death) may seem a relatively small and unimportant point, but I want to argue that there is a particular reason why it matters. There is an argument, which we will explore more fully in Chapter 3, that evil actions done against us can be experienced as messages, something that makes a claim about us, and this hidden claim can have a major influence on our sense of ourselves. At this point, I simply want to reflect on some of these potential claims. What messages do the injuries that we do to one another potentially convey?

- To the abused spouse – it is your fault this is happening, you provoked me.
- To the victim of racism – you matter less than people of other races and you always will.
- To the sexually abused – you want this and it is your fault that you aroused me.
- To the victim of a con trick – you are an idiot to fall for this.
- To the victim of a hate crime – who you are justifies what I am doing to you. (Adapted from Radzik, 2009)

These are false but pernicious and dangerous ideas, and if the victim is left silent then there is a sense in which the messages stand. We are becoming increasingly aware that these messages can be internalized and therefore contribute to the injured person's shame; this is why it matters that the victim has a voice. Abel's voice cried out even after death and denied Cain's version of events; God listened to the voice of the victim, not just that of the offender. The fact that Abel's blood rang as loudly as Cain's voice in the ears of God matters, because for Abel and those who come after him there can be no gospel if these messages are allowed to stand. There can be no gospel without some form of justice, which means giving a lie to the idea that the offender's needs matter more than those of the injured. A gospel that does not take seriously the story of the injured person is the gospel of a God who does not care and of sin forgiven too lightly, and ignores the reality that some people live with every day. Such a gospel does not reflect the God who heard Abel's blood crying out and asked Cain, 'What have you done?'

## A Summary and a Warning

So let me try to bring together what we have seen so far. In the story of the creation we saw the importance of seeing ourselves reflected in the gaze of God and knowing that God saw that it was good. This means that how we perceive the gaze of God, as judgemental or as warm and welcoming, is a profoundly theological issue; eventually we will see that, for the Christian, it matters that we see God through Jesus. In the stories of Adam and Eve and Cain and Abel we saw that there is no one single root to sin (everyone is different), and there can be a complex mix of motives leading people astray and to which we respond in different ways. The problem in the garden was not simply pride and overreaching authority but also being passive and simply conforming. What is more, we have seen that sin is greater than just the individual actions of individual people; the serpent exists before Adam and Eve do anything and sin is represented as a power waiting to take over Cain's life.

Which brings us to the warning. The idea of a single root for sin (normally assumed to be pride) has strong roots in the Christian tradition, although feminist theologians have been arguing against it since 1960 (Saiving Goldstein, 1960). It seems that there is something about human nature that finds the idea of a single root (and presumably therefore a single solution) extremely attractive. Modern pop psychology has gone for an equivalent that appears to be the opposite to the Christian tradition, but which in fact has much in common with it. Today we are constantly assured that most, if not all, destructive human behaviour is caused by low self-esteem. It seems now that the most important trait we can instil in our children is a sense of their own worth and the belief that they can do anything. There is a measure of truth in this; we have already seen, and will return to, the idea that shame is at the root of a great deal of violence. However, it is not the whole truth. We will also need to grapple with those situations where shame is good and necessary and helps us to live together with suitable mutual respect. As we move through Scripture, especially as we do so deliberately looking for all of the ways in which Scripture speaks about shame distorting life and preventing us from flourishing, we will need to be alert to the danger of reverting to a single root for sin. Sin, according to Scripture, is a multi-headed monster; shame can be an overpowering problem, but it is not the *only* cause of *all* problems.

While resisting the idea that pride is somehow the main root of all sin, we do need to take seriously the idea that pride can be a problem. This raises the issue of language and what pride means in the twenty-first century. Black Pride rightly celebrates black culture and African heritage, and equally Pride rightly celebrates the LGBTQ+ community. Pride in this sense is good and important, especially when used by those whom others have wrongly tried to shame. How, then, do we speak of pride when it is problematic? We must distinguish carefully between a healthy pride that recognizes that you are loved and valued, and an unhealthy pride that topples over into arrogant self-obsession and that can blind you to the need to respect others. God looked at *all of creation* and saw that it was good; she did not look at one single human being somehow placed above all others. I will use arrogance or hubris for problematic pride, and we will need to return to why arrogance (and shamelessness) is dangerous.

Going back to the two exits, if Genesis resists the idea that there is a single root to sin, it also shows us that sin has any number of results and that shame and self-judgement become part of the story before God gets a chance to say or do anything. Our problem is not simply the judgement of God, but our tendency to judge and blame ourselves and others (and, of course, to project those feelings on to God). Shame can lead to any number of pernicious results – blame, division, withdrawal and aggression all spiral together to lead us to the first murder. In Genesis we are catapulted remarkably quickly from the blissful first garden with the happily naked couple who are in complete accord, into a blood-soaked field with one dead brother and the other denying all responsibility – in other words, we soon encounter a world that looks much closer to the one that we have to navigate.

Finally, having spent a chapter on these two stories, we might just mention that they are not so important for the rest of Scripture as Christians sometimes assume. The First Testament never refers back to the story of Adam and Eve (and the story is correspondingly less important in Jewish theology than in Christian). For the First Testament, it is the Exodus that is the salvation event shaping Israel's imagination, and which they are constantly commanded to remember and celebrate; it is the Exodus that is recalled in the Passover and, when the disaster of the Exile struck, it was the Exodus, not Genesis 3, to which the Israelites returned to renew their theological vision. In the next chapter, therefore, we move on to look at two more very different stories of sin, and how sin shapes both the world in which we live and our own inner life – the Exodus and the Exile.

# 2

# Exodus and Exile

> Shame can burrow into you so deep that it shrinks the brain and constricts the heart. (Parkinson, 2019)

## The Exodus

It is one of the great stories of the First Testament; the weak and oppressed people of God are rescued from the power of a ruthless tyrant by the power of God, working through a reluctant leader. It is also one of the definitive stories of the First Testament; it is the founding narrative of the people of Israel, one that they remember and celebrate every year, and to which they return when they are in trouble. It is a classic story of salvation; it is celebrated as salvation in the song given in Exodus 15: 'The LORD is my strength and my might, and he has become my salvation', sang Moses and the Israelites (Exod. 15.2). Jesus was crucified at some point during Passover (in Matthew, Mark and Luke the Last Supper is a Passover meal; in John, Jesus dies the day before and is killed at the same time as the Passover lambs), giving a clear connection between Exodus and the Christian understanding of salvation. In this chapter, then I want to examine what the story of the Exodus (and then the Exile) has to tell us about what it means to live in a world of sin and shame.

In one sense the story of the Exodus begins at the end of Genesis 47. There is a famine and this has two major results. First, Jacob and all his descendants (that is, all of the ancestors of the people of Israel) move to Egypt where they join Joseph (one of Jacob's sons), who had been sold as a slave but has managed to rise to become one of Pharaoh's trusted servants. Then Joseph, acting for Pharaoh, exploits the famine to buy all the land in Egypt and to demand that, in future, one-fifth of all harvests should be given to Pharaoh. In other words, soon after the Israelites settle in Egypt, Pharaoh becomes the absolute master who has an iron grasp on the main sources of wealth. Joseph plays a major role in this and there is a certain irony that someone who is presented as the hero of the story up to this point is responsible for a situation that will cause such problems in a later generation. The stage is set for a story of conflict between Pharaoh, who is in a position of absolute power allowing him to oppress ruthlessly, and the Israelites who are weak and vulnerable and who are, like so many immigrants, dependent on the goodwill of another.

By the beginning of the book of Exodus the situation has deteriorated quite badly. The generation who move to Egypt have died and their descendants have committed the ultimate sin of any migrant population – having too many children. There is a new Pharaoh on the throne; Joseph is forgotten, and Pharaoh fears that the Israelites may one day turn against him. The Israelites are cruelly exploited and eventually Pharaoh even resorts to infanticide so that their newborn children are under threat. It is clear from the beginning of Exodus that the Israelites have done nothing to deserve this; Joseph may be responsible for creating the situation, but this generation has been left to struggle with the consequences of other people's actions. It is a story of sin – but one in which the people of God are more sinned against than sinning.

The people of God are portrayed as helpless and oppressed by the sin of another; not only do they not deserve their suffering, they are unable to help themselves. The only thing that they do to initiate their own rescue is to cry out to God, in just the same way that Abel's blood once cried out to God. Exodus 2.24–25 appears to say the same thing several times: God hears their groaning, God remembers his covenant with their ancestors, God looks upon them, and God takes notice of them. At first this repetition appears to add little to the story, but it reminds us of Abel and underlines one issue that will be repeated throughout Scripture: the struggle for attention. Just as when God heard the blood of the murdered Abel, so here also we are reminded that it matters to be heard. Knowing that your cry for justice has attracted attention may not be all that the oppressed need, but it is still important. In Scripture this issue becomes focused on one question – has God heard me or is she deaf to my cries?

So this is the salvation that the Israelites need in the story of the Exodus. As Brueggemann puts it:

> What Israel requires as sinned-against is not guilt, punishment, and repentance, but an intervening advocate who can and will work justice,

and extricate Israel from this unwarranted suffering. (Brueggemann, in Park and Nelson, 2001, p. 30)

In other words, this is a story of sin (and shame) but it is a story from the point of view of the one who is sinned against – that is, the one who is too often ignored in the Christian tradition. In this story God does hear the cries of the Israelites and becomes the advocate for whom they have pleaded. God intervenes, Pharaoh is defeated, and the people are able to escape oppression and begin their journey to the Promised Land. They are able to sing their song of salvation in Exodus 15 because they have been set free from the sin of another.

However, the story of Israel's redemption is not complete at this point. They may be exultant because they have escaped the clutches of Pharaoh, but they are not yet free. It is possible to see in the story that the people of Israel have been shaped and affected by their experience of oppression, and that changing their outer circumstances is only one part of the change that they need. The movement out of powerlessness and away from being oppressed is going to need more than the ten plagues and the dramatic escape through the Red Sea. Once away from Egypt, they do not immediately act like free people; rather, throughout the rest of Exodus and beyond they struggle to escape the scars that remain from their time as slaves. As Gutiérrez put it, 'they remain bound by subtle and powerful complicities' (Gutiérrez, 1985, p. 74).

There are signs of the ways in which the Israelites carry the scars of their experiences from the very beginning of the story. When they are first offered the hope of salvation they vacillate between belief and despair. At first things appear to go well; Aaron and Moses meet with the elders of the people, they deliver the message that God has given them, perform the signs that they were told to perform, and we are told that the people bowed down and worshipped (Exod. 4.31). God has spoken and the people have responded with trust and adoration so all appears to be well. However, this does not last. The first attempt to stand up against Pharaoh goes wrong (which feels just a little predictable – did anyone think that he would give way instantly?) and the result is that the difficult circumstances in which the people have been working are made even worse. When this happens, the people of Israel do not blame Pharaoh but turn against the easier targets of Moses and Aaron (Exod. 5.20–21). Moses, by the way, does little better; his immediate response is to blame God (Exod. 5.22–23). It then seems that the people are so discouraged and alienated that they refuse to listen to Moses at all (Exod. 6.9 says they would not listen because of their 'broken spirit'). In fact, there is very little sign in most of the story that Moses is supported by the people whom he is attempting to liberate; instead, the next few chapters are a confrontation between Moses and Pharaoh with only Aaron in support. The people become active and supportive only at the point at which the battle with Pharaoh is over and permission has been given for them to leave (Exod. 12). It is tempting to see all of these behaviours as in some way the outworking of the Israelites' fig leaves; they have lived with oppression and shame for so long that they have learned destructive ways of living that they find difficult to abandon.

It comes as no surprise to find that the escape from Egypt is not the end of the struggle. The people continue to find it very difficult to believe in their own freedom and in the power of God that has achieved such freedom. When Pharaoh pursues them into the desert they are terrified and, once again, blame Moses, now claiming that they never wanted to leave Egypt in the first place (Exod. 14.10f.). When that crisis is over and they have begun to settle down to life in the desert, as soon as difficulties strike their first reaction is to begin to dream of the slavery from which they asked to be rescued. Liberation is too uncertain for them and their past situation looks more and more attractive (Exod. 16.3) – or we could say that learning to live without their fig leaves proves a long and difficult process. As Gutiérrez points out, they need to learn; they have to struggle through success and failure in order to become aware of the roots of their oppression and to truly understand what it means to be liberated and to be the people of God (Gutiérrez, 2001, p. 154).

Let us look at this final story a little more closely. By Exodus 16 the Israelites have reached the Wilderness of Sin. They are tired and hungry and worried that there is no food, so they begin to complain and, once again, blame Moses and Aaron for their situation (the cycle of shame and blame continues):

> The Israelites said to [Moses and Aaron], 'If only we had died by the hand of the LORD in the land of Egypt, when we sat by the fleshpots and ate our fill of bread; for you have brought us out into this wilderness to kill this whole assembly with hunger.' (Exod. 16.3)

Compare this statement with the reality of their life in Egypt as described in Exodus 1.14, which talks about hard labour, not sitting at leisure by pots of meat. It is true that the early part of Exodus does not mention that the Israelites suffered from a lack of food, but it seems highly unlikely that slaves were allowed to eat their fill – particularly of a luxury item like meat. Whether their memory about how much food they had was correct or not, it is clear that everything that was difficult about their life in Egypt – all those issues that caused them to call out to God for help – has been forgotten. Freedom, with its attendant risks and responsibilities, no longer looks attractive and they prefer the familiar situation of slavery. For these people, liberation is going to mean more than just a change in circumstances; something needs to change inside as well. Somehow, they need to get to the point where they can begin not simply to be free externally, but also to believe in their own freedom and act as a free people.

In other words, the people of Israel are recognizably human. We know that we are shaped and formed by our experiences and that a person who is treated cruelly or abused during childhood is likely to be affected by that abuse in their adult life. We know that the effort to deal with the effects of abuse can continue long after the abuse itself has ended, and trauma of any kind can shape perceptions and reactions and even cause major personality changes. It is part of the vulnerability of the human condition that we are influenced by our experiences and respond to our circumstances. Exodus is not just about God's concern for and liberation of the oppressed; it is also a vivid story of how long and difficult the struggle to overcome the results of the oppression can be.

However, even though we know this, it often seems that the story of the Exodus has had little influence on our understanding of sin, for nearly all talk of sin is concerned only with the offender. It is as if we listen to Cain but not to Abel. In hearing only Cain and not taking the Exodus into account, we have restricted our understanding of sin – which in turn means we have not grasped the fullness of the gospel. We know that the gospel is reduced when it is restricted merely to whether or not our sins are forgiven, but too easily that version of Christianity becomes our default.

By limiting our attention to the offender we also miss one of the sad realities of sin that the Exodus highlights. When a bad act takes place, the offender may respond with guilt, but the injured too often experiences shame and is left struggling with major issues around why this happened to her and whether she provoked it. We need salvation from this result of sin as much as from the sins we commit.

For the Israelites, the Exodus was the great controlling image of salvation and what it means to be God's people – they re-told the story and celebrated it regularly, until it became part of their sense of who they were. They were, and are, literally an Exodus people, constantly re-living that journey out of oppression and captivity into new life with God. In the words of Rabbi Michael Goldberg, this is the Jewish 'Master Story', through which we 'get our bearings for the rest of Scripture' (quoted in Rutledge, 2017, p. 223). Even more than that, it is a story that helps us to understand our own story, and can give us an image to describe the Christian life. Faith is often described as a journey, but it is often an exodus. The word 'exodus' comes from the Greek for 'way' (*odos*) and 'out of' (*ex*); it describes not just a journey, but a passage out of one way of life lived under an unwanted power (sin? shame? our own fig leaves?) and into a life lived under a very different power, the love and grace of God. We are on an exodus in which we seek to be free of what binds us so that we may be more fully ourselves under the gaze of our loving God. The biblical Exodus reminds us that this is not a simple journey; the people were bound in ways that they did not at first fully recognize, and they had to learn how to be free.

This is a powerful image for the exodus out of shame-ache. Much as we might like a simple healing (say a prayer, and God will take the feelings away), it may in fact be more like a continual emerging from captivity. Just as with the Israelites, there may be painful work to be done by recognizing where we have made fig leaves for ourselves, or where the cycle of shame and blame is still affecting us. Also like the Israelites, it may be necessary to recognize that the sin done against us has so shaped us that we then sin against others and God. A realistic understanding of sin will encompass this reality.

We will come back to this issue in a later chapter – but first there is one more story from the First Testament that can deepen our understanding of sin and what it means to flourish in the face of sin and shame.

## The Exile

Let me introduce you to Rebecca, a totally fictional character who we will imagine living in Jerusalem in the year 587 BC. She lived, we might say, at the other end of the story of the First Testament from Adam and Eve, Cain and Abel, and even from the Exodus. Rather than the founding stories of Israel we are now looking at much later history and have come to history that we can date from external evidence. The year 587 BC would prove to be a turning point in the history of Israel, but to fully understand how devastating it was we need to give Rebecca's life a little more historical context.

Let us imagine that in 587 BC Rebecca was 25 years old. This would mean that she was brought up during a time of extraordinary political instability for the people of Israel, which would, of course, have a huge impact on her own daily life. By the time that Rebecca was born, Israel had been divided into two kingdoms: Judah in the south and Israel in the north. Over 100 years before Rebecca was born, life in both Israel and Judah had been dominated by the ruthless power of the Assyrian Empire, a brutal and threatening superpower that had twice invaded the land of Israel. The northern kingdom finally collapsed in 722 BC. Many refugees had fled south into the kingdom of Judah while many others were transported (Smith-Christopher, 2002, p. 56). Judah was made a client state of the Empire. Then something entirely unexpected happened and we can imagine that the story of this event was told and re-told during Rebecca's childhood. The Assyrian Empire collapsed and, for a brief, golden moment, Judah experienced a return to power when King Josiah was able to reassert some independence for the southern kingdom. However, this time of hope did not last as Egypt rose to prominence and Josiah was killed (2 Kings 23.29–30). He was replaced by a puppet ruler under Egyptian control. Things changed again when Rebecca was seven years old; at the battle of Carchemish, Egypt was defeated by another rising superpower – the kingdom of Babylon.

What this meant for Rebecca was that most of her life was dominated by one geographical fact: Judah lay directly between the two rival powers of Babylon and Egypt. King Nebuchadnezzar of Babylon continued to regard Egypt as a threat and Judah became a pawn in his foreign policy. Rebecca would have grown up watching her government vacillate between submitting to Babylonian demands (including paying taxes, which was about as popular then as it is now) and attempting to resist the power of Babylon, normally by creating some kind of alliance with Egypt (Birch et al., 2005, pp. 330–1). When Rebecca was 14 Judah paid the price for all of these attempts at independence. Nebuchadnezzar punished Judah by invading and decided to ensure that they would be more compliant in the future. All the leading citizens (in other words, everyone whom the Babylonians assessed as most likely to cause them problems) were deported and taken to live in Babylon, with the aim that those left behind would be docile and easy to rule.

We have an inscription from the time of Nebuchadnezzar which states that he appointed in Jerusalem 'the king of his liking, took heavy booty from it, and brought it into Babylon' (Smith-Christopher, 2002, p. 57). The attitude of the conquerors was plain; the people and the property of the land they conquered became theirs, which meant that they could loot, massacre or transport into exile at will. It is worth remembering that being a victim of someone else's power can increase the sense of suffering. Your pain is not the result of a natural disaster or an accident, and somehow the knowledge that an adversary has inflicted the pain upon you can increase the agony that is felt.

Let us imagine that Rebecca's own family has been divided on the question of how Israel should respond to Babylon's demands. Her brother and her husband dream of the glory days of King David when Israel was a great and independent kingdom and want to stand up to Babylon. Her father thinks this is dangerous and overestimates what Judah (even allied with Egypt) can achieve, and wants to pacify the brutal superpower. He keeps reminding the rest of the family that if one country unsuccessfully attempts to stand up to another it is often the ordinary folk who pay the price. It is possible to get a sense of just how confusing and painful this time was by reading Jeremiah 28, which tells of an argument between two prophets about how Israel should respond.

In 587 BC Rebecca and her family, along with the rest of Judah, faced a far more terrifying invasion. This was a key moment in Israel's history when it seemed that all hope collapsed and their worst fears came true. During this second invasion everything that Rebecca and her fellow citizens of Jerusalem most valued was destroyed:

- The king was dragged away in shame and the dynasty of David came to an end.
- Jerusalem itself was utterly destroyed. Since Rebecca lived in Jeru-

salem she would have been defenceless before the invading army and subject to attack and rape. Her husband and father were killed. Her home and all her most beloved possessions were ransacked.
- The Temple of Jerusalem, which was seen as the symbol of the assured presence of God with God's people, was totally devastated. (Adapted from Birch et al., 2005, p. 334)

What did this mean to Rebecca herself? It is difficult to describe just how devastating it must have been when everything that was most precious to her was taken away. This happened after a lifetime of dread and insecurity; the worst that she had feared for so long had now happened. As an individual, Rebecca herself endured physical abuse, the loss of family members, the destruction of her possessions, and possibly a life as a refugee in a foreign land (historians disagree about just what percentage of the population were taken to Babylon). As part of the people of Israel she also faced the death of the national dream of greatness. The great symbols of her faith had been destroyed along with any illusions she might have had about the power of her country. God's people were not the celebrated country to which others looked in awe and admiration, but a small and insignificant nation caught up in the power politics of empires. We could describe this as a corporate experience of shame as the people of Israel discovered that they were far weaker and less important than they had thought. It is hard to imagine the misery and psychological devastation this must have brought. Rebecca lived in a sinful world and had become one of its many victims – and being a member of the people of Israel had not protected her.

Rebecca is, of course, just a convenient way to describe what, according to the First Testament, happened to thousands of people. Telling one person's story is one way to make the struggle of the many others more real, and it matters that we remember just how horrific that time was. It is easy for us when reading the First Testament as Scripture, and looking for God to speak to us today, to spiritualize the story and somehow downplay the fact that it describes devastation and suffering.

So having tried to grasp just how appalling a tragedy the Exile was, we now need to ask how the people of Israel reacted to this suffering. What can we learn from them about what it means to have faith when you are faced by oppression from powers that are greater than you? We start with one idea that most biblical scholars agree about and that helps us to better understand the First Testament. It seems that the Jews responded to the crisis of invasion and of the dispersion of their population by editing and writing down their stories of faith and their most precious literature. Ancient culture was an oral culture in which only a few people could read and write, so the stories of Israel – as well as their laws and guidance for living – were first handed on by being told and re-told again and again. We must distinguish between the first telling, the repeating through time and the last edit, and writing down of the same. Scholars estimate that something like two-thirds of the First Testament reached final form either during or immediately after the Exile. In particular, the Pentateuch and the histories of Israel were edited and written down by different schools, and the disciples of various prophets wrote down the teachings that they had preserved.

It is worth pausing and thinking about how remarkable that assumption is. Faced with an overwhelming crisis and experience of national shame, the Jews responded with an amazing outburst of creativity. It would have been easy to have decided that God had abandoned them, or that he had never existed or cared for them in the first place. They could have turned to other, apparently more powerful, gods – especially those of their conquerors (and, indeed, some did). Instead it seems that many Jews responded by turning to their stories and resources of faith and telling them over and over again, writing them down so that they might be preserved and carried wherever the people of Israel might find themselves.

Knowing this tells us something remarkable about the very nature of the First Testament. One of the most common clichés about history is that it is always written by the winners. It appears that the First Testament is one of the great exceptions to this rule; the vast majority of it was written down either at a time when the Jews had most conclusively lost everything that they most cared about, or as they were beginning to recover from the loss. It was written down, therefore, by people asking themselves the kind of questions that all people who are suffering ask themselves. Why is this happening to us? Will our suffering ever end? How is it to be borne? Alongside those questions were the doubts that suffering throws up for people of faith. Where is God in all this? If she is a great God, why has she not looked after us and prevented this happening?

Here I might mention those parts of the First Testament that my neat summary has passed over. If we emphasize only Two Exits, an Exodus and an Exile, this misses out the story of the Patriarchs that is told in the rest of Genesis and the story of Israel after the Exodus. We have passed over the taking of the Promised Land, the rise of the monarchy and the reign of David in particular, along with the division of the land into two kingdoms and the events leading up to the Exile. If scholars are correct about when Israel re-told, edited and wrote down these stories, then what we have in the First Testament are stories of Israel's greatest times and tales of their illustrious heroes and heroines told during their worst times, while meditating on what had gone wrong.

How, then, did the people of Israel respond to this crisis and what can we learn about living in a sinful world from the stories and the literature that they have left us? It is not surprising that they responded in a variety of ways and we can find within the First Testament – and particularly in the stories of the Exile itself – a number of reactions to what happened. I want to suggest that each of these responses is useful in terms of our project of seeking to help those with shame-ache and seeking to understand Abel as much as Cain:

- Total and utter rage alongside profound expressions of misery.
- A grappling with the sense that this was all their fault, and that if they had only done better this would not have happened.
- A call to live differently.
- A re-interpretation of suffering and the very way that God is seen in the midst of suffering.

Let's look at each of those reactions in turn.

## Rage, Utter Rage and Lament

We start with the most human of responses: it is quite clear that the people of Israel responded to the devastation of what had happened with expressions of rage and misery. The depth and clarity with which they expressed this can be quite a shock to those who are expecting that Scripture will be full of spiritually uplifting sayings (and nothing else) and who read these for the first time. Rather than somehow rising above what had happened, the biblical writers give full vent to bitterness, resentment and the open desire for revenge. The one thing that they did not do was put a brave face on it and pretend it did not really matter. They gave voice, before God, to their anger and their misery and did not hold back. We can imagine Rebecca herself crying out the first few verses of Lamentations:

> How lonely sits the city
> that once was full of people!
> How like a widow she has become,
> she that was great among the nations!
> She that was a princess among the provinces
> has become a vassal.
>
> She weeps bitterly in the night,
> with tears on her cheeks;
> among all her lovers
> she has no one to comfort her;
> all her friends have dealt treacherously with her,
> they have become her enemies.
>
> Judah has gone into exile with suffering
> and hard servitude;
> she lives now among the nations,
> and finds no resting-place;
> her pursuers have all overtaken her
> in the midst of her distress.
>
> The roads to Zion mourn,
> for no one comes to the festivals;
> all her gates are desolate,
> her priests groan;
> her young girls grieve,
> and her lot is bitter.     (Lam. 1.1–4)

Compare this with the profound pressure in so many churches for Christians to always emphasize the positive and talk about the good things that God has done. The Bible is much more honest than we are about the feelings that such experiences can evoke. There is something here about honesty before God and with ourselves and those around us, as well as the reality that the exodus of faith can be hard and confusing.

But there is more to be said since the above passage deals only with the feelings and experiences of the Israelites themselves. How were they supposed to respond to those who injured them? If some Christians struggle to admit that life is difficult and to give voice to lament, it can be even more difficult to be honest about another possible reaction: anger towards those who hurt you. The pressure to always be 'nice' can be immense in some churches; it is simply not acceptable to admit that you are feeling angry or bitter about the actions of another.

In comparison with the struggle of many Christians to avoid admitting just how deeply angry they really are, the ancient Israelites appear to have had no problems in admitting to, and even writing, psalms about, their bitterness:

> By the rivers of Babylon—
> there we sat down and there we wept
> when we remembered Zion.
> On the willows there
> we hung up our harps.
> For there our captors
> asked us for songs,
> and our tormentors asked for mirth, saying,
> 'Sing us one of the songs of Zion!'
>
> How could we sing the LORD's song
> in a foreign land?
> If I forget you, O Jerusalem,
> let my right hand wither!
> Let my tongue cling to the roof of my mouth,
> if I do not remember you,
> if I do not set Jerusalem
> above my highest joy.
>
> Remember, O LORD, against the Edomites
> the day of Jerusalem's fall,
> how they said, 'Tear it down! Tear it down!
> Down to its foundations!'
> O daughter Babylon, you devastator!
> Happy shall they be who pay you back
> what you have done to us!

> Happy shall they be who take your little ones
> and dash them against the rock! (Ps. 137)

The book of Psalms is commonly seen as the prayer book of ancient Israel, a collection of words used in prayer and worship over thousands of years, and adopted by the Church for the same purpose. It contains some wonderful words of praise and exultation, but it also contains this expression of bitterness and desire for revenge. This is not an easy psalm to handle in worship; imagine responding to the last couple of verses with 'This is the Word of the Lord'! However, the very fact that it entered and was retained in the prayer book of Israel and of the Church tells us something very important about what it means to live in a sinful world where we might be the ones sinned against by someone else.

First, it reminds us that genuine interactions with God must include the whole range of our experience. If we can only ever tell God about the good things in life, then we become voiceless or, even worse, complicit in the kind of faith that is more about coercive obedience than trusting faith in a loving God (Brueggemann, 1986, pp. 60–1). If we propagate the kind of faith where God is all-powerful and must be praised whatever happens, we risk pushing people further into shame and resentment; it is easy to assume that if God is always right then I must always be wrong – and therefore responsible for sins done against me. This is not a biblical faith; in Scripture God is powerful, but does not use that power against us – and arguing with God, as well as expressing lament and anger, are both positively encouraged.

Second, it reminds us that expressing our anger before God can be healing. Brueggemann puts it like this:

> Such cathartic utterances are also an honest and courageous practice of prayer. They offer an opportunity for turning brutalizing loss into an act of faith that may in turn issue into positive energy. These speech practices give us a way to vent our rage at loss without letting it escalate into actions that will hurt our neighbors. (Brueggemann, 1997, p. 631)

I think that I would want to go further and say that the inclusion of such words in Scripture tells us something very important about such emotions and how we should deal with them. They are part of the human condition and it is too easy to be ashamed simply because of how we feel. In too many churches the implication of much of what is said is that good Christians should not have such experiences and feelings, and there is a very strong pressure to pretend or to suppress any hint of anger or hurt at what has happened to us. Church and prayer therefore become exercises in hiding the emotions we feel, which risks isolating us from the worshipping community and increasing our sense that we are only acceptable if we conform to a particular understanding or way of being (Boulton, 2002, p. 59).

Psalm 137 (alongside other psalms) encourages us to believe that such emotions belong before God. It is possible to be frightened and shamed by the depth of our own anger. Yet those who do struggle with an anger they think they should not feel can be shocked by the rage expressed in this psalm; it is unlikely that they are experiencing anger that strong. If God can cope with a psalm that wants revenge by smashing the brains of children, then God can cope with the very worst that we feel. There is something here about the appropriate way to own and express our anger, while knowing that we are loved; this brings us back to the knowledge that anger belongs before God with whom we can be totally honest. As Brueggemann says, owning and expressing our anger is a way of preventing it from escalating into actions.

## It Was All Our Fault

Rage is not the only response that we can find in the story of the Exile. Now we come to one of the most common themes of the First Testament and one of the reasons why it is vital to read about sin and shame together, rather than assuming that the only way we can deal with shame is to deny the reality of sin. The First Testament speaks of sin quite regularly and we cannot avoid this. The prophets of Israel regularly reminded the people that God had called them to be holy and gracious to the outsider and generous to the weak and vulnerable. This was their calling, but they had failed to live up to it. The disaster of the Exile had overtaken them because God was punishing them for their sins.

We could read this as a variant of what is a common reaction among people who are oppressed by others or who become refugees; they look back on their own history and assume that this disaster came upon them because they are cursed, sinful or doomed. Daniel Smith-Christopher gives a number of examples:

- Cambodians in the late 1970s who argued that Cambodian culture had bad karma.
- Cree Indian Christians in Canada who lamented that their shamans had lost their powers because they had abused them in the past, using them for self-gain rather than the good of others.
- Armenian clergy who explained that they suffered at the hands of the Turks as a result of their own sinfulness. (Smith-Christopher, 2002, pp. 80–1)

We remember again that those sinned against can often respond with shame and self-blame even when, in fact, they were innocent and did nothing to cause what happened to them. It is commonly noted that such an attitude can be seen as a form of coping mechanism that offers a strange kind of hope. After all, if our suffering is our fault then there is some kind of hope that by acting differently we can do something about our situation. In this way even the oppressed can find some kind of power and self-definition and grounds for optimism about their future.

The Israelites, however, were often told by their prophets that the Exile was their fault, so we are dealing here with something other than the Israelites' own instinctive assumptions. Running through the First Testament (remember that most of it was written down while thinking about the Exile) is a persistent warning that the people of Israel cannot assume that, because they are God's people, they will somehow be protected whatever. They are given the Torah and warned that they must live according to the Torah in order to prosper (Deut. 4). When the Exile comes, the prophets keep saying that the Exile happened because the Israelites forgot this most basic command. To give just one example:

> For from the least to the greatest of them,
> everyone is greedy for unjust gain;
> and from prophet to priest,
> everyone deals falsely.
> They have treated the wound of my people carelessly,
> saying, 'Peace, peace',
> when there is no peace.
> They acted shamefully, they committed abomination;
> yet they were not ashamed,
> they did not know how to blush.
> Therefore they shall fall among those who fall;

> at the time that I punish them, they shall be overthrown,
> says the LORD.
> Thus says the LORD:
> Stand at the crossroads, and look,
> and ask for the ancient paths,
> where the good way lies; and walk in it,
> and find rest for your souls.
> But they said, 'We will not walk in it.'
> Also I raised up sentinels for you:
> 'Give heed to the sound of the trumpet!'
> But they said, 'We will not give heed.'
> Therefore hear, O nations,
> and know, O congregation, what will happen to them.
> Hear, O earth; I am going to bring disaster on this people,
> the fruit of their schemes,
> because they have not given heed to my words;
> and as for my teaching, they have rejected it. (Jer. 6.13–19)

So, we are faced with a number of issues. Is this simply another version of the response mentioned above, with the prophets (who, after all, were also part of the people of Israel) joining in – in other words, this disaster was our fault and therefore we can do something about it by returning to the Torah and living differently? Is this an example of blaming the victim? If we return to the story of Rebecca for a moment, are we really saying that, having suffered a childhood made insecure by the power politics of different nations and having now been raped, looted and separated from all she loves, the response that God demands from her is to repent of her sins and accept that it was all her fault? This seems on the face of things to be a return to the judgemental God that some Christians assume is the God of the First Testament – the one who has only the law to offer and who punishes those who do not keep it. In terms of our theme this would make God someone who inflicts shame on the weakest and most vulnerable as well as anyone who does not live as he wants them to live.

We need to be abundantly clear that our image of God matters. It is possible to read the First Testament and find a God who demands that people grovel in their sins and who keeps insisting that they should have listened to her, the all-knowing, all-perfect supreme being, but only if we focus on a selected group of passages. If this is the God we find, then this is exactly the God that a person suffering from shame-ache will do everything to avoid. However, we cannot ignore the fact that one prominent theme is that the people sinned and, as a result, were sent into Exile – how are we to deal with this? This is where it matters that large parts of the First Testament were written down either during or after the Exile.

Remembering the connection between the writing down of the First Testament and the Exile, it is not surprising that the issues raised by this disaster shaped the way that the stories were told. What went wrong? How did we end up here? As they re-told their stories of faith, the Israelites emphasized that God had given them the Torah – guidance for how best to live and laws to shape their society and their living together – but that this guidance had often been ignored. The people turned away from God and suffered the consequences. However, this is not the whole story as they grappled with their crisis. In Chapter 5 we are going to look at Job and we will discover there a theological battle. The theology of his friends says, do right and God will be with you, do wrong and God will punish you. The conclusion they draw is that things have gone wrong for you, therefore God must be punishing you. Job's complaint in return is not that his friends were wrong – but that their understanding of God was truth but not the whole truth. God cares about justice and right living because he cares about Abel and victims of sin and because living by the Torah was a way for the Israelites to flourish. Job does not deny that sin is real and has real consequences, nor that a just God should punish an unjust person. His argument is more subtle – the problem lies in the idea that this must be universally applied, so that we can always assume that if there is suffering, it is the person who suffers who must have sinned.

Whenever the prophets denounced the sins of the people of Israel they were speaking to all the people or to the powerful leaders who had, in their eyes, led the people astray. The bitterest complaints in the First Testament are not addressed to individuals, inviting them to an internal psychological response of shame and self-blame, but are addressed to those who failed to lead the people of God in the ways of God, commanding them to lead differently in future. Those leaders have, it seems, become caught up in that most complacent form of faith that assumes that God is always on the believer's side and will protect the believer regardless, no matter how evil their behaviour or how carelessly they may live. The prophets demand that they return to what is good, and eventually begin to argue that God himself will come to replace those leaders:

> The word of the LORD came to me: Mortal, prophesy against the shepherds of Israel: prophesy, and say to them – to the shepherds: Thus says the Lord GOD: Ah, you shepherds of Israel who have been feeding yourselves! Should not shepherds feed the sheep? You eat the fat, you clothe yourselves with the wool, you slaughter the fatlings; but you do not feed the sheep. You have not strengthened the weak, you have not healed the sick, you have not bound up the injured, you have not brought back the strayed, you have not sought the lost, but with force and harshness you have ruled them. So they were scattered, because there was no shepherd; and scattered, they became food for all the wild animals. My sheep were scattered, they wandered over all the mountains and on every high hill; my sheep were scattered over all the face of the earth, with no one to search or seek for them. (Ezek. 34.1–6)

There is no hint here that each individual involved in the Exile was being punished for their own personal sin; instead, the issue is that the leaders of Israel have let down the Rebeccas of their world and have failed in the most basic part of their leadership. The complaints of the prophets reflect the idea that the Exile was a national tragedy before it was a personal one.

Our issue, therefore, is how to read these passages today. We live in a culture in which faith is seen as a profoundly personal issue; it is all about my individual relationship with God, and membership of the Church or attendance at worship is seen as a choice that I make, not part of being a good member of society. We need to recognize that this is a profound change in understanding, not just from when the Scriptures were written down, but even, for example, from the sixteenth century when some of our traditional prayers were either written or re-shaped for public worship. Our culture encourages us to read the Bible individualistically and, in particular, to read everything that the Bible says about sin as a personal condemnation. If the Bible speaks about sin and judgement, then the issue has to be *my* sin and whether or not *I* will be judged. It is this culturally conditioned reading of Scripture that can lead us to the assumption that if the Exile raises the issue of who sinned, God must be blaming Rebecca for the tragedy that overtook her. What we miss if we are not careful is that the question in the Exile is that of the identity and behaviour of the whole people of God, not of one chronically shamed person. The expected response to the great prophetic pronouncements is not to mire a single person in guilt, but to challenge a nation to find a different way of seeing and living.

This brings us to a key verse in the passage from Jeremiah quoted above: 'They acted shamefully, they committed abomination; yet they were not ashamed, they did not know how to blush' (Jer. 6.15). If shame is damaging when it becomes shame-ache and distorts a person's whole life, then so is being shameless – particularly if it is a leader, a nation or a powerful organization that does not know how to blush. We will look later at the concept of honour and the importance of a person who has power demonstrating that they have integrity and a sense of what behaviour is appropriate and what is not. This is intimately linked with the ability to feel proper shame. That sense of what is shameful and what is not can apply to nations and organizations as well as people (see Jacquet, 2016, for a passionate argument that the shame and the ability to shame the most powerful is a vital tool in the face of our current climate crisis).

It is not difficult to think of times in the history of the Church when the idea that we are the people of God, and therefore God must always be on our side has had the most appalling results; the Crusades, the encouragement of antisemitism and the Inquisition spring to mind. Equally, we can name some examples when a nation's refusal to accept appropriate shame has had disastrous consequences. Daniel Smith-Christopher cites the Turkish refusal to acknowledge the massacre of Armenians or the way in which the Serbian Orthodox Church refuses to acknowledge the savage genocide of Bosnia. Having been born in Britain, I need to acknowledge the evil of the British Empire and what was inflicted on others in the name of a supposedly civilized society, along with our part in the devastation of the slave trade. Smith-Christopher quotes the Turkish social historian Taner Akçam, who comments:

> A society, a state does not like to confront an imagery that is at variance with its self imagery, and, as such, is likely to destroy its world

fantasies. Herein lies the reason for our sharp reaction to those who call our attention to that reality. (Smith-Christopher, 2002, p. 122)

Compare this to the picture of Israel that we find in the First Testament. When the people of God tell their history it is clear that they are not indulging in the fantasy of being a people who are always right, and they are not defining patriotism as 'my country right or wrong'. The story does not hesitate to lay bare the weaknesses of even their ultimate heroes. David, Israel's greatest monarch and the symbol of all of her hopes, is an ambiguous figure who is both full of faith, courageous and capable of the deepest of friendships, but also corruptible, using his power to have sex with Bathsheba and to murder her husband. In one of the iconic stories about David, the true hero is Nathan, the prophet who dares to confront even Israel's king when that king does not live as a king should (2 Sam. 12). We will return to this story later. In other words, the entire First Testament denies what has often been the delusion of religious people – that somehow God is always on our side and so we must always be right and successful. To put the matter at its simplest, the issue in the First Testament is: does our behaviour demonstrate that we are on God's side – and do we know how to blush when appropriate?

The First Testament gives an example of an ancient people who were willing to read their own history critically. We need to think carefully about how we read this today in our much more individualistic society that tempts us to read the constant denunciations of sin and the regular prayers of penitence as addressed to us personally. The result can be that we respond with 'paralysing personal guilt' rather than seeing them as a call to recognize alternative values and to read the history of the people of Israel with eyes open to the weaknesses of Rebecca's ancestors as well as their strengths. The issue in the First Testament is not feelings, or even the psychological scars of shame-ache (although this can make a huge difference to how we respond), but how we shape our behaviour and identity and the shame that makes us sensitive to our mistakes and determined to live differently in the future (Smith-Christopher, 2002, pp. 120–1), as well as the issue of holding our leaders to account. There is a way of interpreting shame as being about a proper concern for others and a form of modesty that is vigilant to one's own tendencies. When nations or organizations are powerful, it matters to remember how to blush. In this way, what comes out of the Exile is a form of hope,

hope that asks us to imagine a new way of living that will not repeat the mistakes of the old.

However, we can go one step further in asking what came out of the Exile.

## Thinking Again about God and Suffering

The book of Isaiah contains four passages that are now commonly referred to as the 'servant songs' and that you will find in Isaiah 42.1–4, Isaiah 49.1–6, Isaiah 50.4–9 and Isaiah 52.13—53.12. They are often read alongside several psalms, especially Psalm 22. My guess is that it is the passage from Isaiah 53 that Christians know best; the opening verses of that chapter read as follows:

> Who has believed what we have heard?
>     And to whom has the arm of the Lord been revealed?
> For he grew up before him like a young plant,
>     and like a root out of dry ground;
> he had no form or majesty that we should look at him,
>     nothing in his appearance that we should desire him.
> He was despised and rejected by others;
>     a man of suffering and acquainted with infirmity;
> and as one from whom others hide their faces
>     he was despised, and we held him of no account.
> Surely he has borne our infirmities
>     and carried our diseases;
> yet we accounted him stricken,
>     struck down by God, and afflicted.
> But he was wounded for our transgressions,
>     crushed for our iniquities;
> upon him was the punishment that made us whole,
>     and by his bruises we are healed.
> All we like sheep have gone astray;
>     we have all turned to our own way,
> and the Lord has laid on him
>     the iniquity of us all. (Isa. 53.1–6)

This is a passage that we read most commonly during Lent or when thinking about the suffering of Jesus, and for many Christians all we need to say about this passage is Isaiah prophesied that Jesus would suffer to save us from our sins and that this prophecy was fulfilled on the cross. Often it seems that we believe that is all that we need to say about this and similar passages.

For biblical scholars, however, the picture is quite different. A huge amount has been written debating who, exactly, this servant is and the significance of this sense that an innocent suffered as part of a divinely inspired mission. In fact, Westermann argues that the biblical text is deliberately mysterious on the issue and that we should take this into account when interpreting the passage (Westermann, 1980, p. 95). It is, however, generally noted that when Jews read this passage they assume it refers to the entire people of Israel, not to a single figure.

So, here is a question. Can we bring these two worlds together and learn something by not leaping too quickly to the notion that this is a prophecy about Jesus and that is all that is being said? We can acknowledge that this is a remarkable description of what Jesus endured, written a long time before his birth, and that it would be true to say that in this sense he fulfilled this passage, but that does not need to be all that we say. This is the truth but not the whole truth about Isaiah 53. If we pause to read this passage as coming from a prophet who did more than just forecast a life that was to come, then we will have a richer reading of the passage itself and also understand Christ and his mission more fully.

As part of doing this, we can highlight the following.

The passage begins at the end of chapter 52 with Isaiah promising salvation and the coming reign of God. God is going to return to Jerusalem and redeem his people and therefore people should rejoice. What is more, God has 'bared his holy arm' before all nations, so this is not simply about what will happen to Israel – it is greater than that (Isa. 52.7–10). This salvation is going to be astonishing; people are going to be startled and kings will be silenced because of what happens (Isa. 52.14–15).

The servant lacks one of the traits most commonly associated with being blessed. He is not physically attractive and there is nothing about him that would command the attention of others, and this is in contrast to some other biblical heroes such as Joseph (whose good looks get him into trouble (Gen. 39.6)) and David, where the writer does attempt to have things both ways. In 1 Samuel 16, Samuel is told in verse 6 that the outward appearance does not matter because the Lord looks on the heart, but when David appears in verse 12 he is immediately described as handsome with beautiful eyes. Not only is the servant in Isaiah 53 not physically attractive, he is also despised and rejected and others do not hold him in high regard (Isa. 53.3). In fact, when awful things happen to this servant, the general assumption is that God has struck him down (Isa. 53.4). He becomes a victim of injustice in verse 8 and is buried with the wicked in verse 9. It might appear therefore that God has turned against him but Isaiah's point is the exact opposite. Isaiah is doing something remarkable here and redefining what it means to be a servant of God. To be God's representative and to do God's work on earth is not going to mean glory, riches, power or even the esteem of others – it is going to mean shame, suffering and injustice. This is not how we assume that God will work and yet, somehow, God brings healing and salvation not despite this suffering but through it.

So what happens if we reflect on this passage as not simply a prophecy about Jesus but as a description of what it means to be a servant of God (which Jesus exemplified), and even as a passage that challenges our understanding of what it means to serve God in a sinful world? What if we allow these servant songs to shape our understanding of the very ways of God in the world and even of the nature of God herself? What if this radically alters our sense of how God responds to sin and shame and to the human victim of both? Might this provide a vital background for understanding the God and Father of Jesus?

I believe it does and we will pick up this theme again in later chapters.

# 3

# Recovering Abel and Learning from Cain

> I have yet to see a serious act of violence that was not provoked by the experience of feeling shamed or humiliated, disrespected and ridiculed, and that did not represent the attempt to prevent or undo this 'loss of face' – no matter how severe the punishment, even if it includes death. (Gilligan, 1996, p. 110)

When Cain murdered Abel he thought he had got rid of his brother. Knowing that his brother was gone, it was natural for him also to assume that Abel had been silenced; after all, we do not expect that dead people will speak. What a shock, therefore, when he discovered that this was not the case and that, according to God, Abel's blood was 'crying out to me from the ground' (Gen. 4.10).

When Cain murdered Abel (if my reading is correct) he was reacting (in the most extreme way) to his own shame and hitting out at the vulnerable to avoid his own pain. Naturally, his story does not mean that all people who struggle with shame-ache will respond in the same way, but it does challenge us to think deeply about how we respond to shame. Would Cain have reacted differently if he had had greater self-respect? Or do we need to reflect carefully on what Genesis 3 says about the multiple causes of sin and to avoid falling into the trap of believing that all anyone needs in order to behave better is more confidence and a greater love for self? The relationship between sin and shame is multi-faceted and we will need to return to it. However, one of my arguments in this book is that, in general, Christian theology has said too much about the sinner and not enough about those damaged by sin, so we are going to start this chapter by paying attention to Cain's victim and try to turn down, for now, the overly loud voice of the offender.

There is comfort in the thought that the voice of the victim of sin is not silent before God; Abel's blood cried out from the ground and God listened. I want to suggest, though, that knowing this also raises major issues for us. If it matters to God that the silenced one is enabled to speak and be heard, should it not matter to us as well? The quiet, the passive, those whose lives have been fundamentally shaped or even destroyed by the bad acts of another, do they also have to live and die knowing that *only* God hears their cry, or do we need to work harder at recovering their voices, even as we read Scripture itself? For the purposes of this chapter I have called this the 'recovering Abel' project. The ways in which we understand sin and forgiveness have been shaped by our excessive attention to the voice and the needs of Cain and our lack of attention to the voice of Abel. On my reading, Abel was also struggling with shame and his response was to become quiet and retreat into himself. My thesis throughout this chapter is that being sinned against does something to us and that we need to understand what this is before we can begin to speak about the interrelationship of sin and shame, let alone the thorny issue of what forgiveness might actually mean. We need to examine carefully why it is that the offender may respond to what happens with guilt, but far too often the injured party experiences shame, even when they have done nothing to deserve what has happened to them.

However, let us start with a fundamental question that might seem to undercut my argument from the beginning. Doesn't the Bible say that we can only sin against God?

## Psalm 51 versus the Lord's Prayer

Consider these three Scripture verses:

> Psalm 51.4: 'Against you, you alone, have I sinned, and done what is evil in your sight.'
> Luke 11.4: 'And forgive us our sins [*hamartias*], for we ourselves forgive everyone indebted [*opheilonti*] to us.'
> Matthew 6.12: 'And forgive us our debts [*opheilēmata*], as we also have forgiven our debtors [*opheiletais*]'.

The two verses from Matthew and Luke are, of course, slight variants on one line of the prayer that Jesus taught his disciples and which Christians pray on a regular basis. That prayer is fundamental not simply to Christian prayer, but also to Christian living. It would seem obvious, therefore, that Jesus' own prayer, taught to his disciples, which is clear about the basic assumption that we can sin against other people as well as against God, would dominate Christian theology and provide the context from which we then interpret Psalm 51 – in which the speaker claims to have sinned only against God. Instead, for some at least, it seems that the opposite has happened: the statement attributed to David has dominated our understanding so that it has become commonplace to ignore the Lord's Prayer and to assert that sin can be committed against God only.

It is worth pausing and reflecting on how convenient this is to both the sinner and the most powerful. What really matters in faith, we tell ourselves, is our relationship with God. When I sin, therefore, this is the only relationship that needs attention and I can find forgiveness by means of an entirely private transaction between me and God (and possibly a priest). With my conscience thus relieved, I can continue on my way without ever having to deal with the person who has been injured by my actions. This is, of course, something of an exaggeration and is by no means a description of how all Christians act, but it is a potential weakness to which we need to give attention.

But what of Psalm 51? This psalm is traditionally attributed to David and is said to have been written while reflecting on his appalling actions in using his position as king to coerce sex from Bathsheba and then to cause the death of her husband Uriah. We are going to look at this story more fully in the next chapter, and one of the ideas that we will examine then is the difficulty of holding an ancient king to account. The action of Nathan the prophet in standing up to the king and declaring his actions sinful is extraordinary when seen in a historic context. However, while it might be a step forward to say that if an ancient king simply took what he wanted without thought to the consequences, this was in fact a sin for which God would hold him accountable. Therefore we do need to ask questions when we simply take that idea and make it generally applicable to everyone, and conclude that all sin is committed against God only. This is particularly the case when in doing so we contradict Jesus.

So that is my first argument. The Lord's Prayer makes it clear that it is possible to sin against another human being and that God cares deeply when we do, and therefore our understanding of sin and forgiveness needs to take this into account. This is not all we can learn from these verses, however. Notice that the metaphor used to convey what sin is like has changed. In the First Testament sin was seen primarily as a weight or a burden and this gave us one useful way to speak of what sin does to the sinner. In the New Testament, however, the image changes and sin is often pictured as a debt or as creating a debt, and I am going to argue that this is a helpful metaphor if we want to look at what sin does to the person who is sinned against. We will come back to this.

For now, I am going to take it that it is appropriate to speak of sinning against another human being and that, since this is the case, it matters to explore the impact of other people's sins upon someone like Abel. This is a vital part of the project to recover Abel and to listen to the voice of the sinned against, particularly if we want to be attentive to issues of shame. Being sinned against can shape who we are and how we act in profound ways and we need to be able to take this into account. This will also begin to raise for us some fundamental questions about who we are.

## On Vulnerable Vines and Impervious Islands

We have already seen that a basic theme of the First Testament is that understanding sin and how it influences us means more than just the issue of forgiveness. According to the First Testament:

- Sin creates a cycle of shame and blame that corrupts human life and behaviour.
- Being oppressed by the sin of others shapes who we are so that liberation involves more than just the ending of the oppression. It also needs an exodus, a continual struggle out of one way of life and towards another.
- Living in a sinful world involves a number of different faithful responses, including bringing our anger before God, praying for and imagining a different world, and seeking to live differently.

Sin in biblical language is a *power*; it traps us and distorts our living in any number of ways. What this means is that the First Testament has a far more nuanced approach to human identity than a great deal of what passes for Christian discussion about sin.

To open this up more fully I want to look at an idea that theologians have explored when discussing how to speak of sin today. Let's start with an image of human life that most of us will be familiar with:

> No man is an island entire of itself; every man is a piece of the continent, a part of the main. (Donne, 1624)

John Donne lived in the seventeenth century (hence his non-inclusive language) and it is worth pondering the fact that since his death he has been much quoted, and yet the temptation to try to live as an island has only increased. Society has, as is regularly pointed out, become more and more individualistic. If we accept Donne's point and agree that we are not islands, can we say something about what we are? Is there another image that might give us some sense of how to describe *both* our interdependence *and* the importance of responsibility for our own actions? Donne himself suggested that we are part of a continent, an image that works well to give a simple contrast with being an island but that, taken on its own, might imply that all we are is a part of the whole. We need an image that both reminds us that we are not isolated beings, but also that we are not totally determined by outside forces either. For a more nuanced picture of human life I have gone for a different image, even while I recognize its weakness.

In some ways human beings are like vines. Jesus used this image, telling us, 'I am the vine, you are the branches' (John 15.5). He used the image to emphasize the disciples' dependence upon him and to urge us to 'abide' in him. We can stretch the image a little further. A vine is 'true to itself' when it grows; nothing from outside can make it a vine or force it to grow grapes. Its shape and existence are not totally defined by outside forces. Equally, however, it will normally grow up against or be entwined with something else and its final shape will generally be determined by whatever that 'something else' is. It needs food from the soil, water and sunshine in order to bear fruit and if one of these elements is missing it is likely to be stunted. As Jesus reminded us, it also benefits from the attention of a gardener.

What I am trying to describe with this image is what theologians have, with less descriptiveness but rather more accuracy, called 'the situated being' (McFadyen, 2000, p. 35). Describing people as 'situated beings' is an attempt to recognize the two different issues mentioned above. We are responsible beings, and any definition of sin that implies we are helplessly driven by factors entirely outside our control is deficient. At the same time, though, we live in situations that were created by outside forces, and both those situations and our inner lives have been distorted by sin – sins committed against us, sins we have committed, and the sinful forces and structures that shape the world in which we live. Human life is messy and complicated and we need to make sure that our theology reflects this.

Rowan Williams puts it like this:

> For human activity is misunderstood if it is seen as a sequence of responsible decisions taken by conscious and self-aware persons in control of their lives. More often it is a confused, partly conscious, partly instinctive response to the givenness of a world we do not dominate, a world of histories and ideas, languages and societies, structures we have not built. More perhaps than we ever realize or accept with our minds, we are being acted upon as much as acting. If our assumption of 'responsibility' rests on the belief that we can construct the patterns of our own lives, it is an illusion – not the child's evasiveness this time, but the infant's assumption of omnipotence. It is a hard lesson, this; we should all like to believe otherwise, but intentions are not enough. Reality is stronger. Our uncertainty about the degree of our responsibility need not be cowardly or self deceiving; it can be an honest acknowledgement of the way in which reality, even human and personal reality, resists the mind's desperate attempt to organize it reasonably. (Williams, 1995, p. 75)

In other words, a realistic assessment of our day-to-day lives will help us to see that we are not autonomous – or at least not always. The extent to which we get to decide our own actions is likely to be dependent upon circumstances and character, but even those of us fortunate enough to be relatively free from outside forces are still not totally self-sufficient. What is more, our behaviour today is influenced by what we did yesterday; I can build up habits, good and bad, and once a habit is established it can be remarkably difficult to break (at least the bad ones are; we all know that it is harder to form good habits and easier to forget them). In addition, we do not always recognize the extent to which we are influenced by those around us. Most adults like to consider ourselves to be independent thinkers, but there are plenty of studies that show that many of us behave differently in groups of people than we do when we are on our own. We are more conformist than we often realize.

Those who have read some Liberation Theology will recognize some of these themes. Liberation Theology has always insisted that structures can be sinful as well as people, but also that there is an interplay between our inner lives and our situations; personal sin and structural sin can feed each other (Gutiérrez, 2001, p. 74). As Gutiérrez argued:

> Sin, the breach with God, is not something which occurs only within some intimate sanctuary of the heart. It always moves into interpersonal relationships, and hence is the ultimate root of all injustice and oppression – as well as of the social confrontations conflicts of concrete history. (Gutiérrez, 1985, p. 147)

This can be a hard reality to face for those of us who live relatively privileged lives. We are insulated from the struggles of others by our wealth and/or race, gender, etc., and by having sufficient power and resources to live independently of others can make it easier to believe in our ultimate autonomy.

Genesis reminded us that there are many ways in which sin can shape our lives, but I am going to remain focused on shame and the effects of sin on those sinned against. How does the image of being a vulnerable vine help us when reflecting on our response to a world distorted by the cycle of shame and sin? Cain became aggressive and dominating; when things did not go his way he resorted to violence. We might argue that he needed to be reminded that he was his brother's keeper and that they were both formed by their experiences and that they would find a richer life in co-operation rather than competition. He needed to know that vines are vulnerable, shaped by outside forces for good or ill, and also that God cares about the impact of his actions on others. Abel, on the other hand, responded to shame by withdrawing into himself and becoming quiet and passive; we might argue that he needed to know that he was a vine and nothing else, and that being a vine comes from within and is important. He needed to be empowered and to be encouraged to believe in his own responsibility to shape and influence the world around him. We need a theology that is capable of speaking to both brothers and that can speak to those of us who are Cain at some times and Abel at others.

All of this may appear to be relatively straightforward and just common sense, until we begin to compare it with the ideas of sin that are preached in our sermons and suggested by our prayers and worship.

There, far too often, we imply that God is only interested in our personal sins and not in the sins done against us or in the situations that formed us and in which we live. Let's try out a concrete example.

Peter has an extremely difficult day at work; his immediate superior manages by bullying and today Peter bore the brunt of her anger. What is more he has always struggled with his memories of a distant and frequently angry mother who rarely offered any encouragement or expressions of love. On the way home he is cut up by another driver and drawn into a dangerous race which only ends when the other driver pulls off the motorway. On walking through the door at home he is met by his exhausted wife who wants to hand him the fractious toddler who has run her ragged all day. Peter shouts, walks out, and only returns two hours later.

Next Sunday, Peter goes to church. It is likely that in the prayers he will be encouraged to confess his own sins (so he might include the race on the motorway and his poor treatment of his wife), but it is much less likely that he will be given an opportunity to pray about the sins committed against him (so does God not care about his bullying boss or the actions of the other driver?). The emphasis is likely to be on whether his actions were sinful, and all his actions will be assumed to be wholly his fault, rather than allowing him to see himself as a vulnerable vine who both contributes to and struggles with the sins of the world. It is also unlikely that he will be given any time to reflect on the ongoing damage from his childhood, nor will he hear any reassurance that God cares as much about the damage done to him as she does about the damage he has done.

We absorb the theology that shapes our lives and our relationship with God from more than just theories, ideas and books. How we pray and worship, our own experience and thinking, our reading of Scripture and how Scripture is proclaimed in sermons, all of these profoundly influence our basic sense of who God is and how God sees us and we have already seen that our perception of how God sees us is both profoundly theological and basic to our struggle with shame. Peter is unconsciously absorbing something about what really matters to God from what is (and is not) mentioned in worship. There is too much within the Christian tradition that encourages him into a very narrow view of what sin is and too little that reminds him that his personal actions are the truth – but not the whole truth – about sin. We need a broader and more biblical theology that takes seriously how sin and the sinful world in which he lives has shaped him.

## Sin as a Debt

Let's return to the Lord's Prayer for a moment. When we first looked at the prayer, we saw that both Matthew and Luke use the idea of sin as debt. To be more specific, Matthew speaks of sin as both our debt to God and to others, while Luke makes a distinction, when speaking of God forgiving, by using a traditional word for sin that emphasizes loss; this word is sometimes translated as 'missing the mark' and he uses the image of debt when he speaks of us forgiving one another. The First Testament does use other images for sin – most notably *paraptoma*, which means a false step or a lapse and is often translated 'transgressions' – but this idea of sin as debt became key in the later part of the Bible. Anderson has shown that the image for sin moved from being a burden to be borne in the early part of the First Testament to being a debt to be repaid in the later part (particularly after the Exile), which is then taken up in the New Testament (Anderson, 2009, p. 27). This idea that sin creates a sense of debt can be fruitful in thinking about sins committed against other people and can help in the recovering Abel project by enabling us to reflect on what sin does to Abel and also what is involved in forgiving others.

We will now examine how other people's bad actions affect us. I am going to concentrate on those times when the injury is serious. When people live, work and play together there are likely to be one-off small insults, petty wrongdoings and general thoughtlessness; these matters may cause minor hurts, but can simply be laid aside and forgotten (although we will come back to those times when a small sin is constantly repeated). We are going to look at the injuries that damage us and that we cannot easily ignore, while acknowledging that dealing with injuries that are truly traumatic is another matter again, and take a greater expertise than I can offer. Linda Radzik, in her book *Making Amends: Atonement in Morality, Law and Politics*, argues that wrongdoing affects the injured, the offender and also the communities in which they live. She contends that when a wrong action is seen from the point of view of the injured it can be interpreted as both an insult and as a threat.

I admit that when I first read this argument it seemed a weak way to describe a potentially traumatic injury; however, as I lived with the idea for a while its usefulness began to become more apparent, not least because it demonstrated one way in which shame and injury might be intertwined. The concept of an insult, after all, relates to our sense of status and how we are valued and how we value other people; therefore it touches exactly on those parts of our self-understanding that are raised by shame. This is the heart of Radzik's argument – when she analyses wrongdoing as an insult she argues that the offender is, in effect, acting as if the injured has a status so low that the action does not matter. Jeffrie Murphy has put this particularly powerfully:

> One reason we so deeply resent moral injuries done to us is not simply that they hurt us in some tangible or sensible way; it is because such injuries are also messages – symbolic communications. They are ways a wrongdoer has of saying to us, 'I count but you do not,' 'I can use you for my purposes,' or 'I am up here high and you are there down below.' Intentional wrongdoing insults us and attempts (sometimes successfully) to degrade us – and thus it involves a kind of injury that is not merely tangible and sensible. It is moral injury, and we care about such injustices. (As Justice Holmes observed, even a dog notices and cares about the difference between being tripped over accidentally and kicked intentionally.) Most of us tend to care about what others (at least some others, some significant group whose good opinion we value) think about us – how much they think they matter. Our self-respect is social in at least this sense, and this is simply part of the human condition that we are weak and vulnerable in these ways. And last when we are treated with contempt by others it attacks us in profound and deeply threatening ways. We resent (or worse) those who so attack us, and want to separate ourselves from them – to harm them in turn or at least to banish them from the realm of those whose well-being should be our concern. (Murphy, in Murphy and Hampton, 1994, p. 25)

The idea that sins committed against us convey a message about how we are seen (and a threat that we might be treated the same way again) helps us to see why it is that so often the person who has been injured responds with shame. Let's illustrate this with some case studies.

Imagine for a moment that Angie kidnaps Bob. The range of possible injuries that he might suffer is wide – physical injury and possible mental and emotional trauma spring to mind. According to Radzik, there is an additional injury that Bob may never verbalize but that nevertheless matters. Angie has treated Bob as if he is available for her own ends and therefore demonstrated in her actions that he does not matter as much as whatever motive caused her to kidnap him in the first place. As far as Angie is concerned, her needs and ideas outrank Bob's.

Suppose, on the other hand, that Bertie pushes ahead of Andrea in a queue. Clearly, in this case the injury is much less serious, and it is highly unlikely that Andrea might be traumatized. However, the basic message behind the action remains the same. By pushing into the queue Bertie is declaring that 'My time is more important than yours', or 'It is fine that you have to wait but I matter more and therefore I should not have to'.

It is likely that Angie and Bertie gave no thought at all to any message that their actions might send; they were presumably so focused on themselves and their own needs that they simply did not think about Bob or Andrea at all. But this is part of the problem – the message was still sent. As part of the recovering Abel project we are deliberately concentrating on the viewpoint of Bob and Andrea; when we see the action through their eyes, we can also see that at some level this is what they are likely to pick up. Angie and Bertie have failed to treat them with the basic courtesy and respect that a human being deserves. When we are treated as unimportant – or at least as less important than the person who is mistreating us – there can be a blow to our self-respect, leading us to instinctively feel that the offender should do something to make it up to us. Another way of saying this would be to state that being treated badly creates a debt. There can be problems if either the offender or the injured prove unwilling or unable to acknowledge that debt.

Radzik provides a list of some of the damage that wrongdoing can cause (which I have amended slightly). The injured person may:

- doubt her own worth, either in her own eyes or the eyes of others;
- wonder whether he shares the blame for the wrongful act. He may criticize himself for being a bad judge of character or for failing to protect himself and/or others. He may also come to believe that he contributed to the wrong act because he is unlikeable or a fundamentally bad person;

- be left struggling with an apparently overpowering sense of resentment and anger. (Radzik, 2009, p. 78)

It is worth pausing for a moment and noticing that the first two responses are also descriptions of shame and the third can contribute to a sense of shame. Part of my argument is that those suffering from shame-ache are likely to be particularly vulnerable to the 'messages' that sins committed against them convey, and may have the greatest problem in rejecting the message and standing up for themselves. Instead, if they are Abel, they may simply accept that the action conveys the truth about their value and remain passive in the face of the insult or, if they are Cain, may find the message unbearable and react with an overwhelming anger that leads them to take revenge and inflict physical violence.

Let's take the analysis a little further. Radzik (and others) also argue that the insult offered by bad acts makes a claim and that there is a sense in which this claim is ongoing unless and until it is withdrawn. Past wrongs are not as easy to forget as we would like precisely because of this claim that the offender simply matters more than we do and, furthermore, if the injury is not acknowledged as wrong, there is an inherent threat that the offender will act in the same way again – which means there is an ongoing message that the injured person is inferior. The claim of the action is only nullified when another action makes a counterclaim that recognizes the evil of what was originally done and acknowledges that an injury occurred. This withdraws the threat of repetition, and is the significance of apologies, atonement, retribution, punishment, restitution, etc. Any of these actions make a counterclaim in that they demonstrate that the original action was wrong (Hieronymi, 2001, p. 546). Another way to say this would be: they pay back the debt and recognize the equal worth of the injured party.

This analysis of the effects of wrongdoing and the image of debts can help to explain another phenomenon that is rarely acknowledged in churches. Debts can accumulate slowly and incrementally as well as being created all at once. It seems to be the case for at least some people that being mistreated in a small way, and having that mistreatment constantly repeated, causes as much or even more damage than a single bad action. Anne Atkins is a broadcaster and journalist whose daughter disappeared for 37 hours before being found safe and well. She once commented:

> And why are some acts easier to forgive than others that may seem much worse? Some years ago, our 12-year-old went missing, we thought probably murdered (the police were scouring the Thames for her body). Yet in the two days before she turned up safe again, I felt no anger: I assumed her 'murderer' was sick, deprived and depraved. But being repeatedly wronged by a friend or Christian can be infinitely harder to bear. (Atkins, 2006)

Recognizing that moral injuries send messages and that they are both an insult and a threat gives us a way of beginning to answer Atkins's question: why should it be that 'some acts [are] easier to forgive than others that may seem much worse'? As she notes, the acts that she particularly struggles with are those that are done repeatedly by someone she knows, in that the debt slowly builds up. We are all aware of the difference between being hurt intentionally and being hurt when the injury was accidental, and of the difference it can make to know that the act in question was not done on purpose. If the act was accidental, then the message we receive from that act about our value in the eyes of the offender is correspondingly less personal and less threatening to us.

Equally, there is a difference in the message received from a major traumatic injury that is done only once (and done by a stranger) and a much less serious offence that is repeated over and over again by someone who ought to respect us more. There is something particularly harmful about a message that is replicated constantly; it is as if the drip, drip effect has a greater result than a single assault. Not only does the insult acquire greater power as it is repeated, but the ongoing threat that the injured will always be of less importance than the offender becomes clearer and clearer. Since we naturally care more about the opinion of those we know than we do about those we do not know, the insult feels correspondingly more personal. The debt accumulates and it becomes more and more obvious that the debtor intends to ignore it because he regards both it and the person injured as unimportant. What is more, the situation can only be made worse if the injured party attempts a conversation with the offender to deal with the issue, but is then brushed off as this adds yet another insult to the one that has already been dealt. I might add that comparisons are often less than helpful and nothing I have said is meant to downplay the horror of being the victim of a traumatic one-off crime.

What I do want to look at is the number of sermons that have been preached holding up a single appalling act that was forgiven as some kind of inspiring example – with the obvious message that your injury was so much less. This person forgave, why can't you? This leaves the injured person struggling not only with the miserable anger resulting from the original problem, but also with the guilt at being such a poor Christian in comparison with the hero or heroine described.

This is why many have argued that anger and resentment are moral emotions and that forgiveness offered too easily is dangerous. Resentment can be seen as a proper form of protest that makes a counterclaim to the original act. Resentment acknowledges that the act was wrong, that the offender was responsible for his actions and, most importantly, that the injured party is just as valuable as the offender (Hieronymi, 2001, p. 546). If someone does not respond to being treated badly with resentment, this may indicate that he has shame-ache and does not value himself sufficiently – leading him to simply accept the message that the offender matters more.

The problem, of course, is that if we respond to bad treatment by acting equally badly or even worse, it becomes quite possible to create another cycle – a cycle of revenge that can escalate. It has often been pointed out that this is why the First Testament talks about 'an eye for an eye' not to encourage revenge, but to limit it (Exod. 21.23–25). The other possibility was, 'You take my eye, I kill you, your family wipes out mine, and then my tribe … etc.' Jesus replaced 'an eye for an eye' with 'turn the other cheek' (Matt. 5.38) and the Christian response has always been to insist on the importance of forgiveness – both from God and for one other, as the Lord's Prayer makes clear. But this is not as straightforward as is sometimes suggested. What if our insistence on forgiveness only adds to the sense of a debt created, and the offender being valued over the injured? How do we clarify God's (and our) equal love and concern for both Cain and Abel? How is the victim of traumatic and repeated injuries to build her own sense of self-worth if it looks as though the debt will go unpaid? It is all very well attempting to recover Abel – but what are we asking Abel to actually do?

In order to answer this question it is time to move on from Abel's viewpoint for a moment and to begin asking about shame's opposite – what does Scripture have to say about a flourishing life in which shame is put in its place?

## Human Flourishing

They call it the Golden Rule, 'In everything do to others as you would have them do to you; for this is the law and the prophets' (Matt. 7.12). For many people this is the very heart of Jesus' teachings and it is so important that we have three versions of it in Matthew's Gospel alone. The second time Matthew includes it is in chapter 19 when, asked to define which commandments the rich young man should keep, Jesus first names several of the ten commandments and then adds, 'You shall love your neighbour as yourself' (19.19). The third is in chapter 22 when Jesus is asked which of the commandments is 'the greatest'. He replies, '"You shall love the Lord your God with all your heart, and with all your soul, and with all your mind." This is the greatest and first commandment. And a second is like it: "You shall love your neighbour as yourself." On these two commandments hang all the law and the prophets' (Matt. 22.37–40).

In other words, I take it that this idea was fundamental to Jesus' sense of how human life truly flourishes. It is not just that it is a good thing to love others as we love ourselves and to treat others as we would want them to treat us; for Jesus, this sums up the very heart of God's commandments and Paul picks up the same idea in Romans 13.8-9, adding that 'love is the fulfilling of the law'. For Jesus and Paul, I take it, the goal of life was not simply an individualistic relationship with God but rather a life in community in which love for God, love for neighbour and love for ourselves are in balance and support one another. I also take it that the assumption behind Jesus' words is not only that this is how we should act towards others, but also that this is how we should be treated by those around us: our neighbours will ideally also love us as they love themselves.

Today it is virtually impossible to quote the Golden Rule without being reminded of the truism that we cannot love our neighbours unless we love ourselves; the corollary of this tends to be that we need to learn to love ourselves first and then look to love others. This is not what Jesus said. He said, 'Love your neighbour as yourself'; the picture that Jesus presents of a flourishing life is one in which love for God, love for neighbour and love for self are inextricably intertwined and we cannot have any one of the three without the other two. Rather than regarding one as somehow first, then causing and enabling the others, it is healthier to expect that they will grow together. So I would want to nuance this most common of all claims by saying that we should love our neighbours as ourselves but this is most likely to be possible for us if we also have the vital sense of God's love for us, a community around us who are also trying to live by the same commandment and a proper self-love. It is unlikely that our experience of any of these will be perfect, but we need to work at them together. This, I believe, is an image that takes us closer to a scriptural picture of a flourishing life.

On the whole, we thrive in relationships where the other person pays attention to us and tries to grasp our dreams, fears and aspirations – in other words, what matters to us and makes us truly ourselves. At the heart of such a relationship is the quality that we call empathy – that is, the ability to 'put ourselves into the other person's shoes' and to see things from their perspective, even when their perspective is very different from our own. Psychologists have noted that empathy, therefore, has an important moral role because it helps us to remain focused on the other person (even when we are in conflict) rather than treating them as less important than ourselves or as simply an object to be used for our own ends. If Cain had had some empathy, he could not have treated Abel as he did, no matter how deep his own shame. However, psychologists have also noted that shame blocks empathy, shame encourages us to draw into ourselves (remember Cain turned his face away), and to focus only on our own feelings, which ultimately means focusing only on ourselves. The other person becomes not a person but an object or competitor for whatever it is that we want (Tangney and Dearing, 2004, p. 83).

This is where we need to pay close attention to the role (both good and bad) of shame in relationships. Shame is not just a damaging emotion that makes us feel terrible, it is intimately related to our sense of other people and how they see us – it can therefore have an impact, for good or ill, on how we relate to other people. When we become overly concerned with the possibility that others are judging us or that they see only our faults, or when we feel exposed in a difficult way and simply want to hide, then shame is destructive and damaging. It blocks empathy and turns us inward. But this is not the whole truth. If we are to love our neighbours as ourselves, there is a right way to be concerned with other people's (and God's) view of us.

If we do something wrong it is appropriate that we feel guilty and that our sense of guilt prompts us to act, for example, by making amends and by avoiding such behaviour in the future. If sin creates a debt then we need to take the debts we owe as seriously as we do those owed to us. Jesus made this an extremely high priority in the Sermon on the Mount:

> So when you are offering your gift at the altar, if you remember that your brother or sister has something against you, leave your gift there before the altar and go; first be reconciled to your brother or sister, and then come and offer your gift. (Matt. 5.23–24)

Unpleasant as the experience of guilt is, the guilt itself can be valuable if we use it as Christ commanded and work to be reconciled to the one we injured. This is fairly easy to see, but it is equally important to recognize that the same is true of shame. Shame also has an important function in helping us to love our neighbour as we love ourselves.

Fraser Watts is particularly helpful here when he speaks of a difference between 'being ashamed', in the sense of 'feeling disgraced in front of another person', and 'a sense of shame', in the sense of instinctively understanding what it is 'proper to be private and reticent about' (Watts, quoted in McFadyen and Sarot, 2001, p. 63). In this sense, experiencing shame is closely related to respect for other people (Pattison, 2000, p. 83). It is shame that helps us to treat other people as we would want them to treat us, to maintain proper boundaries and act with tact and consideration.

Because shame is both valuable and potentially destructive, many commentators have attempted to distinguish between different experiences, using phrases such as 'situational shame' or 'reactive shame' to describe this emotion that prompts a necessary sense of consideration for others. Robert Karen puts it nicely when he says: 'Situational shame keeps us bathing regularly, dressing appropriately, eating with utensils, and able to work in close proximity to others without acting on every aggressive or sexual impulse' (Karen, quoted in Pembroke, 2010, p. 27).

The danger of the popular assertion that we should not worry about what others think of us is that it forgets that there is a good and proper way to be concerned about how we appear to others. Once again, it is the truth but not the whole truth.

We normally use 'shameless' as an insult that says that someone has behaved badly because they lack an appropriate respect for people, institutions, values, ideals or expected behaviour (Pattison, 2000, p. 84).

We are reminded that one of Jeremiah's accusations against the leaders of Israel was that they had 'forgotten how to blush'. There was nothing to keep their behaviour in check and, as Jeremiah made clear, power in the hands of one who has lost all contact with shame is extremely dangerous. In addition, we could reflect on the way that social media gives us the possibility of interacting with people whom we do not see face to face. It seems that for some people being able to be anonymous, or at least not having to deal with the other person in real life, allows them to lose a sense of shame and they become surprisingly comfortable with attacking someone they do not know.

It is all too easy in an individualistic society to downplay the positive social results of guilt and shame and concentrate solely on the unpleasant or even destructive results of the emotions that we experience. Without in any way denying that shame – and particularly shame-ache – can distort human living, it matters that we remember that their absence can be equally problematic. The command is to love our neighbours *as* ourselves and being alert to good shame is part of fulfilling that command.

However, we can go further in understanding the importance of how love for others and for ourselves are intertwined.

I have already noted that psychologists argue that *shame blocks empathy*. There is something about shame-ache that focuses us entirely upon our own pain and encourages us to see the other person as serving our needs (after all, our needs can feel overwhelming). This is one of the ways in which shame can trap us in cycles of increasingly poor behaviour. Equally, we can note that *empathy blocks shame*. Working to recover a sense of empathy for the other person (or, as Jesus would put it, to love the other as we love ourselves) is a vital part of tackling shame. If shame encourages us to focus entirely on our own feelings and needs, then – in the right circumstances – working on empathy for others can encourage us to break the cycle. Empathy specifically resists the temptation to withdraw into our own heads; it makes us focus on the other person.

There is even more that we can say about the flourishing life in relationship that Jesus encourages. Empathy blocks shame not only when we practise it, but also when we receive it. Brené Brown calls experiencing empathy from others 'the ladder out of the shame hole.' She tells the story of receiving a nasty email and attempting to unload her anger by forwarding it on to her husband, complete with her own unexpurgated commentary. She hit 'Reply' rather than 'Forward'. Tempted to give in to the shame that insisted that she was stupid, she instead contacted her husband and a friend about whom she says: 'They gave me what I needed the most: empathy, the best reminder that we're not alone. Rather than judgment (which exacerbates shame), empathy conveys a simple acknowledgment, "You're not alone"' (Brown, 2015, p. 71).

The issue, as Brown points out, was about not feeling alone in her shame. Empathy allowed both her husband and her friend to stand with her and create a connection between them, and that sense of connection to another who had also experienced shame helped her to acknowledge her error without being overwhelmed by it. She comments, 'Shame dissipated the minute I realized that I wasn't alone.'

Brown's comment that judgement exacerbates shame should also remind us of Jesus' stern warning, 'Do not judge, so that you may not be judged. For with the judgement you make you will be judged, and the measure you give will be the measure you get' (Matt. 7.1–2). Not judging others is a key part of building flourishing relationships, yet this verse seems to receive far less attention than the ones about forgiving.

It matters, therefore, to take note that in Scripture a flourishing life includes flourishing relationships and flourishing relationships are built when everyone takes seriously the command to 'love your neighbour as yourself'. A relationship in which one person does all the caring while another acts like Cain is obviously distorted and likely to damage both parties. On the other hand, someone who is struggling with shame-ache is likely to find that working on empathy for other people and experiencing empathy from other people is healing and helps her to break the cycle of shame and sin.

However, recognizing the vital role of empathy is only part of the work that we need to do in order to describe a flourishing life in scriptural terms, which means we now need to turn to another vital question – if shame is our issue, then how are we to describe its opposite? How might experiencing the opposite of shame have prevented Cain from murdering his brother?

## The Opposite of Shame?

Let's start by clearing some ground – when I speak of the opposite of shame, I mean the attitude towards ourselves that lifts our chins and comes from knowing we are valued, not the practices or attitudes that we need to adopt to get there, nor even the way in which God heals us. So the opposite of guilt is innocence, but when we sin God heals us through forgiveness. God heals our shame in different ways and there are definitely practices that we can adopt to work with that healing, but we will come to those later. Our question here is how do we describe the attitude towards ourselves that is part of a truly flourishing life and, closely related to that, how do we read what the Scriptures have to say on the same subject?

This is where we need to do some translation work – after all, it may seem to you that the answer to my question is obvious: the opposite of shame is either pride or self-esteem. Read the Bible, however, and we see that pride is often used in the toxic sense of arrogance while self-esteem is rarely, if ever, mentioned. In the Bible, the opposite of shame is honour, and honour is not exactly the same thing as self-esteem. In particular, the Bible has some very different assumptions about how a person might work towards honour from our ideas about how to gain self-esteem.

That means to really understand how the Scriptures urge us to find a sense of self-worth we need to do some work. In particular, we need to think carefully about the way in which our society tends to focus on the individual, and therefore assumes that self-worth is ultimately individual. But the Scriptures were written in a very different society, which focused on the group and therefore linked honour much more with belonging to your group, and behaving like them. So I could just say that honour is a much more collective notion, but I want to use an illustration that I hope will flesh that idea out a little. This next section may, therefore, feel like a bit of a diversion, but it provides some vital background for the next few chapters.

Let me introduce you to four, totally fictional, characters. We will call them Marcus Claudius and his sister Claudia, and Julia Claude and her brother Mark. We will make them as alike as possible with just one huge difference. Marcus Claudius and Claudia were born in ancient Rome (we will make them contemporaries of Paul) while Julia and Mark were born at the end of the twentieth century. Other than this difference, their backgrounds are very similar; they all come from reasonably prosperous families and their parents did their best to bring their children up to be happy and to be good people by the standards of the society in which they lived.

Their names, and the way in which their parents chose them, begin to give us an idea of their different worlds. The way in which Romans used names varied quite a lot over time and can get a little complicated so I have simplified it a bit (I am not a specialist, so this is my best shot). We will start with the men. We find Mark Claude easy to interpret: Claude is his surname or his family name which he shares with many members of his family, and Mark is his first name or his personal name. His parents may have chosen to call him after a member of the family or a close friend, or they may simply have picked a name that they liked. Increasingly, in our society, he is likely to be known as Mark and to use his surname only when necessary. What matters to us is Mark the individual, and how much his family matters may vary between individuals.

For Marcus Claudius the situation is roughly similar in some ways; although, as he is the only son, it is much more likely that his father was also called Marcus Claudius. Marcus is his *praenomen,* or first name, and was used only by close family members and friends, although it sometimes came in useful when Marcus was in public to distinguish him from another member of the Claudius family. It was considered to be so unimportant that he would probably write his name as M. Claudius. The second part of his name was by far the more important. This was the *nomen,* and it marked him out as part of the Claudius clan. He might also have a third name (the *cognomen*), which might be a nickname or some other personal name that again helped to distinguish him, because the Romans, particularly the aristocracy, tended to keep using a limited number of names over and over and there were probably quite a lot of Marcus Claudiuses around. What mattered to the Romans was the name that marked him out as being a representative of the Claudius family, although Marcus the individual also did, of course, have a part to play.

By the way (just to appease all those people who know more about Roman history than I do), Claudia and Marcus lived at a point in the Roman Empire when the classic system of three names was beginning to change and the number of names increased. As the Claudius family became bigger, you would have needed to indicate which branch of the

Claudii you came from. So a person's *cognomen*, which had originally been some kind of nickname, could end up being passed down to their ancestors. Or if your mother came from a particularly illustrious family you might add her name in with your father's. I opted not to start playing around with double-barrelled surnames in an illustration. (However, in case you share my love of historical novels, here is a general rule of thumb. If a Roman character has a lot of names, the author has either done their homework and wants you to know that the character lived later on in the history of Rome, or the author thought 'Romans – they had lots of names ending in "us"' and has just chucked a few down in the hope of sounding authentic.)

A specific example of this would be if I were to mention a famous Roman whose *praenomen* was Gaius – you may or may not be able to guess who I mean. However, if I say his *nomen* was Julius and his *cognomen* (inherited from an ancestor) was Caesar, you will almost certainly have heard of him. This most famous of Romans is remembered by a name that says he came from the Caesar branch of the Julii.

So far, the two societies – ancient and modern – do not sound very far apart, and it is important that we acknowledge this. There are similarities as well as differences between the two worlds and we are discussing a difference of degree. It matters that we do not go in for the simplistic expectation that they will always be complete opposites, so that if Marcus and Claudia believe one thing then Julia and Mark will believe something completely different. Our society tends to be individual oriented (but is not 100 per cent so) while the ancient Mediterranean world tended to be group oriented (but also was not 100 per cent so) (Crook, 2009, p. 599).

Where we do begin to see some differences is in the two men's attitude to their names. Let's assume that both of them want their name to be remembered after their death. For Mark this desire is likely to be mainly linked to his own achievements. No doubt he will want to make his parents proud, but to have his name remembered after his death implies to him that *he* will be remembered after his death. Family pride may be a factor, but is unlikely to be central to his thinking. For Marcus Claudius, things were very different. The desire to have his name remembered would have been much more linked to his responsibility to enhance the family honour:

> The names a Roman man bore were shared with his father and male ancestors, as well as with his own sons and male descendants; like the family's political fortunes, economic prosperity, and religious obligations, his name was his only for a lifetime, and he must pass it on enhanced, or at least not diminished, to the next generation. (Potter and Mattingley, 2006, p. 25)

Note the sense of obligation that the name must be passed on to the next generation in such a way that it is honoured by other Romans. This was an inescapable duty for the Roman male that was also an embedded part of his identity – he could only have a sense of self-worth if the honour attached to his family name had been upheld or, even better, increased. We will soon come to see how Marcus was expected to do this, but for now it is worth reflecting on the pressure this created for him to act in a certain way. The dread of shame was a powerful motivating force in Roman society. We are used to sympathizing with the way that women so often seem to be shamed for what seems to us reasonable behaviour; we are not always alert to the way in which a collective society obsessed with honour created burdens also for the men.

And what of the women? Once again, Julia's name is easy for us to interpret as she has been treated exactly the same as Mark, but Claudia was in a very different situation. You will probably have noticed already that her name is simply the feminine form of the family name. Roman women (at least at one point in history, as it did vary) gradually lost the use of the *praenomen* and were simply given the family name. When she married, she would be called Claudia plus the possessive form of her husband's name, so that in effect her name was 'member of the Claudia family, wife of so and so'. What, then, did her family actually call her? Again, it varied over time and probably nicknames would be used, but it is possible that her formal name would have worked like this. If she had one younger sister, she would be Claudia major and her sister would be Claudia minor. If she had more than one sister, they would be numbered. The next couple of girls would, therefore, be Claudia III and Claudia IV. For the Romans it was more important that a woman bore the name of the family into which she was born than that she had her own name. A key part of her identity was that she was a representative of her family. Julia's parents, of course, simply would not think that way and I have therefore given her a name of her own.

The names may feel complicated, but they are just an illustration of the different emphases of a group-oriented society as against an individualistic one. They demonstrate the issue of what has the highest value – the group (which leads to a much greater emphasis on the family name) or the individual (which means that the person's own name is given more attention). Now we need to explore the ways in which both societies encourage their members to pursue the opposite of shame and the different ways in which this is described. For Mark and Julia we can, for now, talk about self-worth. For Marcus and Claudia, however, the vital quality that governed their behaviour throughout their lives was honour.

## Self-respect and Honour

All of our characters have good parents who love them and who want the best for them. We can, therefore, assume that they have been brought up according to the values of the society in which they live. For Julia and Mark this is likely to mean that one of the values that their parents have attempted to instil in them is that of respect, both the importance of respecting themselves and also that of respecting others. Mark and Julia will also have learned a particular relationship between self-respect and respect for, and from, other people. To keep things as simple as possible I am going to assume that their parents are on the extreme end of individualism and that they have, therefore, constantly reminded Julia and Mark that self-respect comes from within and that it is not possible for others to respect you unless you first value yourself. Being good parents, they also have emphasized that it matters to treat others with respect but they have not linked self-respect with how others treat and regard Mark and Julia – in fact, they have emphasized the importance of not caring what others think. Julia and Mark have also grown up valuing independence, both in themselves and others, and have learned to expect that whether or not others respect them should be based on their own character and actions, not on any group to which they belong or on the family from which they come. This means that they will at least attempt to avoid stereotypes and to treat others on their own merits. They also assume that the same standards should apply to both of them, and if Julia is treated differently as a result of her gender she will experience this as an injustice and feel able to protest.

For Marcus and Claudia the situation is both the same and different. It is the same in that self-worth does matter to them. Some attempts to examine life in a group-oriented society have implied that people have no sense of themselves as individuals, which seems highly unlikely. Individual desires and indeed self-worth did matter to them; it's just that they were less important than communal expectations (Crook, 2009, p. 599). What is different is that they were clear that the opposite of shame is honour and they had a clear understanding of what it means to live honourably.

According to biblical scholars who have studied the idea of honour, it is to be understood as partly about the person's sense of themselves but also partly something else. In a group-oriented society it is not possible to have a sense of honour unless the group to which the person belongs acknowledges that person's value. Honour involves an intricate and intimate relationship between how others see us and how we see ourselves. Malina put it like this:

> Group-oriented persons internalize and make their own what others say, do and think about them because they believe it is necessary, if they are to be human beings, to live out the expectations of others. They need to test this interrelatedness, moving the focus of attention away from their own egos and toward the demand and expectations of others who can grant or withhold reputation or honor. (Malina, quoted in Neyrey, 1991, p. 73)

In the world of Marcus and Claudia it would be impossible to have a sense of your own honour unless the group around you also honoured you. To have the group honour you, it was important to live by the values of that group. An honourable person embodied and followed the codes of their family, patron, group and nation. This means that they assumed that being honourable was not simply about how they felt about themselves; it was also closely linked with honourable actions.

This affected many of their other values in life. Mark and Julia are likely to admire independence, self-reliance and personal liberty. Marcus and Claudia were more likely to value interdependence and family loyalty. What is more, they accepted that bad behaviour from one member of the family affected the honour of the whole. This meant that Marcus was under particular pressure to bring honour to the family name in all of his dealings with those outside the family. The list of norms to which he would be expected to conform was long, and there was a sense in which he was always being judged. Claudia also was expected to honour the family by how she lived, but the expectations of honourable behaviour were different for her. She was expected to be chaste, faithful to her husband, and to care for her family and her house (Lendon, 2005, p. 46). To fail to live up to these expectations brought shame on her entire family. This assumption that honour and shame could spread out to entire groups meant that Marcus and Claudia were much more comfortable with stereotypes. They lived in a world in which everyone knew that Cretans were liars (that one made it into the Bible, see Titus 1.12) and all Barbarians were, well, barbaric.

Finally, for Marcus and Claudia, honour encompassed what we (sometimes at least) tend to separate. Honour included reputation, your own sense of self-worth, and what we would describe as integrity. Neither the Greeks nor the Romans thought of morality and prestige as being distinct from each other (Lendon, 2005, p. 41). Honour, therefore, was impossible without honourable actions. Increasingly, I suspect, our society separates these out, so that when we read about honour we think that this is related only to what others think of us while integrity is becoming more a matter of personal choice and linked to that more modern value of 'being true to yourself'. This can potentially create problems, especially when linked to our modern sense of self-esteem which can be interpreted as seeing yourself as better than anyone else. If our sense of self-worth becomes disconnected from behaving well towards others, we need to ask some serious questions. There is something to learn from Marcus' and Claudia's profound sense that reputation, good conduct, integrity and self-worth are all part of the same concept of honour.

Equally, we need to acknowledge the major problems, from our point of view, with the world that Marcus and Claudia inhabited. They had little sense of individual rights, for example, and saw no problem with stereotypes or treating people outside of their honour group very poorly. What is more, honour was a competitive business and the assumption was that if a Roman male bested another in some way then the winner's honour rose while the loser's correspondingly fell. For Marcus and Claudia an attack on a person's honour was an attack on that person and their family, meaning that they (Marcus in particular) were under an obligation to defend and promote the family honour at all costs. Marcus was expected to compete openly for honours from society and it was unthinkable that he would not be concerned about his honour.

This can cause huge problems when the Bible uses the language of honour to speak of God; for many readers today, God just looks petty when she demonstrates a concern for her honour. In the world in which the stories were first written, people could not conceive that God could be God and not respond to attacks on her honour, because an attack on her honour was an attack on God herself. What is more, the Bible and later Christian tradition has been shaped by the assumption that God's honour increases when that of human beings is brought low (honour is competitive, remember). So we get language like 'we are unworthy to even gather up the crumbs under your table'. Such language can be highly problematic for a person struggling with shame-ache. Stephen Pattison has pointed out how much of our language about God only heightens people's feeling of inadequacy and powerlessness.

Throughout the rest of this book I am going to argue that we need to understand how honour works and shapes the biblical worldview if we are to read the Bible well on issues of shame. I will also assume that there is something to be learned from recognizing that in Scripture honour is the opposite of shame, without going so far as to say that we can simply start using honour in the same way again. Honour at its best encompasses not simply self-worth, but also good behaviour and concern for others. Honour at its worst becomes an excessive pre-occupation with how I and my family are seen by others and can even lead to horrors such as so-called 'honour killings'. This is why it is very important to also notice that honour itself needs to be understood in the light of the gospel of Christ. The Bible uses the notion of honour constantly and it is inevitable that what it says has been shaped by the world in which it was written. This does not mean that ultimately the Bible adopts the idea of honour uncritically. Scripture also challenges and redefines human ideas of what is honourable and part of being a Christian is working to shape our idea of honour and self-respect after that modelled by Christ himself.

So we started this chapter saying that we were going to recover Abel, and it may seem that we have travelled a long way from that first idea – that is, how does understanding honour help those hurt by others or struggling with shame-ache? I want to argue that it does so in a number of ways.

First, it raises the question of whether the aspirations of our individualistic society are realistic or whether there is something to be learned from the more group-oriented world of other cultures. It is hard for us to realize just how unusual the world we live in really is. There are many gains from a more individualistic society, such as the idea of human rights, the questioning of stereotypes, and the ability of an individual to transcend their background – but there are also losses. If we are not careful we can fall into the belief that self-worth is entirely independent of the respect of others and treating others well. Once again, Jesus did not say that you have to love yourself *before* you can love your neighbour. We are vulnerable vines, autonomous in some ways, but also inherently social beings, shaped and formed by our relationships with others. Shame blocks empathy, and empathy (exercised and received) blocks shame. It is incredibly difficult to generate a sense of self-worth without empathetic relationships with others and the danger of attempting to do so is that we become excessively self-centred.

Second, it reminds us of the danger of any expectation that we should love ourselves or demand the love of others even when we are behaving badly. Another way of putting this is to remember that good healthy shame is a vital part of flourishing relationships. Good shame keeps us aware of the effect that our behaviour has on others. Good shame reminds us that there is an appropriate way to be concerned about what others think of us, without being dominated by their opinions. There is a danger that since shame is becoming a well-known issue and since it can result in such difficult feelings and in shame-ache, we begin to assume that shame is always bad. Good shame is linked to respect for other people.

Third, it means that we need to think very carefully about how to describe the opposite of shame in a way that works in the modern world. There does not seem to be a single word that can be the modern version of honour. At the very least, though, I want to argue that we need to stop using the idea of self-esteem and replace it with self-respect. This language, I hope, at least hints at the link between self-worth and treating others well (I need to respect others *and* myself) in a way that esteem does not. Esteem carries the idea of high regard and even seeing someone as better than another, which takes us instantly into the world where self-worth is somehow competitive – that is, I feel better about myself by putting another person down. We have already seen that this is a real problem with honour. The point about self-respect is that I can respect myself as a beloved child of God and treat myself with respect (even when I have done something wrong) while remembering simultaneously that other people are also beloved children of God and thus worthy of respect. By doing so I am much more likely to build flourishing relationships.

I also deeply suspect that for those struggling with shame-ache, self-respect is an easier aspiration than self-esteem. Precisely because 'esteem' carries the sense of high regard and even seeing someone as better than most, it can seem impossible to climb out of the slough of shame-ache to the mountain-top of self-esteem. People with shame-ache can bully and judge themselves to a surprising degree. Respect should be built on the idea that you are a beloved child of God (even when you have done something wrong) and should not be put down (even by that bullying voice in your head) in any circumstances. A person struggling with shame-ache can begin the exodus by learning to treat themselves with basic respect and even compassion, when esteem seems well beyond their reach. Learning self-respect may, therefore, be the beginning of the exodus from shame and we may need other ways to describe a fully flourishing life, but it is an important first step.

Recognizing that we read the Bible in a much more individualistic fashion than did generations before us can help us to recover Abel in another way, and underlines some of what we saw when looking at the Exile. Many of us have been brought up to believe in the importance of an individual, personal faith without any attempt to balance the personal aspect with the issues of relationship and culture. The corollary of this is that we are encouraged to read the Bible while always asking what it has to say to us *as individuals.* A large amount of biblical teaching on sin is addressed to the wealthy and the powerful who exploit others. If we are to recover Abel we need to keep stressing this and to recognize it is possible to emphasize the message about sin so much that we lose the message about grace.

If we stick to an individualistic reading it seems to me almost inevitable that people will understand any language about sin as little more than an attempt to push people into feelings of guilt and shame, and possibly also as a way to control their behaviour. No wonder the idea seems irrelevant when so many of the issues that face us are far greater than an individual's acts. The rape of the environment and climate crisis, the horrors of war, a society in which 'alternative facts' are acceptable, the rich growing richer and the poor growing poorer – these are the problems that confront us on all sides and, if we abandon our habit of reading sin individualistically, these are also manifestations of the power of sin in the world.

Let's look at a concrete example of reading sin less individualistically, which I have adapted from Mike Higton (Higton, 2008, p. 269). He suggests that we use racism as our example, for we recognize that racism has many different manifestations. There are deliberately racist acts, but there is also the way in which a person brought up in a racist culture cannot avoid being affected by his upbringing. He may well work hard to overcome the prejudices that he has imbibed, but he may also feel deep shame that this is a struggle for him. What is more, we are also faced with the systems and structures of organizations and of society itself, which are beyond the control of any one person but can still be inherently racist.

Racism seems a particularly good example of the power of sin and the way in which sin can be passed down through the generations, because not only do all these manifestations exist, they also feed one another. If several racist people get together, they are likely to support and encourage one another's prejudice. If people in power manifest unconscious bias and constantly favour 'people like us', the structure is hard to change. It is not an easy thing to combat the prejudices taught us by our upbringing, and even an individual who wishes to do so can be influenced (however, unwillingly) by the racist structure of society.

Once we stop seeing sin individualistically, our understanding of salvation needs to broaden as well. As Higton put it: 'I need saving not just from the consequences of the particular sins I commit, but from the sinful air I breathe and the sinfulness of the world I inhabit' (Higton, 2008, p. 269).

It is worth adding that this understanding of how sin is inherited is not meant to be another simplistic version of blaming everything on our parents. Rather, it recognizes that even good parents were themselves shaped by the sinfulness of the world we inhabit. It also recognizes how difficult it is for any of us to avoid being shaped by the world around us. If we are to recover Abel we need a less individual understanding of sin and a fuller sense of the meaning of salvation.

So, let's return to Scripture and take a look at one example of some of what I have been saying. It is time to turn to a biblical story of a man who is normally portrayed as a hero and a good man, but who became shameless. Put in a position of power, he acted not according to the commands of God nor according to the dictates of honour, but rather he started to act as the world around him said that he should. We need to talk about David.

# 4

# We Need to Talk about David

Oppressors don't just want to do their deed, they want to take a bow: they want their victims to sing their praises. (Mantel, 2016, p. 68)

## We Need to Talk about David (but not quite yet)

Sorry, I know it is going to be embarrassing for all of us, but I cannot put it off any longer. We have swept through the First Testament taking a look at some themes around sin and shame. In doing so, I have focused on the Two Exits, the Exodus and the Exile, but have missed out several other parts. I passed over the story of the conquest and the monarchy, and just offered a few hints that eventually we would need to look at David. We have now arrived at that point. We have to talk about him because he has a starring role in one of the iconic biblical stories about sin – his disastrous encounter with Bathsheba that leads to the death of her husband Uriah and of a baby.

David is quite a divisive figure. The good news about him is that he was the greatest king of the First Testament and *the* ancestor of Jesus; it gets mentioned several times in the New Testament so you really can't miss it – 'son of David' (Matt. 1.1). He was important; he was a hero. In being such a hero David was in a position of ultimate power and privilege, and how he handled all that power and privilege matters. The bad news is that being in such a position gave him a long way to fall – and he did not so much fall as take a running dive into the biggest patch of swill and muck available. David, I am going to argue, lives out for us an example of why healthy honour and good shame matters. Healthy honour and good shame matter for all of us, but they matter particularly for anyone who is in a position of power.

This is a vital story for the recovering Abel project, partly because of the long-lasting influence of the way the story has been told and partly because my basic thesis is that it has been read only through the eyes of the powerful man and the sinner looking for forgiveness. It reads very differently if we pay attention to the perspective of the injured party who is faced with a powerful man who has become shameless. I am going to argue that throughout this story both David and Uriah are deeply concerned about their own honour, but that Uriah acts honourably in the sense of attempting to live by the standards that his society expected of a soldier, but that David seems more concerned with honour in the sense of how others see him. What is more, the two men (and particularly David) are so caught up in the battle for honour that Bathsheba becomes a tool in the war between them. But I am leaping ahead of myself. I want to start with the one person who is key to this story, but who is very like Abel in that she remains strangely silent throughout.

## Introducing the Amazing Vanishing Woman

One of the problems with the story of David and Bathsheba is the way in which Bathsheba vanishes from the report of her own violation. She is presented as a silent, passive figure who only seems to respond to the actions of the dominant men. We have already seen this happen to Abel, so we need to be clear that this is not a problem that is exclusive to women; rather, it tends to happen to the person who holds the least power in a situation. However, the sad reality is that in Scripture, as in life, often the person who holds less power is a woman. To grasp the real horror of what happens, it is important to recover as much as we can of the woman behind the myth. So is there any way in which we can present a picture of Bathsheba that is more fully rounded than the one we get from this story? I believe that there is, by starting at the end of her story – for she did not remain passive and silent all her life.

When David reached old age, there was potential for disaster after his death. His family were at odds with one another and one son, Adonijah, decided to claim the throne before the old king was actually dead. Nathan the prophet turns to Bathsheba for help (1 Kings 1.11) and together they successfully intercede with David to ensure that the throne passes to Solomon. Once Solomon is king, she becomes his adviser (although he did not always take her advice) and the last picture we have of her shows her seated at the right hand of her son, on her own throne (1 Kings 2.19). I want to picture her on her throne, in glory, because this is the woman who disappears in her first encounter with David.

So what of Bathsheba when she first meets David? As the story opens, we are told only that she is the daughter of Eliam and the wife of Uriah and that she is very beautiful. It is important to put her into her proper historical context; we simply have no idea what the state of her marriage was. Certainly, it is unlikely that she was consulted about marrying Uriah, and just because she 'made lamentation' for him after his death (2 Sam. 11.26) does not mean that she was passionately in love. It is possible that this was no more than the mourning that her society expected of her as a widow. What we can assume is that she has constantly been told that her honour is closely tied to her sexual purity, and equally she has also been brought up to believe that she should obey men – and particularly the king. Therefore it is likely that when she was summoned to David's bed she was put in a terrible situation; this violated her sense of honour (which, of course, included her sense of self-worth), but she also had no real idea of having some kind of right to resist.

Bathsheba is treated dreadfully throughout this episode and is silent for much of it, but this has not prevented some parts of the Christian tradition and popular portrayals of the story from attempting to blame her for the 'sin' of catching the king's eye (Gunn, 1996). The story opens with David on the roof of the king's palace from which he spots Bathsheba bathing. The Hebrew simply says that she was washing; in an ancient city that was notoriously short of water, we must be careful not to read our assumptions about a full bath into the text. Nevertheless, Bathsheba is often depicted as also on a roof and deliberately bathing naked in public. When we read 2 Samuel 11 we do not find the story of a seductress, but of a woman overseen doing something private who is then ordered to the bed of a powerful man, without the issue of her consent ever being raised.

It is worth comparing the way in which Bathsheba has been treated with another potential victim of sexual assault in the Bible. In Genesis 39, Joseph has already been taken off to Egypt as a slave and has risen to the position of overseer of the house of his master, Potiphar. Since Joseph is 'handsome and good-looking' (Gen. 39.6), his master's wife decides that she wants to sleep with him. She starts by asking, and when he refuses she attempts to grab him by his garment and he has to run outside, leaving the garment in her hands (Gen. 39.11–12). She then accuses him of attempted rape, and he ends up in prison. When this story is told, the sexual predator takes all the blame; Joseph is never accused of 'enticing' Potiphar's wife. Did he do some of his work topless?

The garment seems to have come off very easily, maybe he should have been more careful about his clothing? Perhaps she was simply overcome with an understandable lust? Girls will be girls, after all.

Of course, it could be that our sympathies lie with Joseph because he is shown resisting and escapes. Bathsheba appears to acquiesce. But Joseph has at least some power of his own as master of the household, whereas Bathsheba is faced with a king. The first she knows of what is going on is when messengers from the palace turn up, so the king has the support of his servants and it seems that everyone just assumes his right to send for her and do whatever he wants. Her husband, of course, is currently in battle under this king's command; what might happen to him if she annoys David? The way the story is written tells us about the brutal reality of power; her consent becomes irrelevant.

So, having introduced the woman who will vanish, let's go back to the start and examine our story.

## Way, Way Back in Time

Let's start by putting this story into some kind of historical context, for it is only when we really begin to understand how ancient this story is that we can also grasp how extraordinary it is. We normally date the story of David to around 1000 BC – that is, somewhere around the early Iron Age. In his day, the brand-new invention that has the older generation sucking on their teeth, and telling the younger generation both that they have never had it so good and that they are going to be corrupted for ever by this terrible new idea, is the ability to smelt iron. Iron is much stronger than bronze and humanity has just worked out how to extract it from the ore. If you were a farmer, in theory at least, you could make the leading edge of your plough a lot stronger and, if you were a soldier, the same applied to the tip of your arrow or your sword. (A minor historical fact is that archaeologists have discovered that iron was used in the Middle East for decoration for quite some time before it was used for these more practical purposes – so David and his contemporaries may just have acquired some nice new jewellery.) The pyramids are looking pretty new, since the last one was completed around 700 years ago and the idea of an alphabet – rather than something like hieroglyphics – is still in development.

The idea of monarchy is also new, at least for Israel. David is only the second king, and the first was controversial. The first book of Samuel is clear that God did not think that a permanent monarchy was a good plan at all, and it was the people of Israel who got the idea from watching the nations around them (1 Sam. 8.5–6). God and the prophet Samuel wanted to stick to the system of Judges, which meant that when a problem arose God chose a leader to deal with it. Actually, to be precise, *God* wanted to stick to the system of Judges. Samuel wanted a hereditary system that would mean that when he died his sons would be Judge in his place (so, rather like a monarchy in all but name). The problem with Samuel's idea was that his sons were not exactly like their dad – they took bribes and perverted justice (1 Sam. 8.3). Faced, therefore, with excellent evidence of exactly what is wrong with any idea of hereditary leadership, naturally the people of Israel demanded a permanent version. They want a king so that they can be 'like other nations' (1 Sam. 8.6). This gives us a major clue as to what goes wrong. The idea of having a king has come from other nations and they do not seem to have noticed that ancient kingship did not usually come with an overwhelming dedication to the rights of everyone else. Samuel gives them a clear and brutal warning of what kingship is likely to mean:

> These will be the ways of the king who will reign over you: he will take your sons and appoint them to his chariots and to be his horsemen, and to run before his chariots; and he will appoint for himself commanders of thousands and commanders of fifties, and some to plough his ground and to reap his harvest, and to make his implements of war and the equipment of his chariots. He will take your daughters to be perfumers and cooks and bakers. He will take the best of your fields and vineyards and olive orchards and give them to his courtiers. He will take one-tenth of your grain and of your vineyards and give it to his officers and his courtiers. He will take your male and female slaves, and the best of your cattle and donkeys, and put them to his work. He will take one-tenth of your flocks, and you shall be his slaves. And in that day you will cry out because of your king, whom you have chosen for yourselves; but the LORD will not answer you in that day. (1 Sam. 8.11–18)

If only they had listened.

## When a King Forgets How to Blush

Ancient propaganda is fascinating. If a king was defeated in battle, he could be portrayed as corrupt and tyrannical (regardless of how he had actually acted) and his successor could be lauded as the honourable hero who triumphed (regardless, once again, of reality). Authority and wealth does not insulate us from a concern about how we are seen; it can simply allow us to surround ourselves with those who will reflect back to us an image we like. The danger of power and privilege is that our voice (and the voice of those who say what we want) becomes the only voice we hear.

The problem is, in an unequal society, the position of the weak can be totally dependent on whether or not the strong act with genuine honour and judge their own behaviour by basic standards of justice and truth. Ancient societies were often very unequal. Scripture is full of commands to the strong to act honourably by treating those dependent upon them with grace. This story demonstrates what happens when this does not happen. In this story honour, particularly as understood by an honour-based society, plays a central but pernicious role and a king forgets what it means to blush.

## It's Not about Sex, it's about Power and Privilege (and making children)

I want to argue that, in this story, David abuses his power and uses sex as one weapon in a series of actions against a perceived rival, Uriah. In order to make that argument I want to do more work to put David (and Uriah) into a proper historical context, so that we can attempt to read the story and interpret the situation as they might have seen it, rather than through the eyes of later commentators (who tend to assume that it is about sex). That means taking a look at one brutal reality of life in the early Iron Age (a reality that existed until surprisingly recently) that had a profound effect on the way in which men and women interacted.

We start with the good news about male–female relationships in the First Testament. Our assumption tends to be that men dominated women in every way, but today scholars want to qualify that assumption. There were many ways in which women did exercise power and contribute to daily life. The First Testament tells us about some remarkable women who were judges (Judg. 4), sages (2 Sam. 14) and prophets (Exod. 15.20f.). Women could make major contributions to the economy of the household and that household was often the centre of the family's economic activity. Gender roles were fixed (and those who crossed them might well be shamed), but generally life was interdependent in many ways and we should not imagine that men were all powerful in every aspect of life (Meyers, 2014). However, it does seem that as power became more organized and was located in the single king, this had a knock-on effect of making it more difficult for women to become leaders.

But it is not all good news. When it comes to sex, the First Testament looks highly biased in favour of straight men. So here is the historical context. The infant mortality rate was horrendous, as was the number of women who died in childbirth. In fact, we estimate that more than half of all children died before the age of five. To put this another way, in order to keep the population steady, every woman would need to have around five or six children, which means that in order to increase the population she needed to have several more. The ancient world faced the problem of too small a population and too competitive a situation. You could generally assume that your neighbours would be less than friendly and, if they had more children than you, your nation would be at a disadvantage in a few years' time. Remember how threatened the Egyptians were at the beginning of Exodus? The Israelites were having too many babies so Pharaoh planned some infanticide to keep his people safe. That was problem number one.

The second issue that dominated the attitude to sex was that of being sure of the father. In a world before DNA testing, there were only a few ways for men to be sure that their children were their own. An obvious way was to marry a virgin and either trust or ensure that a woman remained faithful, and it is this issue that we need to bear in mind when engaging with the Bible's frequent concern for women's virginity.

This situation is the background to some of the 'biblical teaching' on sex that we find particularly harsh, and that we constantly misinterpret. If a man died childless, his wife and brother were expected to sleep together and any children that resulted would be regarded as belonging to the dead man. Onan refused to cooperate with this command and 'spilled his seed on the ground' (Gen. 38.9) and, even though Genesis specifically says that he was trying to avoid giving his brother children, the story has been used to condemn masturbation.

Even worse, the issue of children and therefore access to fertile women could become competitive. Perhaps inevitably, having children became bound up with honour (the more children, the greater the honour) for both sexes. We have already seen that in a group-oriented society, a woman's sexual purity was bound up with the honour of her entire family. It was, perhaps, the combination of these factors that led to another harsh reality of life, which we still see today. Men would strike at other men by taking or raping their women, and this was seen as an attack on the honour of the men rather than concern being focused on the woman's experience (see 2 Sam. 3.6–11). Of course, none of this was right, but it was part of the culture that formed both David and Uriah. David's story, therefore, highlights for us the dangers of allowing your behaviour to be shaped by the attitudes of society and by your own power and privilege.

## Re-reading the Story

One traditional interpretation of this story goes roughly as follows. While Uriah is away fighting, David sees Bathsheba and falls instantly in lust with her. He has a secret affair, which goes horribly wrong when she falls pregnant and he then attempts a cover-up. He calls Uriah back from the front and tries to get him to sleep with Bathsheba so that Uriah will believe the baby is his. This falls apart when Uriah refuses to go home and instead stays at the palace, so David has him killed by ensuring that he will be in the worst of the battle and then claims both Bathsheba and the baby. There are a number of issues with this interpretation:

1 *Secret? What Secret?* David does not meet Bathsheba somewhere private, but acts like a typical king of the time. When he spots her, he sends someone to inquire about her (2 Sam. 11.3), and gets a report back. He sends messengers (plural) to collect her and it seems reasonable to assume that everyone in the palace knew exactly what was going on. David then orders Uriah to come to the palace, so how exactly did he intend to keep what had happened secret?

2 *Whose child is it anyway?* Bathsheba could not exactly pop out for a pregnancy test and, human nature being what it is, it would have been natural for her to ignore any early signs and hold on until the evidence

of her pregnancy became too obvious to ignore. David then has to send a messenger to get Uriah, wait for Uriah to travel back, and when he arrives hope that no one in the palace mentions to him what has been happening in his absence. If David is hoping to convince Uriah that the child was conceived after he left for battle, the timing looks tight. I think he and Bathsheba had a better option available if this was the plan. She could have tried to convince Uriah that the child had been conceived *before* he left for battle. According to 2 Samuel 11.1 the story begins in the spring. In the ancient world it was impractical to fight in winter because of poor roads and lack of grain to feed the army. So David probably slept with Bathsheba not long after Uriah left. We know that she had a period, but not whether Uriah knew this was the case.

Uriah, of course, lived in a highly gendered society in which men positively prided themselves on not getting involved in 'women's issues'. The best evidence I could find about men's knowledge of pregnancy comes from a lot later than Uriah, but Aristotle (384–322 BC) believed that pregnancy could last anything from 7 to 11 months (Aristotle VII, 4) while Pliny (AD 23–79) talks about a court case where a judge called Lucius Papirius was persuaded that a child was the child of a dead man (and therefore could inherit the estate) because the man's wife had been pregnant for 13 months (Pliny VII, 5). Both these authors had set out to investigate human biology, so it seems unlikely that Uriah would have had a better knowledge about the workings of pregnancy – he is still trying to figure out how to get iron smelting to make his sword stronger.

3 *Unwanted pregnancy?* What evidence do we have that this was an unwanted pregnancy, in a world where having children added to a man's honour? What if David wanted the child, but did not want Uriah to be able to claim fatherhood. When the story gives us any indication, David is shown as wanting the child; he claims Bathsheba as soon as he can (and before the baby is born). His punishment includes the baby dying (again this is a very alien world in which the child is not really seen as having a life independent of David) and he fasts and pleads for the child to live (2 Sam. 15.15–23). Of course, human beings are not logical and he could have changed his mind, but the story does not say that this is what happened.

So, what if something very different was going on? My reading is adapted from David Firth (2008 and 2009) who suggests that David already regarded Uriah as a rival before the story begins and that the unfolding events are a working out of that rivalry between the two men, with the woman being used simply as a tool. As Firth admits, we are working from scant evidence, but it does seem to make sense that David might fear Uriah. Uriah is always called 'the Hittite' and is introduced into the story with no explanation of who he is. The only thing that we know about him is that he is one of David's mighty warriors (2 Sam. 23.39). We also know that ancient kings were judged on their ability as soldiers, and the greatest threat to their power often came from members of their own court. We also know that David began as a soldier who won battles for Saul and eventually replaced him (1 Sam. 18.12–16). It makes sense that David might fear that history would repeat itself.

How does the story read if we accept this assumption? David sees Bathsheba when he is on the roof and asks who she is. He does nothing else until he is told that she is Bathsheba, the daughter of Eliam and the wife of Uriah. This is the last time in the story that Bathsheba will be named until Uriah is dead. From now on she is always called 'the woman' or 'the wife of Uriah' – perhaps we should take this as a hint that this is what was significant to David. She is his rival's wife, so what better way to humiliate Uriah than to flagrantly sleep with his wife? Later, when Nathan confronts David, this is the action that is condemned – he has taken another man's wife and the threat is made that another will do this to him. Women are the tool in the power struggle; they are not treated as real people at all.

David then acts very much like a king, with no attempt to hide what he is doing. He sends someone to find out who Bathsheba is and then other messengers are sent to collect her and bring her to him, although she is apparently left to make her own way home (2 Sam. 11.4–5). Only at this point are we given the important information that Bathsheba had been purifying herself after her period. Bathsheba's only action is to inform David that she is pregnant, and she has to do it by messenger, so it suggests he does not seem to have made any plans to see her again.

On hearing the news, David sends again; this time he demands that Uriah be withdrawn from fighting and come back to the palace. Why, though, does David attempt to get Uriah to go home and 'wash his feet' (2 Sam. 11.8)? This has always struck me as a slightly strange euphemism for sex, but a reasonable one for taking your ease, which is likely to include sex. What David is really doing, I suspect, is making sure that his opponent is not seen as too honourable.

## When a Soldier Shames a King

Sometimes the best insults are the most subtle ones. We all appreciate the kind of riposte in which you need to follow a leap of logic, or connect what is said to an unspoken assumption, to work out just how rude the speaker has been. We tend to find this harder to deal with than a direct insult. This was also true for our ancestors, and in a society that was particularly concerned with honour and in which power was unequally spread, the art of the subtle insult was highly developed. Uriah is faced with someone who is far more powerful than he is but who has still decided that he is a threat. He probably already knows that David coerced Bathsheba into sex and interpreted that as a direct attack on his honour. So how is he meant to protest to a shameless king?

Sometimes shame is the only weapon available. If I can do nothing to change events, I can at best appeal to the powerful person's sense of honour in an attempt to change their behaviour or, at worst, attack their sense of themselves as the only form of revenge available to me. The interaction between Uriah and David described in 2 Samuel 11.7-12 can be characterized as an 'honour duel' between two rivals. What I mean by that is a debate in which each is attempting to shame the other and, by doing so, to appear more honourable themselves. David wants to make sure Uriah is not regarded as better than him (such things tend to matter inordinately to the shameless) and Uriah is seeking the only revenge open to him by trying to embarrass the king. The difficulty that Uriah faces is that if he openly acknowledges that David slept with his wife then, strangely enough, it is Uriah who will be humiliated. If he can seize the moral high ground (as we would put it) then he may regain at least some sense of standing and worth. David may already be planning to kill Uriah and it is possible that he is trying to avoid being haunted by tales of the dead hero with whom he could be compared to his own disadvantage.

The conversation is based on some assumptions that we struggle to pick up. One of the most important is that any honourable soldier will be at war with his comrades, not taking his ease at home. There does also seem to have been an assumption that sex could weaken a man and make him impure in a situation where it really helped to have God on your side (Deut. 23.10). Both men are aware that David, who used to be lauded for the number of men he killed in battle (1 Sam. 18.7), has begun to send his troops off to do his fighting for him. Firth suggests that it was a capital offence for a soldier on duty to have sex and that David was seeking a legal reason to have Uriah executed (Firth, 2009, p. 418), but I suspect that the issue is perception. As long as Uriah remains at the palace, he is a soldier on duty and obeying orders. If he goes home, David can argue that Uriah did exactly what David did – he took his ease while others did the fighting.

So let's read the conversation in 2 Samuel 11.7–13 where I have added in what was possibly running through both men's minds but that remains unspoken – partly because this is how the best insults work, and partly because this is a courtier speaking to a king and so Uriah has to be careful about how openly he insults David:

When Uriah came to him, David asked how Joab and the people fared, and how the war was going. [*A little social chit-chat before we really get going.*] Then David said to Uriah, 'Go down to your house, and wash your feet.' [*David attempts to get Uriah to openly rest and take his ease rather than remaining on duty at the palace.*] Uriah went out of the king's house, and there followed him a present from the king. [*A slightly strange verse – but does it mean that David had a spy sent to check up on Uriah?*] But Uriah slept at the entrance of the king's house with all the servants of his lord, and did not go down to his house. When they told David, 'Uriah did not go down to his house', David said to Uriah, 'You have just come from a journey. Why did you not go down to your house?' [*David discovers that Uriah has not obeyed orders, no doubt this adds to his suspicion.*] Uriah said to David, 'The ark and Israel and Judah remain in booths; and my lord Joab [*Notice the way that Uriah refers to Joab as his lord, rather than David. How is a paranoid king to interpret this? On the other hand, Joab is currently doing the heroic job of leading David's army, so David needs to be careful not to insult him.*] and the servants of my lord [*Who does 'my lord' mean here? If it is Joab, is Uriah hinting that the army is now more loyal to Joab than David?*] are camping in the open field [*Unlike their king who has taken to lounging around at home*]; shall I then go to my house, to eat and to drink, and to lie with my wife? [*Like David has been doing.*] As you live, and as your soul lives, I will not do such a thing.' [*Note the passion of Uriah's refusal – this is not a small thing.*] Then David said to Uriah, 'Remain here today also, and tomorrow I will send you back.' [*Just a little reminder that Uriah is under David's command.*] So Uriah remained in Jerusalem that day. On the next day, David invited him to eat and drink in his presence and made him drunk [*If David cannot get Uriah to act dishonourably by sending him home then next best thing is to get him to take his ease and eat well in the king's presence, and get him drunk, perhaps he will also then go home*]; and in the evening he went out to lie on his couch with the servants of his lord [*Even drunk, the soldier remains on duty*], but he did not go down to his house.

So Uriah resists again and David sends again. This time Uriah is sent back to the front, carrying the letter that gives instructions for his death (2 Sam. 11.14). Joab follows instructions and Uriah (along with a few other soldiers who are treated as collateral damage) duly dies. Apparently, another advantage of being king is that someone else does your dirty work for you. David receives word of Uriah's death and sends a message back; it is worth translating that message literally. What he actually says is, 'Do not let this thing be evil in your eyes (or your sight)' (2 Sam. 11.25). This translation is from Brueggemann (2002, p. 57) who points out that English translations tend to be quite weak and cover up the fact that the word used is 'evil'. It is important to notice that the Hebrew literally talks about how the action should be seen. Here we have another danger of power in the hands of the shameless; what David is saying is, 'From my perspective this is not a problem and my perspective is the only one that matters. I am telling you how to see this.' David is now claiming the right to decide what is good and what is evil. When Adam and Eve ate the forbidden fruit, the issue was the knowledge of good and evil, and now David is claiming the right to define it.

But here we must pause and realize something. In one sense what has happened is not at all unusual. An ancient king has taken another man's wife and then eliminated the other man, so what? This story, though, stands out among contemporary stories of great kings because the action is considered worthy of mention. The story is told and then re-told, and then written down rather than it being lost because the king did not want it repeated. The very fact that the story is told at all challenges

David's assumption of power and privilege and reminds us that David's perspective is not, in the end, the decisive one. David has told Joab how to see what has happened, but God sees things differently. Chapter 11 ends by emphasizing that difference. Translated literally, the final verse in the chapter reads, 'The thing that David had done was evil in the eyes of the Lord' (2 Sam. 11.27).

## When Power Hears Truth Spoken

'I am not a crook' (Richard Nixon). 'I did not have sexual relations with that woman' (Bill Clinton). Even in a supposedly democratic age it is not difficult to find examples of the powerful denying or downplaying their wrong actions.

We talk regularly about the importance of 'speaking truth to power' and assume that it takes a good deal of courage because, on the whole, power does not like hearing the truth spoken when that truth contradicts their view of the world. In our world we do at least have some expectation that men should treat women with respect, and yet the #MeToo movement has highlighted how many women have been victims of sexual assault and the problems of holding a powerful man to account. What will happen when truth is spoken to a king who appears to have decided that he not only has the right to do whatever he wants, but can also determine whether an act is evil or not? David has acted exactly like a vulnerable vine and allowed his behaviour to be shaped by the expectations of the societies around him and by his own personal wishes, and in the process he has lost touch with any true sense of honour.

On to the next extraordinary part of the story. A king, totally caught up in his own privilege, has just arranged the death of one of his mighty warriors – one of the most powerful men in the kingdom. So what does the Lord do? God sends a prophet, one defenceless prophet, to confront David and explain that most difficult of topics – what he has done wrong. The odds of Nathan surviving the experience cannot have looked good. In Nathan's case, the consequences of 'speaking truth to power' could have been fatal.

Nathan, therefore, very sensibly opts for the strategy of getting the king to condemn himself. One simple parable about a rich man who nicked a poor man's lamb (2 Sam. 12.1–4), and David decides that this action is definitely evil. Notice again, the parable assumes that the problem is not lust but that one man has taken something valuable from another, an action that makes the king so angry that he declares that the guilty man deserves to die. Again, the issue of perspective and privilege raises its head. David is perfectly aware that justice and integrity matter, so long as they apply to someone else. He walks straight into Nathan's trap and in return the prophet pronounces the fatal words, 'You are the man!' God gave you any number of immense privileges and would have given you more. 'Why have you despised the word of the Lord, to do what is evil in his sight?' (2 Sam. 12.9). The issue is out on the table. As Brueggemann puts it: 'The king and his hatchet men are not the arbitrators of what is good and what is evil. It is evil, and there is no royal privilege or immunity' (Brueggemann, 2002, p. 59). David instantly responds, 'I have sinned against the Lord.' No denial, no excuse, no threat against the defenceless prophet in front of him. David offers nothing but acceptance that he is wrong.

We easily miss how extraordinary that is: the assumption that with power goes some kind of exemption from the rules that govern everyone else was a fundamental part of monarchy. Yet compare this reaction with the reactions that we all too often see today from those with any form of authority. David is shown, a thousand years before Christ, accepting that a prophet had the right to call him out on his actions. Nathan asks, 'Why have you despised the word of the Lord, to do what is evil in his sight?' and we note again the importance that it is God, not David, who gets to define what is evil. We also note David's faithfulness when challenged, and perhaps it is this faithfulness that begins to give us a clue as to how he could be a hero, even though this is part of his story.

Of course, some of us might want to point out that he sinned against Uriah and Bathsheba, but he is a king who is used to seeing himself as accountable only to God. For David this is a major step forward; he has recognized that he should not conform to Samuel's description of how a king acts and that God requires more of him than winning battles and religious duties. God will hold him accountable for the way in which he treats other people.

Furthermore, there are hints within the story that this was a genuine repentance. David does not just *say* the words – we can see ways in which his behaviour changed as well. Up to this point, Bathsheba has been a classic Abel. She has been passive and silent and so insignificant that she was not even named. Once David has been faced with what he has done, he begins to treat her differently. 'Then David consoled his wife Bathsheba' (2 Sam. 12.24). Finally, she is named and her feelings are acknowledged. At last, David seems to realize that this episode is about more than him and his battle with Uriah; there is also a mother who has lost a child and a husband. It is only a small hint and David will struggle for the rest of his life with a family riven by disputes and rivalries, but at least it is a start.

In a world that has increasingly come to see repentance as being somehow about feelings, as if somehow the issue is how bad I feel, these small hints give us a sense of what it means for anyone, but particularly a person in a position of authority, to repent. For each of us, true repentance involves:

- Taking responsibility for our actions.
- Recognizing the value of the other person. He or she is a child of God and worthy of respect; he or she is not an object to be used for our own ends. He or she should be named.
- Making amends and treating the other person differently. Another way to say this is, recognizing that we owe a debt and attempting to repay it. There is no record in the text that David apologized to Bathsheba, but there is plenty of evidence that he treated her differently. She ends up as the honoured mother of the next king. Sometimes a sustained effort to act differently towards the injured person does more to say sorry than an apology.

However, this story can only take us so far. In a book about shame and the way in which shame and sin distort our lives, we have attempted to read this story looking out for the viewpoint of the injured party. While it matters to give a voice to the silenced, it is also frustrating; for no matter how much David changed, Bathsheba still does not say much after this story. If we are to recover Abel, we need an example of someone who is shamed by the actions of others and who responds by speaking up for themselves. What does it look like for the shamed to find their voice and to encounter God? In the next chapter we will read about one man who did just that.

# 5

# Job: The Truth but Not the Whole Truth

> Theology ... involves learning to see the way in which false images of God, ourselves and the world have bound us and taken away the life God intends for us. (Bondi, quoted in Pattison, 2000, p. 297)

Anyone who struggles with shame-ache has a good reason to be somewhat fed up by now. Every time so far that we have looked at a shamed person in Scripture they have been a poor role model. They have given into shame, all of them. Adam and Eve, Cain and Abel, Bathsheba, every one of them has blamed someone else, become aggressive, or retreated entirely into themselves and said nothing. Is that all that the Bible has to offer? How about a good role model who manages to speak up for themselves, resist the pernicious effects of shame, and does that without resorting to violence? If that is how you are feeling, I would like you to meet Job.

If there is one book in the Bible where most Christians assume that they know the major theme – 'what the book is all about' – my guess is that book is Job. We have been told that Job is all about suffering, why God lets it happen, and how we are supposed to respond. That summary is, in part, true but I want to suggest that it is insufficient. Job is about suffering, but not only suffering. Job is also a profound story of one man's reaction when others unthinkingly attempt to shame him. It is also the story of a man doing theology in the most extreme circumstances. The heart of Job is a battle between the unbalanced theology of his friends – which assumes that they understand sin and God and attempts to fit someone's life into the pattern demanded by their understanding – and Job's theological protest in which he refuses to be shoved into the shame box his friends have prepared for him and demands to meet God for himself.

This means that Job supplies a vital balance in the struggle to recover Abel. Abel represents the person who responds to shame by becoming passive and silent, and he reminds all of us how important it is that we listen and make sure that those with shame-ache are able to speak. But for those struggling with shame-ache this is not enough. They do not need simply an encouragement that others listen, but also a role model of someone resisting shame and speaking up for themselves. Job does not simply provide such an example; he also demonstrates what it means to fight back when the people trying to shame you are using theology as their weapon.

In this way, Job will also help us to face from the beginning one possible objection to some of what I want to say. There may be some who think that I am imposing twenty-first-century concerns about self-esteem on to Christianity. Job, I think, demonstrates that the struggle against being labelled a sinner and against the pernicious effects of shame are part of the biblical tradition. To be clear, I am not claiming that sin and shame are the only themes (or even the main theme) in the book of Job, but I do think Job's struggle against shame is an important one and is often overlooked because of our assumption that the book is about suffering.

So let me introduce you to Job. You may have read the book before, but I am not going to assume that you have. Even if you know the book of Job well, I hope to introduce you to a heroic figure. Job is caught up in events far bigger than himself and he struggles to hold on to his sense of who he is and who God is, even while events and his so-called friends seek to destroy both. His story comes straight out of the ancient world and many scholars believe that it was written while Israel reflected on the Exile, and yet Job touches on what we often assume are modern dilemmas to do with self-respect and struggling to find God for yourself rather than accepting what others say. Allowing myself to become caught up in Job's struggle helped to change my understanding of what it means to believe, and taught me more than I expected about sin and shame; I hope you will allow him to do the same for you.

The book of Job has an exciting introduction and emphatic conclusion and a boring middle. Many a reader has got lost in that middle. It is worth doing some work to get hold of the structure of the book because, once we have grasped that, it becomes easier to see the way in which the story is moving forward and how Job, in particular, is working on both his understanding of God and his sense of himself. The simplest version of the structure goes like this:

The introduction: chapters 1—2
The speeches of Job and his four friends: chapters 3—37
God's answer and Job's reply: chapters 38—42.6
The epilogue: chapter 42.7–17

The bulk of the book of Job is taken up with a 'conversation' that is really a series of speeches from Job and his friends. At first sight, the 'conversation' goes round and round in circles until the reader loses the will to … well, read. The characters appear to talk at each other, at great length, with very little listening involved, and it becomes easy to lose track of who is speaking and what point they are trying to make. This is why it matters to have a grasp of the way in which the speeches are structured. However, the introduction provides some vital clues to help us see the points at issue between Job and his friends, so we will look at that first and then come back to those speeches.

## The Biggest Picture of Them All

We all know that sometimes you need the big picture to really understand the detail. The final editor of Job's story knew this and made sure that we start by knowing something about the people who are speaking and the subject they are discussing. If you have not read Job before, it is worth taking a little time now to read the first two chapters, but before you do let me warn you that Job sounds very strange to modern ears and, if it is treated as literal history, it raises more questions than it answers. As a story, it takes us to heaven and lets us witness a conversation between God and Satan, and therefore does a brilliant job of setting us up to read what follows in a particular way. By the end of chapter 2 the reader is absolutely sure of four points:

- Job is a good man. We even have God's description of him as 'a blameless and upright man who fears God and turns away from evil' (Job 1.8).
- God has the highest regard for Job; we can see this not just from the statement above but from the fact that when Satan announces that he has just visited earth, God indulges in a little boasting.
- Life has rained down on Job's head just about every form of suffering possible short of killing him (which might have been a blessing). His

children have been taken away (leaving his none too sympathetic wife) along with his wealth and, finally, his health.
- These disasters happened precisely because Job has been so good.

The stage has been set for a conversation in which the reader knows more about what is going on than the characters do. We know about the divine-satanic bet and that these awful things have happened because Job is good, *but the characters involved do not.* They know only that everything has gone horribly wrong for Job and they are now groping for explanation. This means that they stand where we normally stand, but we have been given a unique view on the situation. In the chapters that follow they do their theology in front of us and there is an implicit invitation to assess how they do this in the light of our superior knowledge. They all believe in God and therefore share the assumption that there must be an explanation, and that explanation must include God.

The friends, it appears, are convinced that their major role is to defend God and stick to the theology that they have been taught. They *insist* on doing this, no matter the harm that is being done to a man who is already hurting. Almost inevitably, given both the situation and the theology that they profess, they speak about sin, guilt and shame – and so give us a classic example of how *not* to do theology. Their very mistakes give us two important issues to highlight from the beginning.

First, the half-truth is harder to spot and more damaging than the outright lie, and it is easy for theology to become unbalanced so that we tell the truth but not the whole truth. The friends could make a good argument that their theology is biblical, and they and Job start with at least some agreement about sin. It is when they push their application that the problems begin to show. I have already argued that our understanding of sin has become unbalanced in just this way – too focused on one particular reading of Scripture, and therefore not so much true as insufficiently true. In Job we meet a man contending with half-truths that his friends keep pressing upon him.

Second, Job reminds us in the most direct way possible that to speak of sin, guilt and shame is, in the old phrase, 'dabbling in the stuff of people's souls'. When theology makes assertions about how people should live, we must take care not to inflict unnecessary and hurtful shame on vulnerable people who are already struggling. Job gives us a magnificent example of a man who is able to fight back, but we have already seen plenty of examples of Abels who could not.

Let us also acknowledge that the whole idea that Job suffers for being good raises huge theological issues. This is why it matters to know that Job is among those books of the First Testament that were written down as part of the response to, and reflection upon, the Exile. The Israelites were struggling with exactly the same questions that the book of Job raises. Did the Exile happen because we have been particularly evil? Job, and the idea of suffering because you are good, belongs to the same stream of theology as the suffering servant songs – and we will come back to this theme when we get to Jesus. For now, I want to read the introduction to Job as a story, and assume that the idea of the bet functions to assure us from the start that Job has not caused his own suffering by sinning.

So, on to the speeches and back to the structure. I am going to adapt the suggestion of John Hartley (Hartley, 1988) and speak of 'cycles' in the speeches. Although at first glance the speeches appear to ramble, Job does respond to what his friends have said and then struggles on to his own conclusions. There are three main cycles in which Eliphaz, Bildad and Zophar take turns in expressing their understanding of the situation, and Job responds to each one, usually protesting against something that the former speaker has said. They can be found in chapters 4—14, chapters 15—21 and chapters 22—31.

These cycles of speeches are followed by a further speech from Elihu. Elihu is a previously unmentioned character who pops up at the beginning of chapter 32, explains that he has not spoken up to now because of his respect for the other characters who are all older than him, and then proceeds to argue that all of them are wrong. I'm sure he was very respectful as he did this. There then follows a cycle of speeches from God with further brief responses from Job.

Within the first three cycles it is possible to see a struggle between Job and his friends. The friends represent the voice of a particular theology that insists that, since God is powerful and just, he will punish the sinner and reward the righteous. The obvious (to them) conclusion from this is that the only way to explain the terrible things that have happened to Job is that he is a sinner who is being punished for his sins. This is their basic position and it does not change throughout the book, and they do not appear to recognize how shaming their theology is for Job. Job, on the other hand, insists with increasing vigour that this simple and unbalanced theology does not suffice to throw light upon his situation. Job's theology does develop throughout the book as he struggles to understand his situation. In one sense, therefore, the first three cycles of speeches are an argument about sin and it is noticeable that at the conclusion of this part of the book the friends are silenced, 'because Job was righteous in his own eyes' (Job 32.1). Job has held out against the shaming and his friends simply do not know how to respond.

Since Job's theology is the only one to develop, it is worth noticing where he begins. In chapter 1 we are told not just that Job is a good man, but also that he worried about his children. Whenever they held feast days, Job thought it was necessary to 'sanctify' them and to offer burnt offerings, just in case. He even tells us why: 'It may be that my children have sinned, and cursed God in their hearts' (Job 1.5). Job, in other words, is afraid of sins that may just possibly have happened and is offering sacrifices on a 'just in case' basis. However good Job may be, we do not get the sense of a warm and trusting relationship with his God.

We will look at each of the cycles a little more closely.

In the first of the cycles the friends give some general statements of their understanding of who God is and how God acts. God, they claim, looks after the innocent and punishes the wicked (e.g. Job 4.7-9) and they urge Job to trust this God and commit his fate to her. If Job is pure and upright then he can be sure that his integrity will be rewarded (Job 4.6) and that God will restore him to his rightful place (Job 8.5-7). At this point they are happy to simply proclaim that God is always just and to hint, ever so gently, that perhaps Job is being disciplined in some way: 'How happy is the one whom God reproves; therefore do not despise the discipline of the Almighty. For he wounds, but he binds up; he strikes, but his hands heal' (Job 5.17–18). Bildad does just mention the possibility that Job's (now dead) children may have sinned in some way but it is not a central part of his argument. As long as Job trusts in God, according to Bilbad everything will be all right.

Job, however, feels that his friends have not grasped the depth of his struggle or the heart of his complaint. He agrees with them on some points; in particular, there is some agreement on the reality of sin and that a mortal is never just before God (Job 9.2). He does not, though, draw the same conclusion from the premise as his friends do. Rather than meekly committing himself to God, he complains that God is so overpoweringly strong that if it came to a divine–human contest no human being could possibly prevail. Job wavers between arguing that a) he is blameless and God is being unfair (Job 9.19–24) and b) accepting that he is a sinner but complaining that, if he is being punished, the punishment is out of all proportion to anything he may actually have done. He demands to know what sin he has committed and why he is being pursued in this way (Job 13.22–26). In this cycle the gap between Job and his friends is not so great, but we begin to see the basis on which it will grow.

Before we move on to the second cycle there is one other point Job makes that deserves reflection. In chapter 7 he quotes (or at least appears to refer to) one of the great statements of Psalms which is normally seen as being good news for everyone. Compare these two verses:

… what are human beings that you are mindful of them,
mortals that you care for them? (Ps. 8.4)

What are human beings, that you make so much of them,
that you set your mind on them,
visit them every morning,
test them every moment?
Will you not look away from me for a while,
let me alone until I swallow my spittle? (Job 7.17–19)

It is not good news for Job that God always notices things or is always present and looking. In chapter 14 Job returns to the same theme and wishes that he could hide in Sheol (Job 14.13). The assumption here is that if God is always looking, then Job can never get any rest. Stephen Pattison has pointed out that for many shamed people these kinds of promises can be highly problematic. He comments:

> It suggests that one is perpetually under a kind of divine surveillance. There are no doors or boundaries that can shield one from the gaze of an omniscient and probably disapproving deity who respects no boundaries or privacy. (Pattison, 2000, p. 239)

Pattison goes on to argue for the theological motif of God's deliberate absence. He argues that God limits himself to show 'sensitivity and respect for human beings and creation' (Pattison, 2000, p. 304). Again, we are faced with the issue of how God's gaze is perceived; as long as God is experienced as persecuting and seeking out sin, the idea that he always takes notice of us will be bad news and we will want to join Job in asking that we be allowed to hide.

The second cycle begins in chapter 15 when the friends start to press their case more insistently. Job has not responded as they expected, and in the first speech of this cycle Eliphaz argues that Job is 'doing away with the fear of God' (Job 15.4) and goes on to describe in rather unpleasant detail the fate of the wicked. The others follow suit, attempting to increase the pressure since Job has not repented of his sin and trusted in God. Job responds by calling his friends 'miserable comforters' and asking plaintively, 'have windy words no limit?' (Job 16.2–3). He insists yet more strongly that God has turned against him. In chapter 21 Job makes a vital move that demonstrates that his theology is starting to shift. He questions the assertion at the heart of his friends' theology: the wicked *do*, in fact, prosper, he asserts, and he does this after Zophar has just spent the whole of chapter 20 explaining in detail the exact opposite. According to Zophar, 'the exulting of the wicked is short' (Job 20.5) and God will punish them for their sins.

Not so, says Job. 'The wicked live on, reach old age, and grow mighty in power' (21.7). In direct contradiction to his friends he paints a picture of people who have turned against God, who refuse to serve the Almighty because there is no profit in prayer, and who enjoy full and happy lives. The chapter concludes with Job's accusation that his friends have offered him 'empty nothings' and that their answers are falsehood. The Hebrew word here is *ma'al*, which is the word used to describe the desecration of the sacred or faithlessness in marriage (Hartley, 1988, p. 322). Job is claiming in the strongest possible terms that his friends are harming him and that this is a violation. Job is now involved in a direct confrontation with his friends; he has denied the very basis of their argument and states that he finds their theology abusive. He has become much more insistent that he is innocent and does not deserve what has happened to him.

The next cycle contains the most emphatic assertions from both sides. Zophar does not speak and Bildad adds little new, so I am going to concentrate on the conflict between Eliphaz and Job. Eliphaz is utterly determined to prove his case, so sure that God must be punishing Job for sins committed that he now starts listing those sins in great detail. Here, more than ever, we see the importance of the introduction, so that we can understand what is going on. Both Satan and God agreed in the introduction on Job's innocence and the peculiar bet made it clear that he was put in this position precisely because he was such a good man. What is more, Eliphaz admitted as much back in chapter 4 where he commended Job because Job had supported and strengthened the weak as well as instructing many (Job 4.3–4). Now, however, out of nowhere, Eliphaz starts to describe the long list of sins that Job committed, and that led to the punishment he is now enduring. Job has abused his own family, refused compassion to the needy, and ignored the needs of widows and orphans (Job 22.6–9). His wickedness is great and there is no end to his iniquities (Job 22.5). Having listed these mythical sins, Eliphaz concludes with a passionate plea for Job to repent and a description of how wonderful life will be when Job is restored to God.

No wonder Job describes his friends' theology as abusive. In effect, they are so determined that their dogma must be right and must apply in all circumstances that they are willing to condemn Job by making him responsible for all of the horror that has happened to him. If we remember that Job's misfortunes include the death of his children and the infliction of boils all over his body (surely a shaming experience), then we can begin to see how evil their argument is. They are not simply suggesting that Job has done one thing wrong and asking him to repent of that action, they are arguing that he is evil enough to deserve all that has happened to him. This is, indeed, *ma'al*, a violation; they are trespassing into a very vulnerable part of Job's soul and apparently have more concern for their theology than for Job himself.

Simone Weil has summed up just how poisonous shame can be, especially when experienced by someone who is suffering as Job is suffering:

> In the case of someone in affliction, all the contempt, revulsion and hatred are turned inwards; they penetrate to the centre of the soul and from there they colour the whole universe with their poisoned light. (Weil, quoted in Ford, 2007, p. 105)

Imagine for a moment being Job at this point in the argument. Exhausted and miserable, he finds himself surrounded by people who had supposedly come to support him but who have in fact blamed him for everything that has happened. It must have seemed as if no one was listening and there was no one to speak up for him. How easy it would have been to give in, to accept that they were right and he was wrong, and to shoulder the blame. Job is involved in nothing less than a struggle to hold on to his own sense of himself. No wonder he begins his reply by attacking his friends. 'How you have helped the one who has no power!' he cries sarcastically, 'How you have assisted the arm that has no strength' (Job 26.2); clearly, Job is describing his own sense of weakness. Yet despite seeing himself as one who has no power, he goes on to make the strongest and most direct assertion of his own innocence so far. He continues to insist that his friends are wrong and that God has made his life bitter, and then gives a most remarkable speech.

This speech is so remarkable I would even suggest that you read it out loud. If you are used to hearing Scripture read in church using the slightly pious monotone that some readers adopt, then it is also worth thinking about how you will read it. This is a passionate angry speech uttered by a man who is fighting for the ownership of his own soul, and needs to be read with all the fervour you can manage:

> As God lives, who has taken away my right,
> and the Almighty, who has made my soul bitter,
> as long as my breath is in me
> and the spirit of God is in my nostrils,
> my lips will not speak falsehood,
> and my tongue will not utter deceit.
> Far be it from me to say that you are right;
> until I die I will not put away my integrity from me.
> I hold fast my righteousness, and will not let it go;
> my heart does not reproach me for any of my days. (Job 27.2–6)

This is the strongest affirmation of Job's sense of his own righteousness and it picks up a point made in the introduction to Job. In chapter 2, God taunts Satan because even though Job has been afflicted, 'he persists in his integrity' (Job 2.3). What is more, at the end of the story God affirms that Job spoke rightly. Job argues for his own integrity and God supports that argument, although before we can get to that point Elihu steps in and piles on the misery a little more. His argument lasts several chapters and concludes with an accusation: 'The Almighty ... is great in power and justice ... Therefore mortals fear him; he does not regard any who are wise in their own conceit' (Job 37.23–24). So it seems that the lines are drawn. On one side are Job's friends and on the other is God and Job – which side should Christian theology join?

It can seem that Job is in a battle not just with his friends but also with the very heart of Christian theology. After all, his insistence on his own righteousness sits uncomfortably with the Christian claim that all have sinned and fallen short of the glory of God (Rom. 3.23). Does Job go too far? Does he insist too emphatically that he is a good and virtuous man? In some commentaries, Job is accused of self-righteousness, pride and of failing to remember that he is a sinner in the eyes of God (e.g. Clines, 1989, pp. liv–lvi). Such commentators are keen to point out that the story continues well after the cycles of speeches; there is also the great encounter between God and Job and, after God has spoken, Job retracts his accusation and does in fact repent. Or does he?

The contrast between Job's insistence on his own righteousness in chapter 27 and his apparent repentance in chapter 42 is so great that I am going to jump to that verse, before coming back to the encounter with God. The supposed act of repentance is so important that it can influence our understanding of the entire book. What is more, the fact that many Christians have found this insistence on Job's integrity very uncomfortable can be seen in the way that verse 42.6, which describes this apparent repentance, has been translated. Here are a few examples:

- 'Wherefore I abhor myself, and repent in dust and ashes.' (King James Version)
- 'Therefore I despise myself, and repent in dust and ashes.' (Revised Standard Version, New Revised Standard Version and the New International Version)
- 'I take back everything I said, and I sit in dust and ashes to show my repentance.' (New Living Translation)
- 'I retract all I have said, and in dust and ashes I repent.' (The Jerusalem Bible)
- 'That's why I hate myself and sit here in dust and ashes to show my sorrow.' (Contemporary English Version)

So, that is helpful. All of these translations attribute to Job the very response that his friends have been urging upon him and that he has been resisting. Here he is, expressing both shame, 'I hate/despise myself', and repentance, 'I take back everything I said'. I can almost see Eliphaz, Zophar, Bildad and Elihu rubbing their hands in glee as it seems that God has finally accomplished for them what they could not achieve for themselves. Job has repented, their theology has triumphed, and all is right in the universe. Except, in the next verse God announces that her wrath is kindled against the friends for what they have said, whereas Job spoke rightly. This does seem a peculiar way to follow a verse in which Job has supposedly renounced his previous argument. No wonder some modern translators have pointed out that there is a huge problem with the traditional reading of 42.6. To understand that problem we need to do a bit of work in Hebrew.

Job 42.6 is actually a very difficult verse to translate. The verse can be split into two parts and neither is particularly clear. The problem is that one word has multiple possible translations and, depending on which translation we go for, it looks as though another word is missing altogether. This means that we have two parts of a sentence and it is not clear how we should connect them. If we were simply to translate word for word what the Hebrew says (leaving, for the moment, one word that is particularly difficult to translate in Hebrew), it would look something like this:

I despise/reject/retract.
I turn away/repent '*al* the dust and ashes.

This leaves translators making a number of choices. The first line has a verb but no object to which that verb applies. The Hebrew word is *ma'as*, which means despise, reject or retract. So Job despises/rejects/retracts something, but he does not tell us what. Faced with half a sentence it is understandable that translators have supplied an object. However, the fact that so many of them have opted to translate the verb as something like 'despise' or 'hate' and have then decided that Job despises or hates *himself*, may say something more about the assumptions of Christian theology than about the text. There is nothing in the Hebrew to support the idea that Job is despising himself.

So what if we opt for a different translation? Instead of having Job despise, we could say that he is retracting something instead. The idea of retracting does at least fit with the fact that earlier in the book he has sometimes used the image of a law court when trying to hold God to account. This is closer to the New Living Translation: Job takes back something and we then supply the idea that what he is retracting is his argument against God. The New Living Translation takes this one step further by having him 'take back everything I said', which does seem slightly depressing for a reader who has just ploughed through 40-odd chapters of very long speeches. Job retracting *something* is a slight improvement but still leaves us with a contradiction in the next verse. Job retracts and then God promptly announces he has been right all along.

My preferred translation is based on a very different meaning for the word *ma'as*, which can also mean 'dissolve' or 'melt' (Janzen, 1985, p. 255). This is a much less common translation but does avoid the issue of the missing object. If this translation is correct, then Job is describing his reaction to meeting God rather than denying everything he has said for the rest of the book, and collapsing into shame. So let's take it for the moment that Job says 'I melt' and then put this with the second half of the verse.

The second half of the verse is equally open to misunderstanding. The verb in this half is *nhm*, which simply means to change one's mind or to turn from one course of action to another. It *can* mean repent, but it does not automatically imply any sense of remorse or that the first course of action was wrong. It can be used of God in those verses of the Bible that speak of God 'repenting' (e.g. Jer. 18.8). Once again there is a problem about the relationship between the verb and the object of the sentence, although at least this time we actually have an object. 'I *nhm 'al* dust and ashes.' A great deal hangs on how we translate the preposition *'al*. To put the issue another way, what do the dust and ashes have to do with the changing of the mind? Most traditional translations assume that Job is repenting *in* the dust and ashes, which is a sign of the depth of his mourning since he has just decided to despise himself. However, this is not the usual translation for *'al*. According to Janzen, in every other case where this form of the verb appears and *nhm* is followed by *'al*, the translation given is 'I repent *of*' or 'I repent *concerning*'. Use this more normal translation and Job changes his mind about the dust and ashes (presumably those in which he sat in 2.8). The difference in how we treat this one little word is huge. If Job repents *in* the dust and ashes then we are left with a man who is abasing himself before God and who is subject to the very shame that his friends have been urging upon him. If Job changes his mind *about* the dust and ashes then he is saying that he is ready to move on from his misery and shame and to begin his life anew.

It may seem strange, but the idea that Job melts before God, and in the melting finds the courage to move away from the dust and ashes that have expressed his misery and are a traditional sign of repentance, also seems to me to be quite evocative. We remember that God first created by breathing the breath of life into us and we will look later at the importance of the gift of the Spirit in our salvation. There is something here about relationship and also about the glimpse of beauty and glory that gives us a sense of being one with God. To melt before a gracious and loving God can build us up rather than dragging us down.

My argument above has been very dependent upon those who read Hebrew better than I do, but my main point is this. Verse 42.6 needs to make sense in the light of God's affirmation of all that Job has said in the very next verse, and it would really help if it did not undercut most of the rest of the book. After Job has made such a heroic attempt to hold on to his own sense of integrity, why has he abased himself so strongly? The Hebrew text does not justify such a translation.

We must, therefore, ask why this translation has held sway for so long? Could it be something to do with our traditional reading of sin? Christians have been so concerned to emphasize the basic message that all have sinned, and the traditional idea that pride is both the worst of sins and the root of all others, that we have found it almost as difficult to read Job as his friends found it to listen to him. We have done exactly what they did and tried to fit him into our theological presuppositions. As Janzen puts it:

> There is an almost universal tendency (as attested already in the friends of Job) to view Job's words and actions up to this point as presumptuous and proud. Similarly, there is a predisposition on the part of readers to expect a resolution in which Job repents of this presumption and abases himself before God. The question, of course, is whether the author of this book intended to present Job in such a fashion as to confirm and reinforce such conventional expectations and predispositions. (Janzen, 1985, p. 256)

Job, I believe, needs to be read as a balance to the biblical stress on the universal nature of sin. Both are biblical and both are the truth, but not the whole truth. To allow David to get away with believing that being king meant that he was somehow beyond sin is as dangerous as battering Job with the idea that he is responsible for his own misfortunes.

But have we rejected one set of 'conventional expectations' only to fall into another? In this reading of Job is he just too modern, fighting for his own sense of integrity and apparently putting God in the dock as he does it? There is more that we can say about Job 42.6 and the relationship between the encounter with a beautiful, holy and all-powerful God and the ability to repudiate the dust and ashes that represent the shame that drags us down. These may appear to be contradictory, but I want to argue that actually they build upon each other.

This means returning to the section of Job that I passed over. In chapter 38f. God speaks to Job 'out of the whirlwind' and at first sight God's reply appears to be a denial of everything that Job has said before.

'Gird up your loins like a man,' says God, 'I will question you, and you shall declare to me' (Job 38.3) and this comes after the accusation, 'Who is this that darkens counsel by words without knowledge?' The stage is set for a very one-sided conversation, far more one-sided than the one with Job's friends, in which God appears to be cutting Job down to size. In fact, it seems that God pretty well flattens Job with the enormity of her power and knowledge contrasted with Job's puny strength and understanding. To read these chapters is to gain some sympathy for the translators who assumed that Job's response must have been to despise himself. 'Where were you when I laid the foundation of the earth?' (Job 38.4), asks God, and from that moment on it is clear that Job has no chance in this unequal encounter. God, after all, runs the universe (chapter 38) and created and understands all the animals (chapter 39). Job attempts to concede that he is 'of small account' (Job 40.4), but by now God is on a roll and continues for another couple of chapters. She, after all, created the Behemoth (an unidentified but apparently very formidable beast, chapter 40) and the Leviathan (a traditional sea monster, chapter 41), and is the only one powerful enough to control either of them. Only when Job concedes for the second time is he allowed to speak. Job 42.6 comes at the end of Job's second concession that he has spoken of things too wonderful and that he did not understand, and that he has now seen God rather than just hearing about her as he had before.

## JOB: THE TRUTH BUT NOT THE WHOLE TRUTH

So is God just flattening Job? There does seem to be something here about the traditional expectations of a shame-honour society that expects God to defend his honour when it is attacked. Job has consistently argued that God has been unfair and has reached the point of arguing that God allows the wicked to prosper. This would be seen by the society around him as an attack on the very being of God, so perhaps it is not surprising that God's answer is such a strong defence of his majesty and power.

Yet, Job does not appear to experience this series of speeches as somehow diminishing him. Throughout the book he has fought for what we would call his own sense of integrity and his value as a human being. He has courageously denied the half-truths that his friends pushed upon him and his reward is a vision of God. He never receives a real answer to his question about why he is suffering, which makes him just like us when we do our theology. Faith is not about having the answer to all our questions, it is about how we live with those things we do not understand. Richard Rohr argues that what Job gains is more important than answers to his questions. He gains a sense of being known:

> At last, Job's desire is fulfilled – to see with his own eyes and not 'by hearsay.' To see and be seen. That's all any of us desire. For some eyes to go through us and understand. For someone to see us naked as God saw Adam, and not call us ugly. To see us naked and not name us foolish. We desire to be seen all the way through. (Rohr, 1996, p. 162)

Rohr rightly sums up one way in which the encounter with God heals our shame, but I want to argue that Job goes further still. In 42.5 Job makes an interesting move from hearing about God to seeing for himself, straight after an encounter that is entirely represented by words. What we actually read is God's description of his power and glory, based primarily on what God does. I think that this is quite understandable as words quickly fail us when we attempt to describe who God is. Job, however, is clear; yes, he has spoken about things he did not understand, but a great change has taken place. Whereas before he had *heard* about God, now he has *seen,* and something deeper than words and concepts has happened. Job has had a vision of God and God's beauty that has gone even deeper than that profoundly important sense that he is fully known and fully loved. God has not healed Job by turning him inwards but by drawing him out, and this is what gives Job the courage to change. In the end, Job's attention is not fixed on his own struggle, but on the glory of God. Job has 'melted' – that is, he has reached a place where God's beauty so surrounds him that he is not entirely clear where he ends and God begins. Important as his fight for his own integrity has been, even that has not been enough.

At the heart of this experience is how the power and glory of God is experienced. God's speeches are all concerned with what seems to be an overwhelming power that could easily devastate a human being. Yet this is not how Job experienced it. He has not been put down or abused by this encounter; instead, he has been lifted up, affirmed and given new strength. He abandons the dust and ashes and is restored to his community. In 42.11 Job's 'friends' are replaced with true friends and his family, and it is noticeable that they offer him comfort and consolation for his suffering. Job's encounter with God has not turned him into a superhero with all the answers and no need of human support. What it has done is drawn him out of shame, fixed his eyes on God, and thereby enabled him to find new life.

All of this brings us back to the theme of how the gaze of God is experienced and what it means to see ourselves reflected in that gaze. Job was not devastated by his encounter with God – but what of us? It is time to move on to the New Testament and to begin to examine how encountering God in Christ might enable the exodus from shame.

# 6

# The Welcoming Messiah

Belonging is the innate human desire to be part of something larger than us. Because this yearning is so primal, we often try to acquire it by fitting in and by seeking approval, which are not only hollow substitutes for belonging, but often barriers to it. Because true belonging only happens when we present our authentic, imperfect selves to the world, our sense of belonging can never be greater than our level of self-acceptance. (Brown, 2010, p. 42)

## Why Stories Matter

Let's talk about the Gospel that did not make the cut. A century or so after Jesus lived, there were a few gospels in circulation (and the number continued to grow). The process by which we ended up with just four is quite complicated, but we do know that a book about Jesus was more likely to make it into our canon if it was linked to an apostle and had been written down reasonably close to when Jesus actually lived. The so-called Gnostic gospels tended to be much later and were never seriously considered as part of the Christian canon. There is one gospel, however, that does not quite fit this rule of thumb, and that is the *Gospel of Thomas*. Its date is disputed, but it may be from roughly the same time period as Matthew, Mark, Luke and John (possibly a little later) and it has the apostolic link with Thomas. But it is not in the canon. Why is that? One of the reasons is probably because Thomas does not tell the story of Jesus. There is no account of how he was born (like Matthew and Luke) or even of how he appeared and immediately caused a stir (like Mark and John). There is no John the Baptist, no teaching ministry, no confused disciples, and no great shocking twist when the once popular teacher ends up on the wrong side of the wrong people and is sent to a humiliating death. Instead, Thomas gives us a collection of sayings that are simply delivered with no context, and with no introduction to the man who said them. It is as if they just appear out of nowhere. The opening line reads:

> These are the secret sayings which the living Jesus spoke and which Didymos Judas Thomas wrote down. (Lambdin Translation)

'So what has that to do with shame?', you may be asking. To which I want to answer, 'A lot'. When the Early Church was deciding which books should be read in church (and therefore be treated as Scripture), they were not interested in secret, disembodied sayings (no matter how wise), even though scholars have argued that it is likely that some of them do come from Jesus himself. One of the issues that mattered to them was that a gospel told a story about a baby born to poor parents, the man who encountered and welcomed a variety of people, and about the final humiliation and shocking death that turned out not to be final at all. It is the stories that allow Christians to be gripped by more than second-hand knowledge and allow us to see how Jesus treated the weak and the shamed.

I want to suggest that those stories are particularly important for those who are battling shame-ache. Shame drives us into ourselves, until it can feel like all of our energy goes into battling our own thoughts and feelings. We are constantly being told that we should love ourselves, and Jesus summarized a flourishing life as one in which we love God, others and ourselves. I have already argued that while we are often told that we cannot love others without first loving ourselves, the opposite is also true. Most of us have a deep sense of wanting to belong and cannot build a proper self-love without the love and support of others. A firm grasp on the fact that God loves us, and the depth of that love, is a key part of the flourishing life that will feed the other two.

Our question in this chapter is, 'How is someone with shame-ache to trust that love and hold that truth at the very centre of their being rather than simply stating it?' The story of the Exodus has already warned us that becoming free is more complicated than we think. We began in Genesis and I suggested then that a flourishing human being sees himself reflected in the gaze of God and experiences that gaze as one of love and approval. As soon as shame entered the picture, Adam and Eve's perception of that gaze became distorted. At the heart of shame is a fear of the gaze of others – we assume that they will look at us and see our failures and our weaknesses, and we easily project that on to God as well. After all, none of us are perfect and we are caught up in the forces of sin. We have damaged others and we have remained silent when we should have protested. This is not the whole picture of our lives, but it is part of it. How then, do those with shame-ache find a sense that God looks at them with love and joy?

In this struggle, facts are not enough. Disembodied teaching, no matter how wise and truthful, can be discounted and ignored. What is needed is a sense of who God is that goes beyond words into a personal sense of knowing and being known; we can only find this if God gives us insight into who she is by action as well as description. We have already noted that empathy helps us to grow out of shame both when we exercise it and also when we experience it. There is something about the connection created when someone stands with us, is open about times when they have struggled, or been hurt, that gives us the important realization that we are not alone. It is so much easier to make ourselves open and vulnerable with someone who is open and vulnerable with us.

This is why the stories about Jesus matter so much. This is why the greatest theologians have always insisted that the restoration of our relationship with God is multi-dimensional and rests on the life, death and resurrection of Jesus, not simply on following his teaching or believing in the cross. The central Christian claim has always been that we see God through Jesus. Sin, shame and sheer thoughtlessness can distort our understanding of who God is, with profound consequences for our faith and our image of ourselves. Certain readings of some of the biblical stories about God can do the same. In the stories about Jesus we have access to a sense of who God really is that goes beyond facts.

Shame can distort our living in a number of ways; it can undermine our trust in other people, which has an obvious impact on faith. Christianity constantly emphasizes the need to trust God, but we need to be realistic about how difficult that is when you struggle to believe that there is anything about yourself that is valuable or worthy. Stephen Pattison has explored the way in which being urged to worship a God who is perfect, while simultaneously believing that we are worthless, can amplify shame:

> The hierarchical, dominant God of much formal Christian liturgy and prayer may seem to promise acceptance and love at the expense of self-negation and sacrifice ... For persons who have an inadequate sense of self, this sort of experience may amplify a sense of powerlessness, uselessness, defilement and objectifying depersonalization. (Pattison, 2000, p. 261)

For the shamed person in particular, it matters to ask careful questions, not just 'Do you believe in God?' but also 'Who is the God you believe in?' and 'Is your understanding of God formed by Jesus?'

But we have not said quite enough. The story of Cain and Abel reminded us that shame can lead to more than issues of self-worth. If both brothers were struggling with shame-ache, then we must also remember that our feelings of shame and our fig leaves can lead us into actions that have disastrous and damaging consequences, not just for us but also for others. Trusting that the gaze of God is one of love and approval does not allow us to simply ignore all issues of sin. A God who is unconcerned about justice or who underestimates the horrific damage that human beings can inflict on one another is no real God. In the stories of Jesus we meet a God who does not simply love and welcome us but who also takes sin seriously, both the sins we commit and those committed against us.

So in this chapter we will look at some of the stories of Jesus that emphasize his welcome for the excluded, in the belief that they demonstrate for us something of the very character of God and give those struggling with shame-ache good reason to believe that when they see themselves reflected in the gaze of God, they will experience love and acceptance. In the second part of the chapter, we will move on to a very different way of thinking about God's welcome to us by investigating Paul's picture of salvation as being adoption by God. Then, in the next chapter, I want to take a look at what forgiveness actually means, hoping to take seriously the needs of both Cain and Abel.

First, though, a detour through the beginning of John's Gospel. This is John's introduction to the stories about Jesus and gives us the foundation for arguing that a key Christian discipline is to see God in Jesus. John will begin to introduce us to the theme of God living with and in us and we will return to this when we examine Paul's metaphor of adoption.

## Choosing a Tent Rather than a Palace

> And the Word became flesh and lived [*eskēnōsen*] among us, and we have seen his glory [*doxa*], the glory as of a father's only son, full of grace and truth. (John 1.14)

This is the classic New Testament description of the very heart of the incarnation and we need to note that it clearly declares that in Jesus we see the glory of God. We could equally well translate this as 'we see the honour of God' since the word is *doxa* and comes from the idea of 'good opinion', meaning God's intrinsic worth. In Jesus we see who God really is and God's true honour. However, John tells us more than this.

As we will soon see, the idea of 'dwelling' or God living with and in us, along with the idea that we live in and with God, is a key theme in John's Gospel. However, John normally uses the verb *menō*, which means 'remain' or 'live with', to describe this. Here, John introduces the idea of God living with us using the verb *skēnoō* and it seems that for anyone who read John in Greek, *skēnoō* would have managed to imply two very important ideas about Jesus, both of which draw on the First Testament.

First, *skēnoō* basically means to pitch a tent or to live in one. For anyone with a background in the First Testament this would call to mind the tent or tabernacle that the Israelites made for the Ark of the Covenant when they were wandering in the desert (see Exodus 35—40). The purpose of the tabernacle was to allow the Israelites to have a place of worship that could be set up when they stopped, but also could be easily taken down and carried with them when they set off again. By using this verb, it seems that John meant to call to mind the sense of a meeting place with God, but one that is temporary and moveable. The First Testament makes it clear that there was some controversy about the eventual choice to move to a different place of worship. David is the one who decides that it is wrong for him to live in a 'house of cedar' while the ark was in a tent (1 Chron. 17.1), and Nathan's first response is to argue that this is not something that God has asked for (1 Chron. 17.3–6). God is more interested in 'building David's house' (that is, establishing his kingdom) and it is David's son, Solomon, who eventually builds the temple. When that temple was built the gain was a permanent and more glorious building as a focus for Israel's worship; what was lost was the sense of the travelling God who had a vulnerable dwelling and was with her people in the struggles of the desert. John says that, in Jesus, God came and pitched a tent with us.

Knowing this matters, particularly for those with shame-ache. We need to remember that psychologists often point out that one of the reasons that shame is so very difficult to treat is because shame is itself shaming. We find it hard to admit that we are struggling with shame. At the same time, empathy from someone who has stood where we stand can be profoundly healing and we are much more likely to be open with, and to trust, someone who has personal experience of the agonies of feeling weak and vulnerable.

Equally, though, in Hebrew, the idea of 'dwelling' (*skn*) is linked to the noun *shekinah*, which means glory; this allowed the rabbis to play about with the idea that God's glory and God's dwelling were interchangeable. Rather conveniently, the Greek word *skēnoō* reflects all of this and therefore manages to convey the idea of 'make a dwelling', 'pitch a tent' and 'glory' all at the same time.

It is easy to see why some scholars have wanted to translate this verse 'and God pitched his tent' among us. It is easy for us, when we read it in English, to miss the radical nature of this claim. The claim that Jesus is the Word of God (and the Word was God, John 1.1) is sweeping enough, but John is also saying that Jesus has become the new meeting place for God and human beings; he is the new tabernacle. There is a hint here that we need to be very careful when we assume that we understand what glory means, for the verb also reminds us that Jesus chose a wandering, homeless lifestyle. He pitched a tent; he did not build a palace.

The God who chose a tent over a palace is not simply a God who understands us, she is the God who comes alongside us. If I were to push the metaphor, this is a God who gets what it is to feel tattered, moveable, open to the elements, rather than solid, beautiful and impervious. This is the God of Isaiah's servant songs and a vital element of the story for those with shame-ache. You are understood, even at your lowest point of self-loathing. God does not gaze at you from the safety of heaven, but comes and stands alongside you, in all of your weakness and vulnerability. There is more to say about Jesus' experience of shame, but that is for a later chapter.

The question for us all, whether we struggle with shame-ache or not, is whether Jesus of Nazareth, the human being who was born a couple of thousand years ago and lived and died in an obscure part of the Roman Empire, is the meeting place between God and human beings. Most of us come to faith carrying with us pre-formed ideas of what God is like. They come from many places, half-remembered sermons from our youth, our own experience and assumptions, what others have said, and the culture around us. The list is endless. Our basic expectations of the nature of glory and what is truly valuable in life also fundamentally shape how we see God. It is more difficult than we sometimes assume to ensure that it is Jesus and Jesus alone who forms our basic sense of who God is and how God will deal with us. In fact, it is a spiritual discipline, and unearthing the less than Christian ideas about God that slip in without us really noticing can take a lifetime. Those who struggle with shame-ache and who can far too easily project their own shamed judgement about themselves on to God may need to pay particular attention to this discipline. Jesus is the new tabernacle; he is the place where we learn what it really means to see the glory of God. This is why it is vital to take note of how he responded to the shamed and the vulnerable.

This is not the last of what John has to say about God dwelling with us. If we move to the end of his Gospel we find something else. Having told the story of Jesus' ministry, John gives us the story of the Last Supper and Jesus washing his disciples' feet – which then leads to an exceptionally long speech that is often called the Farewell Discourse. It is presented as Jesus preparing his disciples for when he would no longer be physically present and he promises them that this does not mean that they will be deserted because they will receive another '*paraclete*', namely the Holy Spirit, who will dwell with them for ever. Throughout this speech Jesus constantly uses the word *menō*, which can mean 'remain', 'dwell' and 'abide'. Here, in contrast with the temporary nature of abiding in a tent, is a word that promises a permanent living together. The thread begins in chapter 14 with the idea of Jesus going to prepare 'dwelling places' (this is sometimes translated 'room', but is taken from the same root as *menō*) for us with the Father (John 14.1–4). It then runs through the rest of the speech; see, for example, chapter 14, verses 7, 10, 11, 17 and 23, and chapter 15, verses 4, 6, 7 and 10.

Put all these verses together and you get a golden thread of interlinked ideas all based around a word that implies both coming to live with someone and remaining with them or creating a long-term relationship. The idea of 'abiding' is used in nearly every permutation. God abides with us, God abides with Jesus, Jesus abides in the Father and the Father in Jesus, Jesus and Spirit abide in us and we abide in Jesus, Jesus' words abide in us. It is all there somewhere in Jesus' last great speech in John's Gospel. This is not a fully worked-out theology (whatever that might be) but a constant reassurance of God's abiding presence, which will be experienced in a number of ways and which we will never be able to describe with perfect logic. According to John, Jesus did not just come and live among us, he created the possibility of God (Father, Jesus and the Holy Spirit, any combination of the three, let's just say the Trinity) living in us; through Jesus, we will be drawn into the love and life of God. For many Christians, of course, this sense of God living in us and us living in God is central to their understanding of the Christian's life, but this is not the case for all and there is work to be done in helping those with shame-ache to grasp the implications of God's life in us and our life in God.

This is not a new approach to Christianity, but I do believe it is particularly relevant for the shamed to reflect on this invitation. If you struggle to believe that you are welcome anywhere, try to grasp that at the heart of the gospel is God's invitation to share a home along with his promise to make a home within us; the very word used implies a long-term committed relationship. Shame is isolating; it turns us in on ourselves until we almost believe that we are the only one who has ever felt like this, and that we and we alone are lost in the pit of shame. I cannot see that the Christian faith offers any easy or instant solutions. I know this has happened for some, but many others experience long exoduses which include quite a few wrong turns. Christianity does offer an important promise – you are not in this alone. Christ lives within you, Christ bears the pain in you and alongside you, and Christ will never leave you. This is not something we cause and there is no instruction to ensure that it will happen. It is something that Jesus promises to all disciples and that we need to find creative ways to remember and live out.

We now move on to the stories. This Jesus who came and pitched a tent with us and who promised the life of God would dwell in us, what image do we get from the stories about him? If we allow these stories to grip our imagination and to form our vision of God, how would we then see God and how would we picture the relationship between God and us?

## Standing with the Shamed and Challenging the Judges

It is common today to point out that Jesus was hospitable and knew how to make people feel wanted and loved. It is an important theme, but I do want to raise an issue with it. So often when we think of being hospitable we think of being hosts or people who invite others into their space. This can be a place of genuine grace and welcome, but it can also be a place of power. The host sets the rules of the encounter and makes most of the decisions. Jesus pitched a tent among us and often found himself the guest. God living with us who had no permanent home of his own still found ways to help the shamed and the hurting to feel that their company was welcome.

One of the notable points about Jesus, the holy man, whom John says is the Word of God incarnate, was the way in which he scandalized the comfortable – and those who simply assumed that they were part of the 'in' crowd – by deliberately hanging out with those who saw themselves as unwanted and marginalized. People who had been put down all their lives, or who had been knocked back by life, people who felt they were not good enough for whatever reason, were likely to be at the top of his invitation list. And Jesus encouraged his disciples to do the same.

The Gospels tend to summarize the people with whom Jesus spent his time as 'tax collectors and sinners' and we may read this as meaning that they were the unwanted ones – at least in the eyes of those who considered themselves honoured members of society. Jesus' world was closer to that of Marcus and Claudia (whom we met in Chapter 3) than to ours; in that world, shame was not just an emotional response or personal assumption about our own value. Honour and shame was based in groups – the honour that mattered came from the group that you were part of, and to spend time with the shamed was to risk shame by association. Anyone who made it clear that they were a friend of 'tax collectors and sinners' risked being judged by the same stereotype, for everyone simply assumed that the company a person kept demonstrated something fundamental about who that person was.

Imagine for a moment the issues that this created for the holy people and leaders of Jesus' day. Jesus, of course, was a Jew and therefore the leaders of his people were also Jewish, but we can see the same phenomenon among people of all faiths and none. Here is a remarkable man, who can apparently perform miracles and who has a profound influence on the people around him. He is gathering large crowds by speaking of God and claiming that God is working through him. Already, people are making comparisons between him and those in authority and he is coming out of that looking rather good (Mark 1.22). Clearly, the religious leaders were drawn to him and were divided in their response. Some supported him, warned him when he was in danger (Luke 13.31), and invited him into their homes. Some, like Nicodemus, became followers (albeit apparently in secret, John 3 and John 19.39) while others were clearly more cautious – and he also ended up in direct conflict with some of them. For others he was dangerous and his actions caused great problems, and we can have some sympathy with them when we realize that if you did invite Jesus round to your house you were likely to find that he took over and some fairly undesirable people would turn up with him. He might even give you a lecture on your failures as a host (Luke 7.36f.).

That mixture of responses from the wealthy, the powerful and the religious leaders matters. Jesus was not, as is sometimes implied, universally against those who did well in life; some of the women who travelled with him had the resources to support his little group (Luke 8.1–3). He most certainly was not antisemitic, since he was a Jew as were all of his original disciples. He had a very specific problem with the way that some people used their power and interpreted his faith. We need to avoid assuming that everyone who encountered Jesus responded in the same way. He welcomed the wealthy and powerful (although the rich young man was invited to come along without his riches), but there was one group that he constantly opposed: those who used their wealth, power or influence to put others down. His issue, it seems, was with the judgemental.

Imagine how this might have been experienced by those who had felt rejected. Here was someone who cared about them and valued their company enough that he was willing to accept the inevitable criticism involved in coming alongside them and spending time with them, even when that criticism came from the most influential people around. He chose to spend time with the rejected, and in choosing this he risked losing the good opinion of those who had more to offer him in terms of both wealth and status.

These stories about Jesus give us an important sense of who he was and of one of the reasons that he attracted such a following, particularly among ordinary people. We could call him the hospitable Messiah; he could see through the shame that other people believed made them less than loveable and was prepared to counter that shame not simply with words but with actions. However, he went beyond being hospitable and made people feel welcome, even though he had no home to welcome them to. As Joanna Collicutt puts it, 'the homeless Jesus seems to have been rather good at hosting picnics' (Collicutt, 2015, p. 38). Several of Jesus' parables centre around how important it is to seek people out and welcome them, and the parables make clear that seeking those who believe themselves to be unwanted is an intrinsic part of who God is.

What is more, Jesus pictured the coming age as a banquet or feast at which people would be surprised both at who was invited and who got to enter first (Matt. 21.31–32).

The Gospels give us numerous examples of Jesus' inclusion of those who had been excluded from their community, either due to their lifestyle or because of some physical or mental health issue. If we examine them closely, we can see that Jesus is constantly concerned with more than the miracle of healing; again and again we see him also restoring a person's sense of self-respect or honour. One example would be the healing of the man with leprosy, where Jesus does more than just cure the illness. According to Matthew 8.1–4 (cf. Luke 5.12 and Mark 1.40–45), once the man has been healed, Jesus sends him to a priest and tells him to offer the correct sacrifices that indicated his healing. This second act allowed the man's reintegration into his community by making his healing public and ratified. This is just one fairly obvious example, but there are other stories that show Jesus' concern for people's honour in a less obvious fashion.

## Words of Encouragement?

It is always fun when Jesus messes with our theology. To give you a specific example, there are several places in the Gospels where Jesus heals someone and then informs them that 'Your faith has made you well'. To make this even worse, when we read the Greek it is possible to see when he says the person has been 'made well', he is using the same word as 'save'. So it would be quite possible to translate this statement as 'your faith has saved you'. Cue, lots of theologians jumping up and down in annoyance because the Church has spent ages (trust me, *absolutely* ages) carefully defining that we are healed/saved by God's grace alone and that faith is our response. This is a very important point. If we do not remember that God's grace is always reaching out to us and working in us independent of our faith, we are quite capable of ending up in the ridiculous position of trying to somehow deserve our salvation because our faith is so deep and strong. (If I close my eyes and believe really, really hard, then I will be saved.) In this way we end up with an image of faith that is almost the opposite to God reaching out to us in love and grace, while we learn to trust and love her in return.

This makes it really annoying that Jesus seems to say the exact opposite in several places in the Gospels. But he does, so rather than sulking I am going to take a shot at arguing that the way in which he does this actually makes a very important point for those with shame-ache, and we need to hold on to that point in balance with the one above: that God's love is always prior to and independent of any faith that we may muster up. I am going to do that by looking closely at not only the word for save/heal but also at the word 'faith' itself. The Greek word for faith is *'pistis'* and it can mean assurance, belief and trust. But it can also mean 'faithfulness', that ability to stand firm and to stick by people or your principles even when life is tough and it would be easier to give way. It is this dual meaning that lies behind the fact that the Bible even refers to 'the *pistis*' of God (Rom. 3.3 – this is normally translated as 'the faithfulness' of God). So here is a reality that I suspect most people with shame-ache know well; it is very difficult to have *pistis* in the sense of faithfulness, moral courage and sticking by people and principles if you do not have *pistis* in the sense of a basic trust that God and other people want you and value you. And it is particularly difficult to have that faith in God and others if you do not want and value yourself. Love for God, love for neighbour and love for self depend and build upon one another. We may have good reason to separate the two in theory but in real life faith and faithfulness are closely related, and shame-ache can lead us into a downward cycle that makes having *pistis* in either sense very difficult.

Human beings being what we are, we can even make faith itself a competitive situation and it is easy to imagine that others have a greater faith than we do. So, just for a moment, imagine what it might be like to be struggling with shame but then to hear Jesus commend your faith. Imagine how remarkable that might feel if all that you can see is that you have managed to screw up enough courage to get somewhere close to him and attract his attention.

It is easy to underestimate the courage that it takes for some people to do something that is apparently just a simple part of everyday life. Approaching someone who is famous and who has a reputation for being good and close to God, when you expect to be rejected, or when you have a long experience of being excluded (especially by people who assure you that they are good and close to God), may take just this kind of courage. If you have never struggled with shame-ache, you may need to pause and use your imagination here in order to grasp the bravery involved. So, what was it like to approach Jesus and ask for healing, when you had every reason to anticipate rejection?

I want to take some of the Gospel stories of healing and put them together because I think they are linked by two factors. First, it took particular courage or determination for the people involved to approach Jesus and to believe that he would listen to them. Second, Jesus commends their *pistis* and annoys a lot of theologians in the process. This statement sets you up to expect lots of easy and encouraging stories in which Jesus acts like a good twenty-first-century therapist and is constantly warm and welcoming. Let me be honest, though, and say that it is not quite so simple in all cases, but I am going to start with one of the more straightforward stories.

The story of the centurion whose servant got sick can be found in Matthew 8.5–14. As a representative of the hated occupying race, the centurion might not have expected much from Jesus, but he asked anyway. There is something extraordinary in the fact that he was one of the powerful invaders who had every reason to look down on those he had invaded, and yet he argued that he was not worthy to have Jesus enter his home. He asked for (and received) a miracle performed at a distance. In response, Jesus commended him, 'in no one in Israel have I found such *pistis*'.

And on to the more difficult one, the story of the Canaanite woman in Matthew 15.21–28. The reason this is the more difficult story is because at first it seems that Jesus is rejecting her in exactly the way she might have feared. She approaches him and he ignores her, so that the disciples have to intervene. The intervention is not based on empathy; they are just tired of the way she keeps shouting at them. When Jesus does speak to her, he starts by insisting that he was only sent to those who are of Israel (sorry, you are a foreigner, so I am not interested in you). He even uses a common insult of the time, talking about children and dogs with the clear implication that she is one of the dogs. This becomes only a little bit more palatable when we realize that the word for 'dog' refers to a household pet. It is a difficult story, one that is just a little more understandable against the background of a group-oriented society that simply expected that people would favour those who are within their own group. So why put it in the list of stories that are supposed to be encouraging for those with shame-ache? I have done this partly because it is there in Scripture and it matches the criteria that I gave above, so we can hardly pretend it does not exist, but I have also included it partly because it has something to teach us precisely because it is so difficult.

For our purposes there are two points to highlight about the story.

In a strange way, this story pays the woman a great compliment. Remember Job and his courageous fight against the supposedly biblical theology of his friends? This female non-Jew joins Job and others in a long line of Jewish people of faith who dared to disagree with God when they simply could not understand how God was acting. In Scripture, faith is not simply accepting God's word and being obedient; it is also struggling and fighting, and sometimes it is struggling with God. See, for example, Abraham (Gen. 18.16–33), Moses (Exod. 3—4), Elijah (1 Kings 19), Jonah (chapter 1) and Jeremiah (chapters 12 and 20). This woman got to argue her case with a man *and she was heard*. It is possible, therefore, that Matthew's original readers would have focused more on seeing this Gentile woman as part of a great Jewish tradition of speaking up and arguing with God, rather than on the initial rejection (which simply fulfilled their natural expectation).

This is where we need to remember Pattison's argument about how deeply unhelpful some of the ways in which Christianity presents God can be. If God is distant and all-powerful, if God is perfect and we are always wrong so that our role is just to accept 'God's will' in all situations, then Christianity can force people with shame-ache deeper into shame. This is common Christian teaching but represents only part of what Scripture has to say. To see God only as all-powerful and always right is to ignore an important stream of scriptural teaching in which people of faith see God apparently acting in ways that contradict mercy and justice, and they stand up to him. *Pistis* does not always mean passive acceptance – sometimes it means having the guts to fight for what you believe in. That is what faithfulness is all about.

The second point to highlight is the ending. The story finishes with Jesus recognizing the depth of the woman's faith and doing what she asked for – healing her daughter. If you have shame-ache, take note that Jesus is not offended in the slightest when she does not turn away after his first refusal; instead, he is impressed by the courage it takes for her to persist. There is something here about the way in which the struggle for faith and God's attention is often experienced. For whatever reason, sometimes we have to keep approaching and asking before we are heard. The story ends on a high note when Jesus commends her, 'Woman, great is your faith.'

A simpler story is that of Bartimaeus who tried to attract Jesus' attention when other people tried to silence him (Mark 10.46f.).

Bartimaeus responded by simply shouting all the louder and Jesus stopped for him. In other words, once again it took a particular mix of courage and persistence to be able to speak to Jesus. After healing him, Jesus also commended him. 'Go, your faith has made you well.'

The next story, and for me one of the more interesting ones, is that of the ten lepers from Luke 17.11–19. Here, Jesus cures ten lepers by sending them to a priest. This means that Jesus is not around at the point at which they are actually cured. Only one of them, who is a Samaritan, makes the effort to return to Jesus and to give thanks for what has happened. If the implication of the story is that he was the *only* Samaritan and that the others were all Jews (which seems the most natural reading of Jesus' response), this means that it is the one most likely to assume that Jesus would reject him, and the one most likely to resent Jesus as a Jew, who is the one who returns to give thanks. Jesus comments on the absence of the other nine and then says to the one, 'Get up and go on your way; your [*pistis*] has made you well' (Luke 17.19). Ten were healed of leprosy and yet this is said only to the one who returned. It seems unlikely, therefore, that Jesus was saying that his faith was somehow part of his physical healing, so what did Jesus mean by commending his faith and saying that it had made him well? Again, I cannot help but wonder if there is something here about Jesus' recognition of the particular courage it took for this one leper to approach him and the faithfulness involved in seeking Jesus out once more to give thanks. When Jesus refers to being made well or being saved, he means more than a physical cure.

My basic thesis, then, is that when Jesus says something about 'great is your *pistis*' or 'your *pistis* has made you well/saved you', we need to hear in this a particular commendation for those who drew on what faith they had and the courage they could drum up to approach him, even though they faced particular difficulties doing so.

By this point, of course, anyone with shame-ache may have a sinking heart because they cannot imagine themselves being able to show the kind of persistence and courage that I have described. What is the point of stressing that Jesus recognized and commended the strength of character shown by these particular people to someone who doubts that they have that same strength of character? The slightest sign that they are unwanted is likely to send them back into themselves, so how are they supposed to draw comfort and inspiration from these stories?

This is why I want to spend a little longer on the last of the stories, a story that strikes me as being a classic account of someone with shame-ache. This is about someone who wants something from Jesus, but who cannot summon up enough courage to actually approach him, and yet by the end we find the same commendation.

In Luke 8.41–56, Mark 5.22–42 and Matthew 9.18–36 we are told two healing stories that are described as being intertwined. Jesus is called to the house of a synagogue ruler called Jairus whose daughter is extremely ill (in Mark and Luke) or already dead (in Matthew). His journey to the house is interrupted by a woman who is clearly doing everything she can to get healed without Jesus actually noticing her ('shame-ache'?), yet Jesus not only stops and helps her but also proclaims that her *pistis* has healed/saved her. For our purposes, I am going to concentrate on the better-known version from Mark and Luke.

What fascinates me about this story is the way in which everything about it is set up to emphasize the importance of Jairus and the relative unimportance of the woman. He is a man and she is a woman, in a society that assumed that meant that he mattered more. He is a key member of his society and she appears to be totally isolated. He is named and she remains anonymous. He has a household who support him and bring him messages about his daughter's condition; presumably it was his choice to approach Jesus in person. In contrast, the woman is forced to act on her own and we get the sense of someone with no support to draw on. Jairus is wealthy but the woman has spent all of her money on doctors who failed to cure her. He leads the local synagogue, and she has an illness that makes her unclean. It is important not to over-emphasize the effect of this illness. There were only certain circumstances in which being ritually pure mattered and there were clear rules about how to achieve this state of purity, so having a permanent discharge of blood would not have led to the woman being completely shunned. Nevertheless, there is a contrast here between a religious leader and a woman whose illness meant that she could not participate in some aspects of religious practice. And, just in case we have read enough of the First Testament to understand just how unimportant all of these factors are in the sight of God, according to Mark and Luke, Jairus' need is also greater. He has a 12-year-old daughter who is seriously ill. The woman has already been ill for 12 years so we can be sure that her illness is not life-threatening and we are tempted to ask what difference it could make if she waited just a little longer. Everything is set up to ensure that the reader will thoroughly approve if Jesus ignores the woman and goes where he is needed most.

Furthermore, her actions demonstrate that she also believes that she is unwanted; she seems to be acting out of desperation rather than any trust that Jesus will be responsive to her need. Her plan is to touch the fringe of Jesus' clothes (which we can read as being the minimum physical contact she could possibly manage, and also as implying she came up behind him; he would have been wearing a tassel that hung to the middle of his back). Presumably what she then intends to do is melt away into the crowd without anyone knowing that she was there. She is the only person in the Gospels who is shown as needing something from Jesus but not daring to approach him face to face. We can take this as an indication of deep shame-ache. Surely, anyone who had lived for 12 years with an illness that ensured that anyone who touched her would become unclean, and who now lives in poverty having spent all her money on doctors, would have internalized a deep sense of being unwanted and despised. She risks the crowd (we are left to suspect that she had no choice) and plans a speedy touch and disappearance.

It is entirely understandable that her focus was on the physical cure; what we easily miss is the way in which her own actions could so easily have prevented Jesus from also offering her a greater form of healing. Shame makes us want to run away and hide ourselves, and it is that hiding that makes it more difficult for us to receive the empathy and acceptance that we need in order to be healed. Once again, we are faced with the destructive cycle of shame and the woman is caught within it. She needs more than a physical cure, but her own actions seem likely to prevent her from receiving all that she needs.

To understand how painful this was, it is worth imagining what it was like to be her at the moment when Jesus turned around. She came so close to making it and escaping unnoticed. Perhaps she believed that the fact that Jesus was on his way to an important man's house only increased her chances of getting away with it. Imagine, therefore, being her and realizing that Jesus has stopped and is looking for the person who touched him. She must have been mortified and, for those who do not have to live with shame-ache, it is worth staying for a moment with that sense of mortification. It is easy to talk about people with shame-ache being 'their own worst enemy' without realizing what it is like to be in the grip of a sense of uselessness and a desire to flee that can be overpowering. So let us pause for a moment and pay tribute to her (reluctant) courage. The Greek of Luke 8.47 literally speaks about her realizing that she 'could not escape notice' and we need to remember that escaping notice was her dearest wish and at the centre of all the plans that she had made. However, when she realizes that it cannot be managed, she makes no further attempt to run away, but rather comes forward and speaks up for herself. Anyone who has struggled with shame and with the primitive instinct to disappear will understand just what it took for her to face Jesus and explain what she had done.

While we imagine being her when Jesus turned and searched for her, we might also ask why he did this. Why not let her get away with it? The only clue we have lies in what he then said.

First, there is the same commendation of her faith that we noticed for others who approached Jesus a little more openly. To be told by Jesus that your faith (which is closely related to being faithful) has been recognized is surely healing in and of itself. In this sense, the woman is part of the pattern we have already noted; Jesus realized that when someone approached him it took extra courage and he commended this, even for a woman who had done everything she could to avoid a direct conversation. Jesus engineered a moment when he was able to look her full in the face (despite her plan to come up behind him and run away as quickly as possible) so that she was able to see his smile and his acceptance of her. In other words, she got her chance to see herself reflected in Christ's gaze of love. But there is more; we should note the full sentence that he spoke to her: 'Daughter, your faith has made you well; go in peace.' This is the only time in the Gospels that Jesus addresses a woman as 'daughter'; he bestows on this woman who has been rejected for 12 years a title that implies family membership – the ultimate acceptance.

## One More Act of Imagination

Try for a moment to imagine what life was like for the woman after she met Jesus. I cannot think that 12 years of struggle and growing poverty faded away instantly just because she had been healed and was now a part of her community again. It seems to me more likely that she experienced a long exodus out of shame-ache, with all of the struggles we have examined, to believe in the new freedom she had been given. I wonder how much it mattered to her that she could look back and remember that time when Jesus refused to let her slink away having received only a physical cure. I suspect she treasured the memory of the way that he stopped, despite the vital call on his time, looked her in the face, bestowed on her the title of 'daughter', recognized the faith and courage it had taken for her even to approach him from behind and offered her the traditional blessing: 'Go in peace.'

Let's pause for a moment before we move on to a very different idea of how we are welcomed and summarize what we have seen so far about how Jesus counteracted shame. He stands with us in the vulnerability of life (he chose a tent rather than a palace), he took a stand against those who judge others or set themselves up as greater than others, and he had a special welcome for those whom his world had rejected. He recognized and honoured the courage that it can take for those with shame-ache to approach and ask for help, and he commended the faith of those who managed it. Faced with the need of an important man and an unimportant woman he made time for both, and gave the woman who had been isolated by her illness the loving title of 'daughter'. Jesus, we might say, was the welcoming Messiah.

There is also a very different way, though, of describing that welcome in the theology of Paul.

## Welcome (to the Family)

In Paul's letters there are three passages that all use the idea of adoption in some way or other. They are:

> For you did not receive a spirit of slavery to fall back into fear, but you have received a spirit of adoption. When we cry, 'Abba! Father!' it is that very Spirit bearing witness with our spirit that we are children of God, and if children, then heirs, heirs of God and joint heirs with Christ – if, in fact, we suffer with him so that we may also be glorified with him. (Rom. 8.15–17)

> But when the fullness of time had come, God sent his Son, born of a woman, born under the law, in order to redeem those who were under the law, so that we might receive adoption as children. And because you are children, God has sent the Spirit of his Son into our hearts, crying, 'Abba! Father!' So you are no longer a slave but a child, and if a child then also an heir. (Gal. 4.4–7)

> Blessed be the God and Father of our Lord Jesus Christ, who has blessed us in Christ with every spiritual blessing in the heavenly places, just as he chose us in Christ before the foundation of the world to be holy and blameless before him in love. He destined us for adoption as his children through Jesus Christ, according to the good pleasure of his will – to the praise of his glorious grace that he freely bestowed on us in the Beloved ... In Christ we have also obtained an inheritance, having been destined according to the purpose of him who accomplishes all things according to his counsel and will, so that we, who were the first to set our hope on Christ, might live for the praise of his glory. In him you also, when you had heard the word of truth, the gospel of your salvation, and had believed in him, were marked with the seal of the promised Holy Spirit; this is the pledge of our inheritance towards redemption as God's own people, to the praise of his glory. (Eph. 1.3–6, 11–14)

This is a powerful image of welcome that can speak to us without any investigation into what it might mean in its historic context. God invites us to be part of his family; this is a profound image of welcome. Set against Paul's assumptions around adoption rather than our own, however, the image has even more to say.

We will start with the images that adoption brings to mind for us. My guess would be that most people living in the twenty-first century assume that the main purpose of adoption is to care for a child and give that child both physical and emotional safety and nurture. So here is the first point to ponder – Paul understood the purpose of adoption very differently. To grasp what Paul is talking about, and therefore to see how this particular image of salvation might be of help to the shamed, our first task is to set aside our understanding and try to grasp something of what adoption meant in first-century Roman culture. As the passages above make clear, adoption for Paul is associated with receiving the Spirit and moving from being a slave to being a child of God. It also means gaining an inheritance in and alongside Christ (notice how important this is – all three passages mention inheriting) and that inheritance is linked with redemption and holiness. We will explore all of these further, but first we need to tackle a major difference between Paul's world and ours, that is, the issue of who gets adopted anyway.

## Why Adopt an Adult?

Let's start with who gets adopted and acknowledge that we are not talking about an orphaned child. In Roman culture the child had an obligation to continue the family honour of the biological family, and therefore an orphaned child would often be assigned a tutor, whose role was to manage any property (Lindsay, 2009, p. 69). Yet Paul still uses the image of adoption and expects it to be familiar to his audience.

We will return for a moment to the story of the imaginary Marcus Claudius and his sister Claudia, and Julia Claud and her brother Mark who we looked at in Chapter 3. Remember, they are an example of a brother and sister living in the ancient Roman Empire and in the modern UK. For the purposes of the next part of their story we are going to assume that they are the only children in their nuclear family; that they have reached adulthood and that their parents are too old to have any more children. We will give their story a tragic twist by sending Mark and Marcus off on a boat trip. For Mark, our modern-day example, this is likely to be about leisure so we will send him off on a sailing trip on a friend's yacht. For Marcus, however, it is likely that he is using the boat because it is the only realistic form of travel available. Whatever the reason, both boats sink and both men drown.

What issues do their families face? We have assumed that both have good and loving families, so both families will be devastated by the tragedy and will mourn their much-loved son and brother. However, Marcus' family faced an extra problem, one that is unlikely to concern Mark's family in the same way. Once again, this has to do with the family name and identity, and the sense that the family name was linked with the family honour that needed to be continued into the next generation. Some scholars argued that for noble families it was more important to perpetuate the family name than to continue the family bloodline (Lindsay, 2009, p. 93). Claudia could not pass the name to her descendants and inheritance laws favoured men over women. The present-day Claude family would have been faced with the possibility that their family name would die out in the next generation, and for someone who lived in a group-oriented society, and particularly Roman society, this was to be avoided if at all possible.

The Romans had a solution to the problem that the Claude family faced. If, for whatever reason, a Roman family found themselves in a position where there were no men to pass on the family name and inherit the family property, they would adopt an adult male. In fact, scholars argue that adoptions in the Roman Empire often involved an adult rather than a child being adopted (Lindsay, 1998, p. 61). It was possible to adopt a minor, but there were strict rules in case the adopter took financial advantage of his charge (Lindsay, 2009, p. 69) and it was also rare for women to be adopted. If you remember what we said in Chapter 4 about how difficult it was to have children and raise them to adulthood, then you will realize that this was an issue that faced any number of Roman families. Not surprisingly, Romans would often adopt a close relative, such as a nephew (Lindsay, 2009, p. 103). A man who had been adopted was able to inherit exactly as he would have done had he been born into the family; in fact, increasingly the benefactor would even use his will to adopt a man, so that the man might inherit.

However, let's concentrate on adoptions that happened when the adopter was still alive. Certain obligations were placed upon the one who was adopted. Men were generally expected to be the public face of the family while women were expected to confine themselves to the domestic world. An adopted man was expected to take seriously his role in representing the family in all that he did, which meant he had to adopt the honour code of that family and the strata of society in which that family moved. Everything that we saw in Chapter 5 about the importance of the family name, and the obligation to pass it on to the next generation burnished rather than degraded, now applied to the adoptee. Naturally, any children he might have would become members of the new family and be regarded as grandchildren of the family who did the adopting.

As Paul was no doubt aware, one family within the Empire had taken adoption to new lengths, and that was the Imperial family. Beginning with Julius Caesar, the family of the emperors had increasingly come to use adoption as a means of ensuring succession to the role of emperor. To give some sense of the history, here is a simplified account of the early Roman emperors and how each came to the throne, beginning with the Emperor Augustus (who according to Luke was emperor when Jesus was born (Luke 2.1)), and ending with the Emperor Nero (it is possible that Paul died in the persecutions under Nero):

- Gaius Julius Caesar (the Emperor Augustus). He was born Gaius Octavius Thurinus and the original Gaius Julius Caesar was his mother's uncle. On his adoption he took Caesar's name, but other people sometimes referred to him using Octavius, his old family name. The Roman senate granted him the name Augustus after his defeat of Antony and Cleopatra. Historians normally refer to him as either Octavius or Augustus. For the rest of the emperors, I have used the name normally used by historians but added other names used in brackets.

- Tiberius, who was the stepson and adopted son of Augustus. (Born Tiberius Claudius Nero, and on adoption became Tiberius Julius Caesar.) Tiberius adopted his nephew Germanicus who died before him. Germanicus was an able general and popular in Rome. Later emperors used Germanicus as part of their name.
- Caligula, son of Germanicus (born Gaius Julius Caesar Augustus Germanicus – Caligula was a nickname).
- Claudius, uncle of Caligula.
- Nero, adopted son of Caligula (born Lucius Domitius Ahenobarbus, but on adoption took the name Nero Claudius Caesar Augustus Germanicus).

In other words, of the five emperors who reigned during Paul's possible lifetime, four of them inherited owing to either their own or their father's adoption and in every case it was an adult who was adopted. In fact, one of the many great political scandals of Paul's day was that of temporary adoptions; this happened when men were adopted so that they could temporarily change social class and be elected to office, only to repudiate the adoption when it was no longer useful.

So let's stand in the shoes of Marcus' family as they have a crucial decision to make. They need to find a man to whom they intend to entrust the future honour of their family. We can imagine that they are going to search carefully and that they will look long and hard at any potential candidates, asking themselves whether he is likely to live up to their expectations. This is another reason why Romans often adopted adults; it meant that they knew what they were getting. Hopefully, the chosen candidate will also regard his adoption not simply as a benefit, but also as a privilege and a mark of the high regard that the family have for him.

We can imagine further that they have made their choice and decide to adopt Antonius Cato, a distant relative from a poorer and less honourable branch of the family, who have other sons to continue the family name. What will actually happen to Antonius as the adoption goes through? Inevitably, the Romans had a ritual to allow this to happen and at the heart of this ritual was the idea of a transfer from one power to another.

The key figure in any family was the so-called *paterfamilias*, or the male head. In this case the *paterfamilias* would be Marcus' and Claudia's grandfather until his death and then their father. It was he who embodied the family's honour and by tradition he had tremendous power over his family, including the power of life and death. I need to say quickly that this was a tradition – we can find no examples of a father actually claiming the right to kill his children in Paul's day. What we can find in the written records are a few references to the power of life and death and the inevitable assumption by some that children were more disciplined when it was exercised. The idea of the power of the *paterfamilias* was embedded in Roman culture and therefore in Roman adoption. The Roman father acted for the entire family and the rest of the family were under his power until he died, even after the children had reached adulthood. The *paterfamilias* owned the family property and acted legally for the entire family. So if Marcus' grandfather were still alive, he would adopt Antonius on his son's behalf (Lindsay, 2009, p. 66). To be adopted meant that Antonius moved from the power of one father and came under the power of another.

If, therefore, Antonius' father was still alive there would be a ritual to formally sever that relationship, and then the actual adoption would include this formula:

> 'May it be your will and command that A. Cato may be to M. Claudius in right and in law his son, just as if he were born from him as *pater* and from his *materfamilias*, and that he [Marcus Claudius] may have in relation to him [Antonius Cato] the power of life and death, as there is to a father in the case of a son.' (Adapted from Walters, quoted in Sampley, 2003, p. 53)

Notice the very strong sense here that Antonius is being transferred from one power to another and is to be treated as if he had been born into the Claudius' family. Antonius would probably then adopt the name Marcus Claudius.

With this background in mind, let's explore a little what adoption as an image of salvation might say to us – and in particular what it might say to the shamed. Adoptions should remind us that becoming a child of God involves being welcomed to the family as a Roman would have understood that phrase. It bestows upon us a new status, a new obligation and a new inheritance.

## A New Status

It is a sad fact of life even today that a child who happens to be born into one type of family is likely to have a greater status than an equally deserving and talented child born into another one. Paul's world did not question this. Today we want to emphasize even more strongly that all are equally valued by God; nevertheless, the image of being adopted can be used as a way to help those struggling with shame-ache to grasp that they now have a new family and therefore a new status.

Paul makes the change of status as dramatic as possible when he speaks of having been a slave and now being a child of God (Gal. 4.7). A slave had no status even as a human being; he was a thing and seen as a possession of his owner. What Paul is asking us to imagine is going from being a possession to being a member of the family with all of the rights and privileges that this conveys.

## A New Obligation

To return to our illustration above, when the adoption goes through the new Marcus Claudius will have gained a new status as a member of the Claudius family, but he will need to remember that they have adopted him for a specific purpose. They are looking for a man who will be the public face of the family and who will ensure that the family name is passed on to the next generation, at the very least generally held in good esteem, and preferably enhanced. He will need to live honourably and to give the rest of the family a reason to take pride in the family name. We might say that he has been given a new status and now is expected to live up to that status.

We need to recognize that for a person with shame-ache this could come across as an overwhelming responsibility, and therefore no one image of salvation can convey everything that it involves; all images need to be balanced by other ways of speaking of salvation. But we also need to emphasize that the Claudius family chose Antonius because they saw in him the qualities they wanted in a son. We will return later to the question of what God sees when she looks at us. This is an image about God's trust in us and ability to see in us what we cannot always see in ourselves. It is also an image that helps us to hold in balance two vital but different ideas. In theory, all Christians recognize that to be a Christian is to be both justified (accepted and welcomed despite our flaws) and to begin a lifelong process of ongoing sanctification (progressively becoming more like Christ as our new identity as a child of God becomes more and more part of how we live). In practice, theologians and preachers have constantly had to look for creative ways to hold them together, and throughout Christian history the emphasis has fallen more on one side than the other. Any version of Christianity that collapses into simply a way to get to heaven has fallen too far in one direction, while any version that constantly emphasizes God's judgement has gone too far in the opposite direction.

I want to argue that adoption, properly understood, helps us to express both ideas in one image. As Burke and others have shown, adoption is helpful because there is a natural link between joining a family and representing that family in our behaviour. Put the image against its Roman background and that becomes even more clear. What Paul was trying to say with the image is, God has chosen you to be one representative on earth of his divine family; now live as a valued and wanted family member would live.

## A New Inheritance

If Jesus annoys theologians in the way he talks about faith, Paul has also got the biblical scholars going in the way he uses the word 'adoption'. Look carefully at the Romans and Galatians passages quoted above and you might see that Paul is unclear about whether adoption leads to the giving of the Spirit, or the giving of the Spirit brings about adoption. Paul is not entirely logical in his use of this and many other images. Personally, I think this is quite understandable when we consider what we know about his lifestyle. Paul did not lock himself away in some room and write nice, tidy theology; he spent his time travelling, preaching, starting arguments, running away when the arguments got out of hand, avoiding being arrested (not always successfully), singing hymns with fellow prisoners (because he failed to avoid being arrested), swimming for shore when yet another boat sank, disagreeing with Peter, founding churches and then trying to advise them because he had moved on somewhere else. In between that little lot, he dictated some letters to a secretary (Rom. 16.22) without the benefit of a word processor. Sometimes his images are not fully worked out. This does not prevent us from drawing out from what he says some key essentials, one of which is that adoption is inseparable from the giving of the Spirit who works within us to bear witness that we are children of God, to pray within us so that we call God *abba* just as Jesus called God *abba*, and who is also the pledge of our inheritance that is to come.

In other words, Paul's image of adoption points us back to where we started with John and the idea of *menō* – God the Father, Jesus, the Holy Spirit will dwell within us, drawing us into the life of God. To be adopted is to receive a new life that begins in us now, but that is also the pledge of an inheritance to come.

None of this is new – and yet all of it seems to be forgotten too easily. In popular theology and in many of our favourite hymns the focus appears to be solely on the need to have our sins forgiven and on the idea that Jesus in some way bore our sins or substituted for us on the cross, but this is not the whole truth of the gospel. If we focus on this too much our understanding of salvation becomes one-dimensional and we leave many Christians struggling to articulate how Christ's death on the cross actually makes a difference to them. Used well, the image of adoption can help to counteract this.

Our potential to live well and to flourish was distorted when we were born as vulnerable vines into a world dominated by cycles of sin and shame. We have already seen that Scripture sometimes sees sin as a power that is bigger than us and that we need to be saved from more than just the result of our own sin. We need to be saved from the sinful cultures around us that warp our thinking and living. For Paul, adoption implied something about how that salvation happens. Adoption rescues us from one power (which Paul sees as being a form of slavery) by placing us under the power of our loving God and gives us both the beginnings of a new life now and the promise of an inheritance alongside Christ to come. All of these are images of how salvation is worked out in our lives.

# 7

# The Demanding Messiah

An act which calls for forgiveness usually causes guilt in the injuring person and shame in the person injured by that act. (Patton, 1985, p. 13)

I first noticed Anna when she arrived late for an evening service. She slipped into one of the rows at the back and left during the final hymn. This continued for several weeks until after one service when the steward came to see me and said that Anna had asked if the minister would mind talking to her. The fact that she had asked somebody else if I would be willing to speak with her said something about her state of mind. So it was that one Sunday evening I sat in a cold church and heard her story.

At the time I had been a Methodist minister for a few years. I had read quite a lot of theology and had some pastoral experience under my belt. I would not say that I felt ready to deal with anything that was thrown at me, but I thought I at least had a good grasp on teaching about God and some ministerial skills. Then I met Anna. This conversation really happened, although I have changed Anna's name and some of the details of the history I am about to describe. Anna turned out to be only one of a number of women with similar stories and questions I have met over years of ministry.

Anna had been abused by her stepfather over a period of several years and her mother had done nothing to protect her. Although she could not be certain, Anna now suspected that her mother had chosen to turn a blind eye to what was happening for fear of losing her husband. Anna finally escaped the abuse by leaving home as soon as possible, with no qualifications and was now struggling to support herself by means of a series of low-paid and boring jobs. By the time she reached our church she had been to any number of other ones and had told her story. In each case she had received a sympathetic hearing and she expressed some gratitude that at least she had been heard and believed. But in each case also, the conversation had then moved to the one imperative on which it seemed all Christians agreed. Anna needed to forgive both her abuser and her mother. No one, it seemed to Anna, fully understood the depth of her sense of betrayal or the struggle she now faced with a shame that, at times, threatened to overwhelm her. She asked the question that I simply could not answer. 'Why, according to the Church, does God care more about my abuser's need for forgiveness than he does about my need for justice?'

All I could do that evening was listen and assure her that she mattered to God every bit as much as her abuser. As I walked away, however, the overwhelming sense that I carried with me was that the theology I had already learned, everything I already knew about reading the Bible and speaking about God, was not enough. Not wrong, necessarily, but not enough. I had plenty to say to someone who had done wrong and was asking for forgiveness, but little to say to the one who had been hurt. I knew that was wrong, but I hardly knew where to start in addressing the inadequacy. Just one thought remained with me: this was an issue about that most old-fashioned of ideas – sin, and how we normally talk about sin. Clearly, what had been done to Anna was a sin. Since the Bible constantly addresses just this issue, why was it that I knew so little about biblical teaching concerning the person who has been sinned against?

But it took me years before something else struck me about the conversation that night. As I look back now, I cannot help but think that Anna was really asking at least two questions at once. On the surface there was the very serious question about forgiveness and why the Church was so insistent that she needed to forgive. However, behind that question was another one, and possibly an even bigger one. Am I wanted? Am I valued? Is my attacker just more important in God's eyes than I am? Do his needs outweigh mine on the divine scale of justice? Christianity had taught me to deal with questions of being saved from the sins I had committed – but I felt adrift in this very different territory.

There is no simple answer to Anna's question about why her attacker's needs seemed to be valued above her own, but we can recognize why the churches she visited emphasized forgiveness so much. Forgiveness was central to Jesus' own message. It is even in the Lord's Prayer – 'Forgive us our sins as we forgive those who sin against us.' It is the subject of several parables and it is often argued that Jesus modelled forgiving others on the cross: 'Then Jesus said, "Father, forgive them; for they do not know what they are doing." And they cast lots to divide his clothing' (Luke

23.34). So we cannot duck the issue and claim that Anna should not have to even think about forgiving.

What we can do is give much more attention to the issue of balance, remembering again that Job's friends were pursuing a biblical theme and could call on plenty of Bible verses to back up their case that all people are sinners and need to repent. The issue was not that their message was not the truth; rather, it was not the *whole* truth. They did not listen appropriately to Job or ask the hard questions about how this biblical truth should be lived out in a messy human life by a vulnerable vine. Could it be that the Church has done the same with the message of forgiveness?

Anna heard clearly the demand that she forgive her attacker. What she did not hear so clearly was that God paid attention to her voice and her needs, even though this is also part of the biblical message. In other words, there was little attempt to integrate Jesus' radical concern for the oppressed, the shamed, and those who had been sinned against with Jesus' emphasis that forgiveness is part of the life of discipleship. This raises the question as to why, when the gospel is supposed to be all about grace, did Anna feel that forgiveness was something that she needed to accomplish all by herself?

So in this chapter I want to try to give forgiveness its proper context and to ask some hard questions about exactly what we mean when we pray that line in the Lord's Prayer. At the very least we need to take careful note that we pray, 'Forgive us our sins *as* we forgive those who sin against us', not 'Forgive us our sins *once* we have forgiven those who sin against us'. The context into which I want to put forgiveness is everything that I have tried to argue in this book so far:

- Genesis 3—4 encourages us to realize that sin traps us in cycles of shame and blame and that sin is not a simple issue.
- God cared equally for Cain and for Abel, for the offender and the injured, and that it is possible that both have been affected by shame in different ways.
- We are vulnerable vines, not impervious islands; this means that we are formed by our experiences and our relationships with others. How others treat us has the power to build us up or damage us and we have a similar power over others.
- Sin can distort our vision and our living so that the other person

becomes less than human and we act as though he exists purely for our own ends, as David did with Bathsheba. True repentance is demonstrated, at least in part, by treating the other person with the respect that he always deserved. An apology and this better behaviour withdraw both the threat and the insult that the original action conveyed.

- Being sinned against creates a sense of debt and leaves us vulnerable to believing that we are somehow less valued that the offender – a message that the gospel of Christ denies. A person with shame-ache is particularly vulnerable to this message. Whatever we say about forgiveness we must not deny the basic message that God values Cain and Abel equally, and we must take seriously that the person who has been injured may be struggling with an acute sense of shame. This shame can either be about what happened or felt in a more general sense, which may make it more difficult for them to insist upon the respect that they deserve.
- Jesus is the welcoming Messiah who pitched a tent among us and shares our vulnerabilities and weakness. He is also fully aware of the courage that it can take for a person with shame-ache to approach him.
- Salvation can be pictured as adoption in which the life of God is born within us and God begins to draw us into her very life.

How, then, does forgiveness and Christ's expectation that Christians will forgive fit into this larger picture?

## Some Opening Work

Before we begin there is some preliminary thinking to do, particularly around our language and the words that we use to talk about forgiving. If you are very practically minded you may be tempted to skip this part, but it is worth remembering that the words and ideas that we use to talk about a subject can have a profound effect on how we think and imagine around that issue. It pays to think carefully and use words clearly.

Let's start with the people involved. Most people are aware that calling someone a 'victim' can be problematic as it traps that person in a passive role in which everything is done to them. In certain situations people prefer to use the word 'survivor' and obviously it is important to respect the ways in which people choose to describe themselves. However, part of my argument is that forgiveness can be a struggle even when it seems to others that the action was an unimportant one; as we saw in Chapter 3, sin can be like a debt that accumulates and a small insult constantly repeated can be difficult to forgive. I have therefore opted to use the most flexible word I can think of, and will refer to the person sinned against as 'the injured'. I find this a helpful description because an injury can be anything from a cut thumb to something life-threatening requiring intensive care.

What about the one who does the sinning? The Christian tradition has the word 'sinner' and I could quite easily have used that. I chose not to do so for two reasons. First, because the word has such difficult connotations that are related to some of the arguments I have made already; we have misunderstood the broader biblical picture of what sin actually is and have used the idea of sinner to shame some people while ignoring the far greater sin of others. Having attempted to recognize the complicated nature of human life and the way in which cycles of shame and blame and sin shape us, and the reality in which we live so that most of us are both sinner and sinned against, I intend to avoid the label of sinner and use the most neutral phrase possible. I have chosen to use 'the offender' on the basis that a person can give offence by a relatively innocuous action, but the word can also be used to describe someone who commits criminal acts.

So if that is how we are going to describe the people involved, what about the events and, in particular, the response that we make to them? I want to suggest that if we are going to acknowledge that we can sin against one another and that a sense of debt exists after an evil action, if we are going to listen properly to the voice of Abel and take seriously all that we learned from the Exile about what it means to live in a sinful world, it matters to be clear about the following.

A desire for *justice* is not the same as taking *revenge*. We have already seen that to be badly injured is to suffer an insult and possibly an ongoing threat that the action could be repeated, and it is not wrong to protest at this injustice. In fact, we could say the opposite and argue that it matters to ask that the injury done to you is acknowledged and redressed. If being injured carries the implicit message that you matter less than the offender, then to demand justice is to ask that the message be denied and the truth that all people matter equally in God's sight be acknowledged. This means that to be pushed into forgiving too easily may only emphasize the message of your lesser importance and possibly exacerbate your struggle with shame. People who suffer from shame-ache are particularly vulnerable to this. We have seen the way in which shame can produce any number of responses, but at the heart of all of them is the sense or the fear that the self is worthless. A person with shame-ache may, therefore, accept the idea of her lesser importance too easily and may 'forgive' too easily because she does not believe that she deserves justice. There is a question, though, as to whether this would be forgiving or condoning, and I explore this below. Covering over the injury in this way may only add to the cycles of shame in which she is trapped. Equally, a person with shame-ache may find any sense of her lesser importance absolutely unbearable and therefore find it impossible to forgive. If she is a Christian and well aware of Christ's teaching on the importance of forgiveness, her own inability may then add to her shame.

To ask for justice is to ask that the injury done to you is taken seriously and that you be valued equally with the offender. To take revenge is to take action against the offender, perhaps in an attempt to prove that you matter as much or more than the person who injured you. Revenge continues the cycle of sin, shame and blame in which we so easily become trapped. However, as we saw from the Exile, to dream and pray about taking revenge is not the same thing as actually doing it; if it were, we would need to remove several psalms from the Bible. The Scriptures generally emphasize *both* God's love and mercy *and* God's belief in justice. When read as a whole, the Scriptures are also realistic about just how difficult it is to keep these two in balance. Christians, on the other hand, have a tendency to label the cry for justice as a desire for revenge, and to push people to forgive too easily.

*Anger* is not the same thing as *aggression* and while one can lead to the other this is not always the case. No matter how we may try, we cannot simply switch anger on and off; indeed, telling ourselves that we should not be feeling whatever we are feeling can exacerbate shame and other mental health issues. We have already seen in looking at the Exile that there is a proper place for the experience and expression of anger and that we are positively encouraged to bring that anger before God. This is, after all, the God and Father of Jesus Christ, who became so angry at what was happening in the temple at Jerusalem that he knocked a few tables over and caused havoc. Anger is the emotion that needs to be recognized without guilt, and managed so that it finds an appropriate expression. Aggression refers to actual behaviour that is hostile to another person or physically attacks them.

*Repentance* is not the same thing as *remorse*. Remorse is the offender's own feelings of regret and/or guilt about what happened, and not all offenders deal with their remorse in a mature fashion. The cynic in me notes how often people are sorry that they got caught, but are not necessarily sorry about their original behaviour. As we have already seen when looking at David, repentance involves not just inner feelings, but also a determination to change behaviour and to treat the other person with the respect that he should always have received.

The Hebrew word for repent is *teshuva*, and it comes from the word *shuv* which means to turn back or to turn away. For example, in Ezekiel 18.21–24, *shuv* is used both of the wicked turning away from wicked behaviour and of the righteous turning away from righteous behaviour. Repentance, in Hebrew, is intimately linked with changing our actions. There is a different word for feeling regret at what has happened, *nicham*. It is vital that we resist any interpretation of Christianity that implies that what God really wants is for us to feel bad about our sin (and about ourselves) while doing nothing to address our actual behaviour and without giving us any sense of how we might change. Remorse can be a very painful feeling for the offender and too often so-called 'apologies' focus on relieving the offender's sense of guilt and excusing her actions, rather than addressing the injury done to the other person and the question of how future behaviour will be different.

Despite the famous saying, *forgiving* is not the same thing as *forgetting* and the two do not necessarily go together. We will say more about this later, but for now let us note that a number of theologians today are arguing that to forgive is, in fact, to remember – but to do so in a different way and in a different context. Attempting to simply forget the injury is not the same thing as forgiving, and 'forgetting may be a dangerous way to escape the inner surgery of the heart that we call forgiving' (Smedes, 1984, p. 39). In other words, forgetting may simply be used to avoid facing the pain of an injury as well as avoiding the real effort involved in genuine forgiveness.

Equally, to *forgive* is not the same thing as being *reconciled*. Ideally, one will lead to the other and we can celebrate when this is the case. However, the offender may be dead or untrustworthy or there may be another good reason why the relationship cannot – and should not – be resumed in this life. This can be deeply distressing when the issue is between family members, but it is important not to be too romantic about the family relationship (there are no perfect families in the First Testament). Sexual abuse, for example, is often committed by a family member and it may be dangerous to push the survivor to continue a relationship with the offender. We also need to remember that sometimes profound injury can be caused by a succession of small acts that constantly underline the offender's lack of respect for the injured. In such cases, there are serious questions to ask about any demand that the injured be reconciled with an offender who refuses to recognize the impact of their ongoing actions.

Finally, to *forgive* is not the same thing as to *condone* or to *excuse* the injury done. In fact, it is not possible to forgive unless the injured acknowledges that a real injury has been caused (Volf, 2005, p. 165). If the injured is unable to recognize the degree of injustice involved or is lacking in a healthy sense of self-respect, then he may say that the injury did not matter or that the circumstances made the action understandable, or that his own actions provoked the offender – *but this is not forgiving*. To help us to see how forgiving is intimately linked with an acknowledgement that the action in question was wrong, imagine for a moment this scenario.

Daisy and Margaret have an argument that Margaret is absolutely certain that Daisy began for no reason. The next time they meet, Daisy announces rather grandly, 'You know, you were completely unreasonable, Margaret, but never mind, I forgive you.' Most of us would find being in Margaret's shoes very difficult; far from being reconciled to Daisy it is more likely that we would be affronted by her presumption in 'forgiving' us for something that we had not done, let alone for an action for which we hold her responsible. In other words, in this situation we instinctively realize that forgiveness only occurs when guilt and blame exist. We also recognize that pronouncing forgiveness can itself be harmful, when it is used as a power play allowing Daisy to claim the moral high ground. James Alison argues that what Daisy is doing is actually a form of retaliation; it is a way of saying, 'You were wrong and I hope that one day you will see the error of your ways' (Alison, 2003, pp. 32–3).

There is an interesting contradiction in the way that many of us think about forgiveness. When it comes to forgiving others, we think it is too easy for the offender. It is 'letting her off the hook'. The very metaphors that we use for forgiving encourage us to believe this. To forgive is 'to let go' or to release the injury. We do not like to forgive, in part because it can feel so close to condoning. However, when it comes to accepting forgiveness from others, we may find it all much harder. Then we realize that to be forgiven involves the assumption that what we did was wrong; being blamed is an intrinsic part of being forgiven and most of us want to avoid being blamed. Forgiveness, at minimum, names the injury and takes the injury seriously even as it offers grace to the offender. When we are the offender, we may say we want to be forgiven when what we mean is that we want our behaviour to be excused.

Theologians are increasingly insisting that forgiveness and justice are not opposites but are intimately related. Furthermore, God's wrath, far from being a hangover from the 'Old Testament God' whom Christians often assume is somehow different to the God of Jesus, is a divine response to the reality of sin and the ways in which it distorts human living. As Volf puts it:

> God's wrath is not primarily an emotional state but a forceful censure of sin. In the face of an offense, God doesn't say, 'I am so furious at what has happened; I better take a walk to calm down.' Instead, God turns to the offender and says, 'You've done something terribly wrong.' Someone was wronged, and God names the act for what it is and condemns the doer. That's God's wrath. When God forgives, God doesn't condemn anymore. That's what it means for God to avert anger. (Volf, 2005, p. 166)

God's wrath against sin (to use the old-fashioned phrase) is part of the good news of the gospel, but we can only see this if we learn to see that wrath not as an annoyance with us for not living up to some petty rules, but rather as a passionate commitment to the value of, and justice for, all of God's children. For the Abels of this world, God's wrath matters.

Finally, we should note that seeking forgiveness from the person who has been injured is part of Jesus' teaching, mentioned in the Sermon on the Mount:

> So when you are offering your gift at the altar, if you remember that your brother or sister has something against you, leave your gift there before the altar and go; first be reconciled to your brother or sister, and then come and offer your gift. Come to terms quickly with your

accuser while you are on the way to court with him, or your accuser may hand you over to the judge, and the judge to the guard, and you will be thrown into prison. Truly I tell you, you will never get out until you have paid the last penny. (Matt. 5.23–26)

Notice that Jesus is very clear that the offender's responsibility goes much further than confessing the sin to God. According to Jesus, being reconciled with the one whom we have injured is more important than worship.

## So, What Is Forgiving Anyway?

It is time to ask about the nature of forgiveness. Can we find words about forgiving that help us to understand what we are asking Anna to do? In doing so, can we take seriously Jesus' insistence that there is a relationship between having our own sins forgiven and forgiving others, without turning forgiveness into a huge burden or stumbling block for those who have been badly hurt by the actions of others? At the heart of Christianity lies the idea that we are forgiven through the life, death and resurrection of Christ and we often focus on the cross as a central part of that action. I want to explore the possibility that being drawn into the life of Christ might also enable us to forgive others and so, having explored the incarnation in the last chapter, I turn now to the death and resurrection of Christ. So we start here: what happened when Jesus died?

At one level we might argue this: Jesus died because the religious and political authorities of his day turned against him. They put him through a series of fake trials at which witnesses lied about him and sentenced him to a public, humiliating death that he did not deserve and that involved a whipping and other physical abuse.

In other words, Jesus stood in the place of the injured, enduring undeserved physical and emotional abuse at the same time as he stood in the place of the offender and was judged and pronounced guilty. What is more, after the resurrection he still bore the scars of the injury done to him; Luke and John agree that he proved to his disciples that it really was him by showing them his hands and his feet, the place where the nails had been driven in, and where the spear had pierced his side (Luke 24.39 and John 20.27). At the very least we can say of Jesus that as he suffered physical violence, he literally absorbed the sin done against him and bore the scars caused by the actions of others. The same could be said of the emotional abuse. Jesus was unjustly condemned only to pray for those who injured him; he accepted the sin done against him which could also be seen as a way of absorbing the sin of others.

What if this idea was allowed to shape the metaphor that we use when we talk about forgiving? I want to argue that, in the case of serious injury, forgiving is not 'releasing' the injury, or 'letting it go', and that these images can be positively harmful as they seem to downplay the cost involved and the genuine threat to our sense of ourselves that is involved. They may accurately reflect part of the emotional experience involved in forgiving, but it is important that we distinguish the healing of emotions from the act of forgiveness. When the injury done to us is serious, we need a different set of metaphors based on the real cost of being injured:

> Any wrongdoing leaves in its wake some amount of damage or cost, be it physical, financial, emotional, relational, or social. This is damage which the offender usually cannot repair ('you can't take it back,' as children learn), and which the offended will, in any case, incur. The persistence of the damage threatens any attempt to leave the past in the past, insofar as the damage testifies to the deed. The persisting damage cannot be addressed in the same way as the persisting meaning or guilt. So here's a further thing left for forgiveness to do: With forgiveness, the offended agrees to bear in her own person the cost of the wrongdoing and to incorporate the injury into her own life without further protest and without demand for retribution. (In some cases forgiveness can be uncomfortably intimate: You must allow me to creatively incorporate the scars that bear your fingerprints into the permanent fabric of my life, and trust that I can do so.). (Hieronymi, 2001, pp. 550–1)

What if we begin to imagine and describe forgiving as 'absorbing' the injury or as 'incorporating the scars' of what was done to us into our lives and our story, and what if we did this by constantly emphasizing that for the Christian this is done in and through the Christ who bore exactly the same cost on the cross? What if we take as our context for forgiving the reminder that to be a Christian is to live in God and to have the life of God implanted within us, and this is why we are asked to bear this cost in and through the power of Christ? How might this change our basic understanding of what happens when we forgive another person? This does seem to have the immediate advantage of emphasizing the way in which forgiveness has a real cost – but can it do more? I want to argue that it can, and do so by returning once more to the story of Jesus.

During his trial, beatings and crucifixion, Jesus appeared to be a particularly passive figure. Mark says at one point that he remained silent (Mark 14.61) and the Christian tradition has often emphasized this silence and said less about the fact that he does sometimes speak up in his own defence. Nevertheless, having been an active and powerful figure, Jesus' arrest seemed to reduce him to a much more submissive role. This has sometimes been held up as an example to those suffering, but we need to emphatically reject the idea that being Christian means always passively accepting the injuries done to us by others. In Jesus' case, the crucifixion was not the end of the story – having been unjustly condemned and abused, he was also vindicated when he was raised to life and appeared to his disciples as a powerful and somewhat mysterious figure. Presumably, after the resurrection he could have rained down all sorts of punishments upon the heads of his tormentors, but instead he lived out the heart of his message about God's kingdom – he did not retaliate against those who had injured him. Even when he was active and powerful, Jesus demonstrated something else about what lies at the heart of forgiveness: the costly act of non-retaliation.

I want to suggest that non-retaliation (particularly when we are experiencing the psychological pain of unresolved resentment or, worse, at what happened to us) is a greater part of forgiveness than we often allow for. Remembering the bigger picture can help us to grasp this; part of the message of Genesis and much of the First Testament shows that human beings are caught in cycles of shame and blame and that these cycles are always in danger of escalating. To refuse to retaliate contributes something to breaking that cycle. This, I suggest, moves us a little closer to understanding what forgiveness means. To forgive is to refuse to take my pain out on the offender, which means, in part, that I bear the cost of carrying that pain myself but also means that I contribute to breaking the cycle.

Here I want to note that the Scriptures do not simply speak of forgiving, but also of 'not rendering evil for evil' (Matt. 5.38–42; Rom. 12.17; 1 Thess. 5.15;1 Pet. 2.23 and 3.9). We have, I suspect, come to overemphasize the importance of healing our memories and emotions while underemphasizing the importance and cost of not retaliating, even while we are still angry and hurt. By equating forgiveness *solely* with the first, we encourage people to judge themselves as having 'not forgiven' an injury and we fail to recognize what they have achieved in not retaliating and living with their own hurt and pain.

So having argued that forgiving is absorbing the injury without retaliating against the offender as well as being healed of our own hurt feelings, we also need to say something about the time involved and the way in which forgiveness is a process and not an instant decision. We can again use Jesus as an example of this. It is common to say that he forgave those who crucified him – but he didn't. What Luke actually says is that he prayed, 'Father, forgive them, for they do not know what they are doing' (Luke 23.24). In other words, he asked God to forgive them. This may seem a fine distinction, but what this means is that the man who caused constant issues throughout his ministry by proclaiming that people were forgiven (something that others believed was for God alone to say) holds back from doing the same thing in this crucial moment. Instead he prays for God's forgiveness. Now, admittedly, even to ask God to forgive at the moment that they are driving the nails into your hands takes more grace than I have, but it is subtly different to forgiving them yourself. This may be a hint that, even for Jesus, forgiveness was not something that always came instantly.

This also raises the question of the relationship between God's forgiveness and ours. Forgiveness should not be imagined as something that God demands of me and then leaves me alone to complete; if the heart of faith is about God living in us and us in God, then forgiveness also needs to be something that we do with God.

## Jesus' Teaching on Forgiveness

With this background in mind, let's take a look at Jesus' actual teaching on forgiving.

We start with Jesus' parable about the unforgiving servant (Matt. 18.21–35). The basic premise of the story is that the unforgiving servant owes his master a huge debt, but that there is a second servant who owes the first one a much smaller amount. Having received forgiveness from his master for his debt, the unforgiving servant promptly pursues the second servant for every penny. This is the shock at the heart of the story – the first servant has received overwhelming grace, but refuses to be graceful in return. According to Matthew, Jesus concludes the story by stating, 'So my heavenly father will also do to every one of you, if you do not forgive your brother or sister from your heart' (Matt. 18.35). In each case, it is worth noting that the person who owes the debt is threatened with a practical result; in the case of the first servant, the order for him to be sold into slavery is given and then rescinded, while the second actually is thrown into debtors' prison. The focus, in other words, is on whether or not there is retaliation. The issue of feelings or dealing with the injured person's anger does not arise.

The constant assumption of those who preach on this parable seems to be that we are all in the position of the unforgiving servant; that is, we have all committed sins that are worse than those committed against us. But Jesus never says that this is the case. He illustrates a lack of grace by telling a story about the disparity between the debt that the unforgiving servant owed and the debt that was owed to him, and concludes that we all need to offer forgiveness. This parable has become caught up in the insistence, by some, that all sins are equally bad in the sight of God, a claim that ignores the fact that Jesus repeatedly distinguished between sins. He censured the religious authorities of his day for being hypocritical and judging others, but he welcomed so-called sinners into his fellowship. It is not clear that Jesus regarded all sins as being equally bad:

> From 'All are sinners' it does not follow that 'All sins are equal', from 'Neither is innocent' one cannot conclude 'The sins of both are equal'. The aggressors' destruction of a village and the refugees' looting of a truck and thereby hurting their fellow refugees are equally sin, but they are not equal sins; the rapist's violation and the woman's hatred are equally sin, but they are not equal sins. The equality of sin dissolves all concrete sins in an ocean of undifferentiated sinfulness. This is precisely what the prophets and Jesus did not do. Their judgements were not general but specific; they did not condemn everyone and anyone, but the mighty and the ruthless who oppress the weak and crush the needy. The sin of driving a person from her possession, from her work, from her means of livelihood, the sin of pushing her to the margins of society and beyond, weighs high on their scales. How could there be solidarity in this sin?

The perpetrators are the sinners and the victims are the sinned against, their non innocence notwithstanding. (Volf, 1996, pp. 82–3)

So let's make one more distinction. The biblical claim is that we are all sinners; it is not that every sin we commit is equally bad. The claim that we are all sinners does not mean we are all somehow rotten to the core (we remember again that God pronounced creation, including human beings, as 'very good'), but that we are vulnerable vines rather than impervious islands – meaning that we are embedded in, and influenced by, a sinful world and unable (by ourselves) to avoid the power of sin to shape us and the way we live. This recognition that we are all sinners matters; there is no room in Christianity for self-righteousness or for the constant assumption that God is always on our side. But this is not the same as saying that God is somehow foolish enough to consider rape and arguing with your neighbour as being equally evil.

The insistence that all sins are equally evil risks silencing the protests of those who have been terribly damaged by the actions of others. The Bible clearly and specifically condemns all evil done against others; it holds sin up to the light and names it as wrong and we need to help the injured do the same. To do this is to listen to this parable – after all, the basic premise of what Jesus said is that some debts are bigger than others. Jesus asks us to reflect on what it says about human nature: that it is possible for someone who has been forgiven a huge debt to fail to have compassion on someone who owes a much smaller one. He does not claim that we are all, at all times and in all places, in the position of the unforgiving servant.

There is another problem with our usual understanding of this parable. The final sentence, which is clearly presented as Jesus summing up its basic message, insists that all Christians must forgive 'from the heart', and it is not surprising that many take this to mean that we must get rid of all feelings of hurt and anger about what has happened. If we continue to be angry and to be assaulted by the memories of what took place, then we assume that we have failed to forgive. But there is a distinction we need to draw between what Jesus may have meant, speaking in the language of his culture, and what we who live in a very different culture hear.

Our culture assumes that we think with our heads and feel with our hearts. Jesus, presumably, made the same assumption as the rest of the Scriptures which means that he would have spoken of the heart as the centre of decision-making, not feelings. In Jesus' world, we make decisions with our hearts while, according to at least some parts of Scripture, we feel with our bowels (think about what happens when you get scared and this assumption might make some sense). We still have traces of this assumption in our language when we, for example, refer to being 'wholehearted' in our decisions or we talk about feeling something in our guts. So where we would say 'make up your mind', Jesus would say something like 'decide in your heart'.

I want to suggest, therefore, that when Jesus said that we must 'forgive from our hearts', what he meant was closer to 'make a real decision and live by it' than 'get rid of all the feelings associated with having been hurt'. Remembering that one of the sins that Jesus did constantly condemn was that of hypocrisy, I suspect that his real target was those who claimed to forgive while in practice they were storing up their bitterness and planning to take revenge. I repeat that I find it noticeable that the parable is concerned with the actions of the unforgiving servant, not with his feelings.

The problem with assuming that Jesus is talking about getting rid of all the emotions associated with having been badly hurt is that we are then left with the issue of how. It is not possible to put away the hurt by an act of will. When it continues to hurt, and when the memories keep coming back, we can too easily take it that we have not forgiven 'from the heart' and that we have failed (once again). How different would the act of forgiveness seem if we followed Jesus in seeing 'forgiving from the heart' as being a willingness to make a genuine decision to forgive, and then saw the continuing struggle with our own anger and hurt as part of bearing the cost of forgiveness in solidarity with the Christ who suffered and died for us.

I should, perhaps, make it clear that I am not underestimating the importance of dealing with the sometimes overwhelming feelings of resentment that can blight the injured person's life. It is, after all, miserable to be left struggling with powerful feelings and greatly to the advantage of the injured person if they can neutralize their own sense of pain and anger at what happened. By proposing a different model of forgiveness what I am really trying to argue is that we need to take seriously that it is God's grace that will ultimately help us to heal the pain caused by the injury, and that our discussion of forgiveness needs to be framed in such a way that the injured person is encouraged to bring that pain to God and, if necessary, to do so again and again. For as long as we imply that forgiveness includes the healing of all hurt and must be achieved by our own efforts, we are more likely to alienate people from God – and therefore make the healing that much more difficult.

So can we now say something about what it means to forgive? I suggest that we have learned that to forgive means:

- Naming the injury as real and wrong and being realistic about the message the injured may have received from the injury (which needs to be denied).
- Refusing to retaliate – even when our anger and pain tempts us to do so. In this way we join Christ in a ministry of non-retaliation, even at the point where we may be feeling a lot of anger and resentment.
- Absorbing into ourselves the pain of the injury and the scars that might result. In the case of a profound injury, this may mean telling our story differently in future. In absorbing the injury and refusing to retaliate we contribute to breaking the cycle of sin and shame in which human beings are so often caught. We also live out in our own lives Christ's experience of death and resurrection; Christian forgiveness is always with and through Christ himself.
- Realising the process of forgiveness does not always happen all at once, and may not start with our emotions being somehow brought under control. It may begin with a prayer that God forgive, and even that prayer may be too difficult for some – after all, none of us is Jesus.
- Making commitment to overcome the resentment that we naturally experience and to find healing from the anger and pain that result from the injury. This is an important aspect of forgiveness – but should not be seen as the only sign that it has taken place. Rather, for many people forgiveness is likely to be a process (which could be long and drawn out) and the commitment to overcome resentment is just one part of that process.

If that is what forgiveness is, what then can we say about how we forgive? Let's assume that we have made the commitment to absorb the injury and refuse to retaliate, but this has left us struggling with those memories that keep returning and bringing with them all the feelings we want to be healed from. How are we to deal with those memories?

## Forgive and Remember Differently

We can start by being honest about our memories of being hurt (and of hurting others). The memories can stay with us and can continue to pester us, but part of being human is that the way in which we chose to remember is not always accurate.

The psychologist Roy Baumeister conducted a series of experiments in the 1990s around the issue of how people tell the story of a difficult incident (Worthington, 1998, p. 285). In one of these experiments, a group of volunteers were asked to read a fictional account of a promise not being kept, with some extenuating circumstances, and then to write down what happened from the point of view of one of the people in the story, with a control group being asked simply to recount the story. The researchers noted that even with a fictional story neither of the groups asked to identify with a character were completely without bias in their re-telling. The group that was imagining being the injured party played down the details that might mitigate the offender's actions in some way, and emphasized – and even added – details about the severity of the consequences. The group imagining being the offender did the exact opposite. The researchers concluded that there is an issue about what information we take on board after the event (in their language, 'encode'); the injured failed to accept information that might help them forgive, while offenders failed to recognize details that might help them be more contrite and motivate them to seek forgiveness.

This happened even though the original incident was fictional and the volunteers were simply imagining a role. It is impossible to say how far the very fact that the incident did not actually happen led the participants to feel free to re-write what happened. We all know the difference in the way we tell a story when we are sounding off to good friends, or re-telling it in our heads, and when we are attempting to come to terms with another person who was actually involved. However, what the experiment asks us to ponder is the reality that being human means that our memories of what actually happened are likely to be biased.

Baumeister has also raised another related issue about how we handle our memories in forgiving. He calls it the 'magnitude gap' and points out that almost invariably the injured will lose more than the offender gains. He gives examples of both murder, where the high value of a human life means that the gap is obvious, but also burglary as the injured loses the full cost of the items but the burglar can only sell them for much less

(Baumeister and Bushman, 2008, p. 302). This exacerbates the difficulty of forgiveness because there is no way to repay the debt in a manner that satisfies both parties. If the injured believes that he has lost £1,000 but the offender believes that she has gained only £500, which amount should be repaid? A repayment of £750 is liable to leave both parties feeling like the injured one.

Remembering, and how we remember, is a key part of forgiveness. This means we need to look very carefully at how we remember. Part of being human is that our memories and our assessment of what happened are unlikely to be clear and balanced. We were involved. If we were injured, then we were hurt. If we were the offender, it is likely that we are keen to play down the impact of what we did (although I have met some people with shame-ache who seemed to exaggerate how awful their actions were). It is part of being human that we re-shape what happened, even as we tell the story to ourselves and to others. We may remember one injury in the light of something else that has happened to us and this may cause us to assess what happened as even more significant and hurtful than might otherwise be the case. Alternatively, some people with shame-ache may take time to realize that the action was not acceptable and that they should protest.

Of course, it will be obvious from everything that I have said that this by no means justifies the horror of abuse survivors who were not believed when they told their stories. What I am trying to do is to acknowledge the human element in how we remember actions that injured us. Part of having compassion on ourselves as we struggle to forgive is not blaming ourselves or feeling excessive guilt if we need to come to terms with distortions in our memory. Equally, part of forgiving may be working to tell the story as honestly and accurately as we can, in so far as anyone can remember a hurtful event accurately.

## When Memories Are Pests

There is a bigger and even more difficult issue with the way in which we remember the injuries done to us, something that I have come to call the 'pester power of memories'. This is a common problem and yet seems to be rarely discussed; memories of what happened can almost appear to take on a life of their own. This is sometimes called the 'uncontrollable cascade of memories'; the injured person wants to forget but discovers that the memories slip unbidden into her consciousness, and once there it is almost as if there is a track for them to follow. The incident is replayed again and again, possibly with a different ending or with an opportunity to tell the offender everything that his behaviour meant. There may be fantasies of violence or, at the very least, of the brilliant put-down that was not thought of at the time. The phrase 'forgive and forget' that is so often used can seem both cruel and impossible to achieve. Many people would like to forget but they cannot, and the memories bring back all of the feelings associated with the original actions.

Miroslav Volf is a Croatian American theologian who has grappled with some of these issues of forgiveness because of his own experience. He was arrested in what was Yugoslavia, primarily because his wife is American, and was subjected to a series of abusive interrogations. This is Volf's description of the pester power of memories:

> For not only do we act on memories of wrongs suffered; these memories act on us, too. They steal our attention, and they assault us with inner turmoil marked by shame, guilt, and maybe a mixture of self-recrimination and self-justification. They envelop us in dark mists of melancholy, they hold us back so that we cannot project ourselves into the future and embark on new paths. They chain our identity to the injuries we have suffered and shape the way we react to others. Such memories are not just clusters of information about the past – not even clusters of information stored for future use. They themselves are powerful agents. (Volf, 2006, p. 69)

Memories have a power all of their own and they are not always under our control; this can make forgiving very difficult indeed. What, then, are we to do with the old cliché, 'forgive and forget'? Volf suggests that we recast it as 'forgive and remember truthfully' (Volf, 2006, p. 93) while also speaking of 'remembering therapeutically' and learning from the past. L. Gregory Jones argues for 'forgive and remember well' (Jones, 1995, p. 147). All of these ideas may be helpful for different people at different stages in their journey of forgiveness, but I want to argue that when speaking of the entire process it is helpful to use a phrase that is as neutral as possible; I will explore below why that neutrality matters. I want to emphasize with Volf and Jones that forgiving does not mean forgetting but the exact opposite and, in general, I tend to think in terms of 'forgive and remember differently'. The important issue, however, is not which of the different phrases a person finds most helpful, but to realize that the overall aim is not to forget but to change our experience of remembering.

One of the ways in which a Christian can begin to change their experience of remembering is by realizing that the Scriptures have a great deal to say about memory and how we remember.

## The First Testament and Memories

Let us start with those memories that have such a power to assault us and convince us that we have not forgiven and never will. The First Testament (and, based on that, the New Testament) has a lot to say about memory and how we remember, so we will start there. When the Jewish people looked back on their experience of being abused as slaves and of being rescued in the Exodus, and also when they looked back at the horror of the Exile, how were they expected to remember? Equally, when the early Christians looked back on the horror of Jesus' execution and death, how were they to remember this event? These are important issues, but when looking at them there is one caveat to bear in mind.

The material we are about to examine, most of which comes from the First Testament, was written for a nation, for a group of people who were living in a world that was much less concerned with psychology than we are. We should not expect to draw simple solutions that can immediately be applied to an individual struggling with memories of being injured. Nevertheless, the First Testament does have a great deal to say about memory that can give us a firm foundation from which to proceed (Volf, 2006, chapter 6). We need to take seriously what the Scriptures say about memory, while also working with insights from psychologists, and from what we have already learned about sin and shame, in order to approach the issue of how to forgive and what forgiveness means.

The Israelites were warned from the outset that they needed to think about how they remembered and that they needed to make an effort to remember in a particular way; we might say that they were asked to recognize that remembering is a spiritual discipline. What they needed to learn was to discipline their memories in such a way that remembering became part of their life as God's people:

> But take care and watch yourselves closely, so as neither to forget the things that your eyes have seen nor to let them slip from your mind all the days of your life; make them known to your children and your children's children. (Deut. 4.9)

In this particular passage the Israelites are being commanded to remember a glorious experience of God in which he spoke to them out of the fire. It may strike us as strange that they needed to be commanded to remember this; surely this experience would be for ever impressed upon their memory? But we are reminded that human nature and human memory can be a strange thing and that an event that appears life-changing at the time can, as time passes, fade and appear less important. Vows that were earnestly meant at the time can be forgotten. Memory, this passage seems to say, even remembering the good and the beautiful, is a discipline and we need to take time out to remember and to recall why something was important to us.

Indeed, it seems that prosperity carries its own dangers according to the First Testament; the danger is that we forget:

> When the LORD your God has brought you into the land that he swore to your ancestors, to Abraham, to Isaac, and to Jacob, to give you – a land with fine, large cities that you did not build, houses filled with all sorts of goods that you did not fill, hewn cisterns that you did not hew, vineyards and olive groves that you did not plant – and when you have eaten your fill, take care that you do not forget the LORD, who brought you out of the land of Egypt, out of the house of slavery. (Deut. 6.10–12)

When life is good, the danger is that we forget God and how we arrived where we are. When we prosper it is easy for us to attribute our success to our own individual efforts and quietly ignore where we were supported by our families or those times when we drew on resources provided by communities. The argument here is not that prosperity itself is a problem but that it carries the temptation to remember badly.

But what of the more difficult memories? What of the Israelites' recollection of slavery and oppression? Again, it is noticeable that they are not commanded to let go of this part of their history; in fact, they are told that it is important that they remember what happened and also why this matters. Naturally, they are asked to celebrate the great redemption from slavery that God worked on their behalf, but it is noticeable that they are also asked to recall what it was like to be weak and to suffer so that they will have compassion on the weakness and the suffering of others. The theme here might be described as 'remember in order to do better':

> You shall not deprive a resident alien or an orphan of justice; you shall not take a widow's garment in pledge. Remember that you were a slave in Egypt and the LORD your God redeemed you from there; therefore I command you to do this. When you reap your harvest in your field and forget a sheaf in the field, you shall not go back to get it; it shall be left for the alien, the orphan, and the widow, so that the LORD your God may bless you in all your undertakings. When you beat your olive trees, do not strip what is left; it shall be for the alien, the orphan, and the widow. When you gather the grapes of your vineyard, do not glean what is left; it shall be for the alien, the orphan, and the widow. Remember that you were a slave in the land of Egypt; therefore I am commanding you to do this. (Deut. 24.17–22)

Compare this with:

> Give liberally and be ungrudging when you do so, for on this account the LORD your God will bless you in all your work and in all that you undertake. Since there will never cease to be some in need on the earth, I therefore command you, 'Open your hand to the poor and needy neighbour in your land.' If a member of your community, whether a Hebrew man or a Hebrew woman, is sold to you and works for you for six years, in the seventh year you shall set that person free. And when you send a male slave out from you a free person, you shall not send him out empty-handed. Provide liberally out of your flock, your threshing-floor, and your wine press, thus giving to him some of the bounty with which the LORD your God has blessed you. Remember that you were a slave in the land of Egypt, and the LORD your God redeemed you; for this reason I lay this command upon you today. (Deut. 15.10–15)

There are other passages on the same theme that I could quote (e.g.

Deut. 5.15; 6.10–12; 15.15; 16.12; 24.18). The Israelites are constantly told not simply that they must remember, but also that they must discipline their memories and ensure that they remember in the right way. They are to remember in order to achieve something. They should not dwell on how bad things were, but rather they should contribute to breaking the cycles of oppression, blame and shame and they do this by remembering at the same time that they were injured and oppressed and that God redeemed them. The Exodus should become their 'master story'. In other words, they should remember the difficult things in the greater context of the action of God in their lives. In order to remember, they are to hold festivals and celebrate together but, equally, in their day-to-day lives they should remember in order to have compassion on the suffering of others.

However, there is more that we can say about the First Testament and memory, which has to do with how memories are passed on through generations. We noted in Chapter 3 that for the Jews the Exodus was the founding act of salvation that created the people of God and helped to forge their identity. Here we need to note how important it is to them that later generations remember the Exodus, and remember it in a particular way through the Passover. This festival is something deeper than a simple annual memorial; the Jews are to remember in such a way that their past as an Exodus people shapes their present as a people of God. Volf puts it as follows:

> The Passover Seder is the paradigmatic Jewish memory in this regard. Its purpose is not so much to convey historical information (though, at some level, it does do so) as to transmit a vital past through time. Rather than simply recollecting the temporally distant event, sacred memory bridges time and draws one into the past event today. All elements of the Seder – drink, food, symbols, prayers, songs, stories, etc. – are 'designed with one overall goal: to take each person at the Seder back to Egypt, to reenact the dramatic Exodus story, to make each one of us feel as if she or he had actually been redeemed from Mitzrayim (Egypt)'. Sacred memory does not simply bring to mind (even the ordinary memory of wrongs suffered does more than that); it re-actualizes. In the words of the Talmud, 'In each and every generation, each person can regard himself as though he has emerged from Egypt.' (Volf, 2006, p. 98)

So, as the generations pass, the Jews are to continue to remember the Exodus and, more than this, they are to re-enact the Exodus in the Passover meal in such a way that each person comes to see himself as actually involved in the original events: oppressed, a slave, helpless in the face of a brutal power, and then marvellously redeemed and brought into a new life. The story of the Exodus is to become part of the story of each individual's life. In other words, the Jews are pressed to remember so that this fundamental story might shape their own sense of identity. As Volf puts it, 'To be a Jew is to remember the Exodus.'

The Jews are to remember the Exodus because the Exodus is to be the context for all of their other memories and everything that contributes to their fundamental sense of their own identity. We could go even further than Volf and say that to be a Jew is to be a person of the Exodus. It is the fact that they can remember their slavery, misery and oppression in the context of God's great act of salvation that will enable the Jews to remember the harm that was done to them differently, and to break the cycle of shame, blame and revenge. They can do this because, no matter how difficult the memory might be, they can be sure that this is not the fundamental truth about their life. The ultimate truth about who they are is that they are a people of salvation, children of the living, loving God.

Of course, no Christian can read the First Testament with its emphasis on remembering differently without thinking of Jesus' command that the Christian should remember him and, in particular, should share in Holy Communion in order to do so. The understanding of Holy Communion is too big a subject for it to be addressed here, but there are one or two reflections that I think are useful. Jesus said we should do this 'to remember him', and remembering has, therefore, always been an important part of our understanding of what happens. The remembering of the Eucharist is often described as 'anamnesis', which can be defined as 'calling into present reality a fresh outpouring of the saving power of the event remembered' ('His Presence Makes the Feast', paragraph 157). This is an idea that explicitly draws on the understanding of the Passover that we have just mentioned; we are encouraged to remember and to draw on the continuing grace of the original event. Equally, though, our understanding of the Eucharist has been shaped by the very theology that I have tried to balance throughout this book. We are urged to remember Christ's death and resurrection for the forgiveness of our sins; however, in the next chapter I want to explore Christ's death and resurrection as an act of solidarity with the shamed and the injured. As I turn now to how a Christian is to remember differently, it seems to me highly appropriate that some may wish to do this specifically as part of their joining in a service of Holy Communion.

However, for now we can draw from the First Testament the general principle that we are to remember, but also that how we are to remember matters. Far from trying to forget the worst times in our lives, we are to remember them before God, but with the great salvation story of Scripture as the context. Whatever message the injury done to us might seem to give, the fundamental truth about our lives is that we are loved, redeemed children of God, adopted into God's family with all that this implies, who are therefore invited to speak to our loving God about all of our struggles.

## Forgive and Remember Differently

Now we need to deal with the more specific question of how remembering differently might affect how we forgive. I start by emphasizing what I have already said; the discipline involved is not switching the memories off (which is in any case a superhuman task), but rather disciplining those memories so that we might remember in the right way. Remembering is part of forgiving, and being assaulted by memories of what happened is not a sign of failure but an invitation to remember differently. Simply recognizing this may give some people a different approach to the pester power of memories that I mentioned before. Rather than trying, and failing, to somehow turn off the 'uncontrollable cascade', we need to seek ways to work with the memories so that they help us to absorb the story of what happened into our sense of ourselves – but without the injury done becoming a dominant theme in our understanding of ourselves. Remembering the injury in this greater context; re-telling the story to ourselves and others while finding creative ways to affirm that the fundamental truth about us is that we are a child of God; working to tell the story as honestly as we can by neither exaggerating nor downplaying the injury done to us – all of these are part of the work of forgiveness.

This is why I want to replace 'forgive and forget' with the statement 'forgive and remember differently' as a way of acknowledging that forgiving is likely to be a process and that all of our attempts are included in that process. Learning to tell our story in a different manner, and within the greater context of God's love for us, may well begin with distorted memories when we are human enough to either exaggerate or downplay the injury, and even this should be included in forgiving. Volf's suggestion of 'forgive and remember truthfully' and Jones's phrase 'forgive and remember well' put the emphasis on where we should aim. I am trying to include in the work of forgiveness even the first painful steps of beginning to rehearse what happened without any fear that we will be condemned if it turns out that our first telling of the story is neither totally truthful nor particularly good. I also believe that using 'forgive and remember differently' as an overall statement allows us to acknowledge that the struggle to forgive can be different for different people.

Telling the story is only one part of remembering differently. We have seen the way in which the people of the First Testament were encouraged to remember in the greater context of being the people of God. For Christians, the obvious context is the life, death and resurrection of Jesus Christ and part of that is everything we said in the previous chapter about the welcoming Messiah who pitched his tent among us and reached out to the shamed. Every act of forgiveness is an act of solidarity with that Messiah, and the journey of forgiveness begins with the trust that the welcoming Messiah turns his face of love and grace towards us, *even while we feel overwhelmed by our own anger and the pestering power of the memories we cannot get rid of.*

More than this, however, I want to argue that the cross and resurrection of Christ should be our greater context and provide important ways to counteract the messages that the original injury implied. It is Christ's death and resurrection that assure us that God has marked out human sin as real and costly, and that forgiving does not in any way downplay that reality. It is Christ's death that shows us that God has absorbed the reality of the cost of sin into his life and it is the resurrection that shows us that God offers a new life beyond the pain of suffering and the struggle of forgiveness. It is Christ's life in us that promises, however painful forgiving might be, that Christ bears the pain with us. Therefore, in the next chapter we turn to Jesus' own experience of shame and how the early Christians, as they learned about him, battled with themes of shame and honour.

# 8

# The Shamed Messiah

> The offence of Jesus Christ is not his incarnation – that indeed is revelation – but his humiliation. (Bonhoeffer, 1993, p. 46)

In 58 BC, Marcus Tullius Cicero fell victim to one of the many power struggles that happened in Roman political life and was sent into exile. While in exile he wrote a series of letters that give us a glimpse of an ancient man struggling with an overwhelming shame and putting that struggle into his own words. He wrote to his wife, his brother and a good friend and consistently stated that of all the difficulties that exile was causing him, shame was the greatest. In these letters we can see that while Cicero lived in a world that is very different from our own, and while that world may have taught him some attitudes to shame and honour that we would not share, there are also some fundamental aspects of the experience of shame that sound very like our own. He wrote to his wife:

> Moreover, I am more miserable than you in this, that whereas the disaster is shared by us both, yet the fault is all my own. It was my duty to have avoided the danger by accepting a legation, or to resist it by careful management and the resources at my command, or to fall like a brave man. Nothing was more pitiful, more base, or more unworthy of myself than the line I actually took. Accordingly, it is with shame as well as grief that I am overpowered. (Cicero, 'Letter to Terentia', 29 November 58 BC)

He repeated this claim to a friend that his greatest struggle was with shame. In this letter, he unpacks a little more of why he feels as he does. He had been fooled by someone he trusted, and he blamed himself:

> Wherefore, when you are told that I am prostrate and unmanned with grief, consider that I am more distressed at my own folly than at the result of it, in having believed a man whom I did not think to be treacherous. (Cicero, 'Letter to Atticus', 29 May 58 BC)

Cicero describes one aspect of shame that we have already explored: that shame is intimately bound up with how we believe others perceive us. Thus, he found himself unable to face his own brother and had to write to Quintus Tullius Cicero to give an explanation:

> Not wish to see you? The truth is rather that I was unwilling to be seen by you. For you would not have seen your brother – not the brother you had left, not the brother you knew, not him to whom you had with mutual tears bidden farewell as he followed you on your departure for your province: not a trace even or faint image of him, but rather what I may call the likeness of a living corpse. And oh that you had sooner seen me or heard of me as a corpse! (Cicero, 'Letter to Quintus', 15 June 58 BC).

Cicero was a powerful and clever man, a politician and philosopher, a poet and a priest, someone who was well known for his abilities in speaking and writing and who is still read and remembered 2,000 years after his death, and yet he tells us that shame brought him to the point where he could not face his own brother. In effect, he says, 'I want to see you, but I cannot bear for you to see me.'

But why start with Cicero in a chapter about Jesus? I've chosen him because Cicero is the person who lived closest to Jesus in time (he died in 43 BC) who has left us his description of a personal experience of shame. We are about to begin the most difficult part of this book, where I want to examine the issue of whether Jesus experienced shame and, if he did, what difference that makes to us. Immediately, it becomes very important to acknowledge that Jesus lived in a very different world to ours and there are some aspects of the way in which that world shaped Jesus and his contemporaries that we will never grasp. At the same time, I want to argue that for anyone struggling with shame-ache it matters to know that Jesus experienced shame and therefore understands the devastation that it can cause from the inside out. Furthermore, for some this knowledge of Christ's understanding will be the only basis on which they can build the ability to trust God and begin to flourish as a child of God.

To make that argument, however, it is important to face the fact that some believe that it is not possible for us to talk about Jesus' own experience of shame. The Gospels simply report his speech and actions; they give us no indication of his inner life, and scholars have often argued that the individual, introspective conscience that we take for granted would not have existed at the time. Pattison quotes a reference in the index of Wright's book *Jesus and the Victory of God* that states 'psychology of [Jesus] (inaccessible to us)'. He goes on to argue:

> It is not clear that the individual personality structure or selfhood of Jesus would have been self-perceived in the same way that a modern Western individual would perceive it, nor, therefore, that his understanding of shame, living in a more corporate 'we-conscious' society, would be the same. (Pattison, 2000, p. 208)

Pattison is, of course, entirely correct that Jesus' understanding of shame was shaped by a shame-honour society and is therefore likely to be different from ours in some ways. We must be very careful not to imply that we can see into his mind in a way that the Gospel writers did not describe. However, I want to argue that we can acknowledge this but still know that he would have experienced acute personal shame, much as Cicero did. This means that, while we have to be careful not to claim too much, we can say enough about his experience of shame to assure those with shame-ache that their struggle is understood. At the same time, as we read the Gospels we will need to be alert to the differences between Jesus' world and ours; in fact, I believe that the Gospel writers deliberately point to one aspect of that difference which would have made his experience all the more devastating. To make that argument we need to explore a little more about the way in which scholars have explored the difference between Jesus' world and ours.

We begin by acknowledging an old misconception that still seems to lurk behind Western attempts to understand shame-honour cultures. In 1946 Ruth Benedict, an American anthropologist, published *The Chrysanthemum and the Sword*, in which she described what she saw as the distinction between the American society and the Japanese society of her day. This was the work that popularized the notion that there is a difference between a shame culture and a guilt culture, and therefore helped to shape the way in which Westerners speak of guilt and shame. Here is the part of her description of that difference that is most often quoted:

> Where shame is a major sanction a man does not experience relief when he makes his fault public even to a confessor. So long as his bad behavior does not 'get out into the world' he need not be troubled.

> True shame cultures rely on external sanctions for good behavior, not, as true guilt cultures do, on an internalized conviction of sin. Shame is a reaction to other people's criticism. A man is shamed either by being openly ridiculed and rejected or by fantasying to himself that he had been made ridiculous. In either case it is a potent sanction. But it requires an audience or at least a man's fantasy of an audience. Guilt does not. In a nation where honour means living up to one's own picture of oneself, a man may suffer from guilt though no man knows of his misdeed and a man's feeling of guilt may actually be relieved by confessing his sin. (Benedict, 2005, pp. 222f.)

It seems that Benedict was arguing here that shame is purely concerned with other people's opinions; in other words, in a shame culture the only issue is whether or not the bad act is known, whereas guilt has to do with our own internal standards and therefore we can feel guilty regardless of whether anyone knows about what we did. It is noticeable that this way of understanding the difference makes guilt the more developed and mature reaction to wrong deeds; guilt involves autonomy and an ability to criticize ourselves while shame is concerned only with the opinion of others. This small section of Benedict's argument seems to have had a major influence on the common perception of the difference between a shame culture and a guilt culture.

However, this was not all of Benedict's argument; she went on to make the point that Americans have learned to build their morality on guilt but that, in American society today, 'guilt is less extremely felt than in earlier generations', whereas shame is 'an increasingly heavy burden' (Benedict, 2005, p. 223). The difference between the two cultures, she argued, is that Americans do not harness shame to their system of morality, whereas the Japanese do. She clearly acknowledged that shame is deeply *felt* and that any Japanese person could experience acute shame if they 'fantasy' what the public verdict on their actions might be.

Benedict's work has been hugely influential but has also been criticized for both her methods and some of her arguments. Nevertheless, it seems that the suspicion lingers that someone from a shame-oriented society is concerned only with the issue of how they are seen by others – and this despite the fact that it does not represent the whole of Benedict's argument. What is more, she was comparing two modern societies, and Jesus lived 2,000 years ago, which can only deepen our suspicion that in his society the sense of an individual self may have been less developed. So, to support my argument that we can assume that Jesus experienced shame as a personal, internalized emotion, I want to point to the work of three scholars who have made a particular study of honour and shame in the ancient societies of Greece and Rome.

Bernard Williams has examined the notion of shame in ancient Greek literature and deals specifically with the issue of whether or not shame was concerned only with the opinion of others. He makes the point that the sense of shame needs to be internalized for a shame culture to even exist:

> If everything depended on the fear of discovery, the motivations of shame would not be internalised at all. No one would have a character, in effect, and, moreover, the very idea of there being a shame *culture*, a coherent system for the regulation of conduct, would be unintelligible. (Williams, 1994, p. 82)

J. E. Lendon has demonstrated the power of the appeal to honour (and shame) in the Roman world. He notes that Rome ruled an extensive empire using a remarkably small army and group of government officials, and yet the empire was governed very effectively. Modern-day America employs one official for every 80 citizens (and this is less than Europe) whereas ancient Rome operated on the basis of one official to 2,000 subjects. Lendon's thesis is that this remarkable achievement was due in no small part to the power that the appeal to honour exercised in the ancient world. He argues for the psychological power that comes from 'the universal human desire for the esteem of those around one' (Lendon, 2005, p. 33) and that this led to the desire for honour and the fear of shame being a huge motivation in Roman behaviour:

> Of course, fear of public shame was internalized to a large degree: shame assailed those even contemplating their undiscovered crimes. An ancient student of the habits of mind of his contemporaries does not see them paralysed by guilt, as a modern psychologist might, but instead diagnoses and prescribes a course of treatment for, those afflicted with a surfeit of unreasonable shame. (Lendon, 2005, p. 41)

In her exploration of Roman honour, Carlin Barton has shown that the Romans walked the same kind of delicate balancing act that we do.

A good Roman valued a healthy sense of shame and knew that it was good to blush at appropriate times and to be properly modest; apart from anything else, they had to navigate public baths and toilets with some dignity. At the same time, Romans were well aware that shame was a painful emotion that could become debilitating. Barton quotes Cicero who notes the problem that I have mentioned several times, 'I am ashamed even to speak of shame' (Barton, 2001, p. 203).

So while it is clear that there are major differences between Jesus' world and our own around shame, the issue is not the lack of an internalized sense of shame that then shaped behaviour. Rather, we need to point to the fact that there was less distinction between your own opinion of yourself and the opinion of others. Someone who lived in Jesus' world created their own sense of self-respect mainly by ensuring that other people regarded them as worthy of respect. This meant that if she failed to live up to the values of the group and lost the esteem of the people around her, that person had no basis at all on which she could found her own sense of self-worth. As Gabrielle Taylor puts it:

> If public esteem is the sole value, to which whatever else may be valued is related as a means to an end, then it follows that where there is no public esteem there is no value. Hence if a man has lost his reputation then he has lost his value in the eyes of all the members of the group, *and this includes himself.* So there is nothing left, no inner quality or whatever, which could be judged to be of value in spite of the loss of public respect. (Taylor, 1985, p. 55, italics added)

There is one other factor that we need to bear in mind and to which we will return, and that is the importance of groups in Jesus' society. What matters is the approval of members of your own group, not respect from simply anyone. When we speak of Jesus and honour, it is the respect of his own people – that is, the Jews – that is integral to his own sense of being valued. The most devastating loss is to lose the esteem and membership of your own honour group. Taylor describes this loss as follows: 'If he loses his status as a member of the group, it is a total loss of identity. Not surprisingly, loss of honour in a shame-culture is the worst that can happen to any woman or man' (Taylor, 1985, p. 56).

What this means is that while shame may be difficult for us, it is possible that it was even more catastrophic in Jesus' day. I am going to argue that the Gospel writers describe precisely this devastation happening to Jesus, but they do so in a way that would be understood by readers in Jesus' time. They do not tell us anything about Jesus' inner psychology, but they do tell the story of a man who first experiences great and public honour, but then the story takes a turn and that honour is stripped away until he is left with nothing. Even more extraordinary, they tell us that Jesus predicted this disaster and insisted both that it was God's will and that he needed to continue on the path set, even though it would lead to great shame and his own people turning against him.

## Confronting Shame

We have looked at one way in which Jesus directly confronted shame, as the hospitable Messiah. The way in which he went out of his way to welcome and honour those who believed themselves to be unwanted clearly fits with our own expectations of how shame can be countered. The New Testament insists that he confronted shame in another way as well: by experiencing and transforming it, and that in the process he has turned our very understanding of shame upside down.

I want to argue that the Gospel writers and Paul both knew that this was a central aspect of Jesus' ministry, but also knew that it was shocking (more shocking in their world than in ours) and that it could lose Jesus followers as easily as it gained them. I believe that once we have been alerted to some of the ways in which they understood shame it becomes possible to see that they were grappling with shame even as they tried to understand what God was saying and doing through the ministry, death and resurrection of Jesus. In the twenty-first century we have lost, or at least played down, much of the horror that Jesus' story originally provoked and therefore have also lost some of the radical nature of the response to shame that the biblical writers were attempting to present. Another way to put my basic thesis is that when the New Testament is read carefully, we will be able to see that Christ does not simply present a therapeutic response to the shame of those around him but rather a radical reinterpretation of the nature of shame itself.

So before we come to look at the story of Jesus as presented by Mark's Gospel and by Paul in his writings, we need to do a little more work on the assumptions about shame that lie behind the words of the biblical writers. Let's start with one point where both Jesus' world and ours agree; we commonly assume that God is glorious, worthy of all honour and above our petty struggles, and there are plenty of biblical quotations to support that view. We also assume that shame is a human experience that cannot possibly touch God, and that it is a deeply painful experience that most people will do anything they can to avoid. The idea of voluntarily accepting an experience of deep shame is a radical one. The notion that God might enter into our experience of shame is completely at variance with our image of who God is, and yet this is exactly the picture that the New Testament writers present.

Our individualistic society has made shame into a more personalized experience than would have been the case in Jesus' society; although we talk about 'public shaming' we also often speak as if shame is mainly about the individual, and that it is possible for the individual to rise above it. Jesus' society had a much stronger sense that a person could be 'put to shame' by those around her and was also much clearer about the importance of a person's honour group. What mattered was that you had the respect of the groups to which you belonged; it could even be a mark of honour to be poorly treated by a member of another group if you were, say, at war. Therefore if a Jew stood up to the hated Romans and, in response, the Romans treated him with contempt, that Jew was likely to be concerned only with the opinion of other Jews. As long as other Jews honoured him, derision from the Romans could even add to his sense of honour. What would be devastating would be to be shamed and/or cast out by your own group. This is exactly what happened to Jesus.

Finally, and most importantly, crucifixion was deliberately designed to be the most humiliating death that could possibly be inflicted, and in the ancient world this was more of an issue than the physical suffering involved. This is such an important point for understanding the New Testament writers that we need to spend a little time on it.

In the year 63 BC (a few years before he ended up in exile) Cicero defended a man called Rabirus against a charge of treason, and we still have part of his speech for the defence in which he is dealing with the issue of punishment. It gives us a vivid insight into how the Romans themselves regarded crucifixion. As you read it, note that the word translated here as 'gibbet' is actually *crucis*, or cross, and that Cicero reflects the common practice of his time that the prisoner's head was covered, which does not seem to have happened to Jesus:

## THE SHAMED MESSIAH

Unless, perhaps, you are fond of such a condition of existence as even slaves would not be able by any possibility to bear, if they had not the hope of liberty held out to them. The ignominy of a public trial is a miserable thing, – the deprivation of a man's property by way of penalty is a miserable thing, – exile is a miserable thing; but still, in all these disasters some trace of liberty remains to one. Even if death be threatened, we may die free men; but the executioner, and the veiling of the head, and the mere name of the gibbet (*crucis*), should be far removed, not only from the persons of Roman citizens, – from their thoughts, and eyes, and ears. For not only the actual fact and endurance of all these things, but the bare possibility of being exposed to them, – the expectation, the mere mention of them even, – is unworthy of a Roman citizen and of a free man. (Cicero, quoted in Hengel, 1977 p. 42)

The Romans regarded crucifixion as so shameful that it was not to be mentioned in polite company. Cicero makes it abundantly clear that the punishment of crucifixion was far worse than the mere threat of a painful death; at the heart of the punishment lay the utter humiliation that was inflicted.

Death by crucifixion was not only physically brutal. The victims were stripped naked and humiliated in every way possible. The Gospels are clear that Jesus was mocked by the soldiers and the crowds which is quite in line with the usual expectations of crucifixion and it is possible that sexual abuse was among the tortures prior to the actual act (Tombs, 1999, p. 104). Then the condemned was either nailed or sometimes roped to a cross and then simply left there, on display, until they died, a process that could sometimes take several days. It usually happened in prominent places, either on a roadside or near a city gate, because it was intended to send a very deliberate message. The process was often finished with the body being left unburied; for a person in the ancient world, being denied burial implied yet another dishonour (Hengel, 1977, pp. 87–8).

Another sign of just how shameful Roman citizens considered crucifixion to be lies in the fact that there are remarkably few references to it in Roman literature, even though we know it was a common punishment. Hengel argues that the Roman literary classes avoided writing about it precisely because it was so shameful. Perhaps the most remarkable fact for readers today to attempt to understand is that the Romans did not always distinguish clearly between the crucifixion of a dead body and that of a live human being – they regarded both with total horror because for them the real issue was the shame inflicted upon the crucified (Hengel, 1977, p. 24).

Part of being a group-oriented society was that the head of the group (the father of the family or the leader of a rebellion) was seen as representing all members of that group. Another reason why crucifixion was designed to be as public as possible was so that all members of the group would be shamed by it. Jesus' disciples would have understood quite clearly the message that the Romans intended to convey via the cross:

> The disciples could not have seen his humiliating and inglorious death as obedience to God, a vindication of his mission, or a heroic martyrdom. On the contrary, precisely because it was a crucifixion, they could have seen it only as the utter discrediting of his claims before man and God. He had been judged a threat to the state by the secular authorities, but far worse in the disciples' eyes, he had been condemned by the religious authorities, the guardians of faith and morals, as a blasphemer deserving of a godless death. It would be difficult to exaggerate the horror of such an unedifying and irreligious outcome to a ministry in the name of God. (Rutledge, 2017, pp. 89–90)

So what can we say about Jesus' own experience? Obviously, since he lived and died in Palestine, we cannot assume that he had exactly the same attitude to crucifixion as a citizen of Rome, but we can assume – with the biblical writers – a pretty similar sense of what it meant. When Jesus was crucified, he was treated with utter contempt and, as someone who grew up in a shame-honour society, he had less belief than someone today in a self-respect that is generated purely from within. In Jesus' world, the only way in which a person could face crucifixion and still hold on to some kind of sense that he was, nevertheless, a person of value would be if he was supported by his own people; the Romans were, after all, the hated invaders. The Gospel writers are keen to emphasize that he did not even have this consolation.

This is where we must pause and acknowledge one aspect of the Gospel telling of Jesus' story that many modern commentators find extremely difficult. This is the constant argument that 'the Jews' turned against Jesus and are the ones who handed him over to the Romans to be crucified. It is important to acknowledge the horrifying way in which this has been read and misread throughout the centuries. Written down at a time when Christianity was a minor sect and Judaism was a worldwide religion, this emphasis reads very differently when it is Christians who are more powerful. The Christian Church and Christian society have been guilty of the most awful antisemitism in which the Jews have been blamed for the death of Jesus and have suffered as a consequence. There is no excuse for this.

Why, then, do the Gospel writers emphasize so strongly that the Jews handed Jesus over? Jesus and his contemporaries would have understood that if he was shunned by his own people then the shame of his death was all the greater. Jesus did not even have the consolation of support from the men around him; some of the women did better but, of course, a woman's opinion mattered less in Jesus' world. His male disciples abandoned him, and the leaders of his honour group judged him, found him guilty, and passed him on to the enemy to be degraded.

We move on now to the story as presented by the Gospel writers. For the sake of simplicity, I am going to focus on one Gospel, Mark.

## Mark's Gospel or 'Where Did it All Go Wrong?'

In this reading of Mark's Gospel I intend to highlight the way in which Jesus is presented as someone who begins in honour but ends in total degradation. In doing so I am drawing on the work of David Watson in his book *Honor among Christians,* which presents a much fuller examination of the role of honour in Mark (Watson, 2010). Although on the surface Mark presents a straightforward story of someone who is revered by those around him until everything begins to change, underlying that story is the mysterious way in which Jesus is seen to insist that somehow God is at work not only when he appears popular and powerful, but also in the disastrous collapse into weakness and degradation. By the end of Mark's Gospel we are left with Jesus apparently dead, the male disciples scattered, and the female disciples running from the tomb in fear and confusion because they have heard the first hints that the story is not yet over.

Let's take a closer look.

Mark 1.1 sets the scene. 'The beginning of the good news of Jesus Christ, the Son of God.' Mark's Gospel is about good news, so we are encouraged to expect it to be hopeful, optimistic and to give us information that is positive and affirming. What is more, this is good news of Jesus 'Christ'; Christ, the anointed one or Messiah, is a title promising us that this man is special and close to God and he is even (in some of the early manuscripts at least) described as 'Son of God'. We do need to be careful with this second title. Years of doctrinal disputes, which all happened after Mark's Gospel was written down, have taught us a particular understanding of the term 'Son of God'. Mark quite possibly saw the idea as a more general way of saying that here was a man who was beloved of God and particularly close to God. But however we read it, the general expectation set up by the first verse is clear; here is a man whom God holds in high regard. So let's settle in and read the good news about him.

The first story we read only supports our expectations as set up by Mark's opening. Jesus has a prophet to introduce him, John the Baptist. It may seem surprising that one so close to God needs to be baptized (commonly seen as a form of washing), but once the baptism is over we are assured even more firmly of his importance and closeness to God. As Jesus is coming up out of the water, he sees the heavens open and the Spirit descends upon him. There is even a voice to proclaim what Mark has already told us, 'You are my Son, the Beloved; with you I am well pleased' (Mark 1.11). We can note that Mark is clear that only Jesus hears the voice and sees the Spirit descend; I would like to suggest, therefore, that we can treat this opening in pretty much the same way as we did the introduction to Job. We as readers are being let in on a secret that is not available to everyone in the story. We know from the beginning that this is God's beloved son, but they have only the evidence of their eyes and ears to establish who this person is. They see only a man who has emerged out of Nazareth in Galilee (both small and unimportant places, as John 1.46 and John 7.41 make clear) with only his own personal authority to commend him. We, the readers, are left to expect that there may be some confusion and conflict at the beginning, but surely there will be a denouement in which Jesus is revealed as he truly is, to the astonishment and delight of all around him.

The next part of the story is, indeed, a conflict story. The same Spirit who has descended upon Jesus at his baptism now drives him out into the wilderness where he is tempted by Satan. A conflict between a representative of God and the devil is only to be expected and sets us up to expect an even greater battle between Jesus and the evil forces that he will naturally win. Mark does not explicitly say that Jesus is triumphant in this battle in the wilderness; however, once Jesus returns from the desert, he is so spectacularly successful that he is nearly overwhelmed by the crowds. What is more, while the men and women around him are just starting to ask the question 'Who is this man?', the demons are already able to recognize him, and he is clearly more powerful than they are (Mark 1.21–28). Indeed, his power over them impresses the crowd so much that they ask more insistently, 'Who is this remarkable man?'

The first sour note emerges with the entry of the scribes. Mark hits an ironic note when they, the religious leaders of their people who are nevertheless just ordinary human beings, accuse Jesus, who we know to be close to God, of blasphemy (Mark 2.6–7). Perhaps we should be surprised that Jesus does not directly confront their accusations, but rather discusses whether it is easier to heal or to forgive. What we can see is that a conflict is developing; the crowd have already contrasted Jesus with the scribes and concluded that he has the greater authority (Mark 1.22), so perhaps it is not surprising that they now question everything he does. Jesus is set on a course that will bring him into conflict with the religious leaders of his own people, something that will feel familiar to anyone who has read the First Testament carefully; prophets often conflict with leaders in the story of God's people. Potentially, Jesus could emerge from this conflict with even more honour as he triumphs over his enemies.

Then comes the first surprise of the Gospel; Jesus calls a hated tax collector to be one of his disciples (Mark 2.13f.). In a world where a person was judged by the company that she kept, this is risky and it is a risk that the Scribes are quick to exploit. Jesus, they point out, eats with tax collectors and sinners, meaning Jesus has made these despised and irreligious people part of his honour group. Jesus' reply signals a very different attitude to spending time with these people; he is here to heal and not to judge and he will go to those who need him, not those who will do his reputation the most good (Mark 2.17).

There follows a series of teaching and healing passages, and Jesus' fame continues to grow until he has to escape the crowd (Mark 3.7f.) because the demand to be near him is so great. By now, Jesus has gathered a number of disciples and from among them he appoints 12 whom he calls apostles. No one who has read the First Testament carefully could miss the reference to the 12 tribes of Israel. This is followed by a greater surprise than even the conflict with the religious leaders; there is more opposition and it comes from Jesus' family who are responding to a general rumour that he has gone out of his mind (Mark 3.21). Suddenly, it is not only the scribes and Pharisees who are against Jesus, but there are hints of a bigger group of people who are asking questions about what he is doing.

Even as those questions are being asked Jesus is shown to have even more power and authority than we have seen before; and at the end of chapter 4 he commands a storm to be still and the disciples' response is the obvious one – they are filled with awe and ask one another who this could possibly be. We, the readers, can be smugly aware that we already know the answer to this question. Even more astonishingly, in chapter 5 Jesus raises a young girl from the dead and again the response of the observers is to be overcome with amazement. We sense the tension rising as more people ask questions and Jesus displays a greater and greater ability to work miracles. This sense is only supported by the beginning of the sixth chapter when Jesus returns to Nazareth and, instead of being greeted with acclamation, finds that the people of his own town take offence at him and he is amazed at their lack of belief.

Next comes what could have been a devastating setback to Jesus' story; we discover that John the Baptist, who was so central to the beginning of Jesus' ministry, has been killed by Herod and Herod is beginning to ask questions about Jesus. He even believes that Jesus might be John returned from the dead (Mark 6.16). Yet another powerful figure has turned against Jesus and, once again, Mark follows the story of a threat with a story of miraculous power. Jesus feeds 5,000 people and walks on water (just an ordinary day in the life of a Messiah). John may have fallen prey to the greater powers around him, but perhaps Jesus is too powerful to be touched? It certainly seems that Mark encourages us to believe this when we discover that people are now being healed merely by touching the fringe of Christ's cloak (Mark 6.56).

Chapter 7 and the beginning of chapter 8 of Mark's Gospel bring us more conflicts and more miracles; it appears that Jesus is continuing to get the better of the argument, although a slightly surprising note is introduced when we discover that Jesus is still trying to keep things quiet while the crowds are determined to proclaim publicly what he is doing (Mark 7.36). A man in those days was expected to compete openly for public honour, so we are left to wonder why Jesus keeps telling those he has helped to stay silent.

Finally, Jesus himself raises the question that has been asked throughout the Gospel, 'Who do people say that I am?' (Mark 8.27). As those who read the opening to Mark's Gospel are privy to what happened at the baptism, we already know the answer – he is God's son, God's beloved, and we are still waiting for everyone around him to acknowledge this properly. Things start well when Peter recognizes him as the Messiah except Jesus again commands secrecy and the disciples are sternly ordered not to tell anyone. By now we should be used to the idea that Jesus wants to keep things secret (although he has never explained why he is acting so strangely in a society that expected him to be very concerned with public honour), but it seems reasonable to expect that he might at least encourage his disciples to offer him the honour he is due.

Instead, Mark introduces an entirely new note. Once Peter has recognized that Jesus is the Messiah, then (and only then) Jesus begins to insist that 'the Son of Man must undergo great suffering', be rejected, be killed and after three days rise again. This statement is met with blind incomprehension on the part of the disciples (Mark 8.31f.) and it is difficult for the reader to blame them. Jesus follows this up by calling the crowd as well as the disciples to him, and a new note begins to enter his teaching. Now, he insists that to follow him means self-denial, taking up one's cross (that ultimate symbol of degradation), and being willing to lose one's life in order to save it. He also begins to raise the possibility that the disciples may be ashamed of him (Mark 8.38). We begin to wonder if the straightforward confrontation in which Jesus triumphs over his enemies is really going to happen.

This is clearly a major turning point, for Mark continues the theme of Jesus' glory set alongside constant commands to remain silent and understand that suffering and rejection is coming. First, we get the ultimate moment of glory in which the disciples are finally allowed to see what we as readers have known from the beginning, except the reader also is challenged to realize that there is more to know about Jesus. In chapter 9, Jesus takes Peter, James and John away from the other disciples and leads them up a mountain, where he is transfigured before them. The Greek word for 'transfigured' is *metemorphōthē*, from which we get our word 'metamorphosis'. Jesus is completely transformed until even his clothes are dazzling. What is more, Moses and Elijah appear, two of the greatest figures of the First Testament who represent the Law and the Prophets. Moses and Elijah speak with Jesus although we are not told what they say. Jesus is portrayed here as glorious, even more glorious than we might have expected from the baptism, as he becomes the focus of the glory of God. As Tom Wright puts it: 'The glory of God comes down, not to the Temple in Jerusalem, not to the top of Mount Sinai, but onto and into Jesus himself, shining in splendour, talking with Moses and Elijah' (Wright, 2011, p. 140).

We need to be careful in interpreting this story, for it is more than the proof of Jesus' divinity that some commentators want to make it. Tom Wright argues that, for the Gospel writers, the story of the transfiguration is a claim that Jesus himself is the place where God's world and our world meet; in that sense, it reminds us of some of the themes we explored in the introduction to John's Gospel. For the purposes of our sweep through Mark we can note this greater claim, but also say that it is a revelation of Jesus' glory and honour that leads us to expect that now he should be able to leave the petty squabbles behind him and reveal this magnificence to everyone so that they can worship him. This seems a natural human expectation, but it is a long way from what actually happens, which makes what comes next even more shocking.

Mark tells us that the first thing is that Jesus swears the witnesses to this glory to secrecy until the Son of Man has risen from the dead. That must have been difficult enough, especially since they promptly get into a debate about what 'rising from the dead' might actually mean (Mark 9.9–10). Personally, I think the options are quite limited, but what do I know? It is perhaps a sign of their confusion that they then start a strange conversation about whether Elijah has to come first. It is Jesus' response to that question that we should focus on, for immediately after the scene of his greatest glory he states:

> How then is it written about the Son of Man, that he is to go through many sufferings and be treated with contempt? (Mark 9.12)

The Greek word translated as 'treated with contempt' literally means to be treated as nothing and it seems that Mark has used it deliberately to contrast with what has just happened. He does not explicitly say this but, in view of the command to secrecy, it seems reasonable to assume that Jesus is saying that the disciples will not be able to fully understand one event until they have seen the other. They must not speak of glory until they have seen the shame. In Jesus' ministry, glory (the true glory of God) and shame (being put to shame by others) are not opposites but part and parcel of the same thing. The transfiguration is commonly seen as a moment of revelation, but I suggest that Mark quite deliberately presents it as a moment of *both* disclosure and of incomprehension and, in doing so, he challenges his readers to realize that they, like the disciples, have so much more to learn about the true nature of both glory and shame.

This moment of both revelation and incomprehension marks a turning point in Mark's Gospel and the story now gathers pace. Jesus begins to confront his disciples on a regular basis with the message that the Son of Man is to be betrayed, killed and to rise again and, again on a regular basis, the disciples do not simply fail to understand him, they appear to be seeking the glory that Jesus has turned his face against. He catches them arguing about who is the greatest and insists that they need to learn about humble service (Mark 9.33f.). The one who wishes to be first must be last and the servant of all, he says, a message that totally fails to get through. The third time he predicts his death and resurrection he includes the details that he will be mocked, spat upon and flogged before he is killed; this story is immediately followed by James' and John's attempt to grab the most prestigious places in glory for themselves (Mark 10.32f.). Jesus has not yet reached the cross, but it seems that Mark is telling us that there is a growing gulf between him and his disciples on the fundamental issue of honour and shame.

Rowan Williams has made a very helpful comment on how we should read these stories when the disciples so conspicuously fail to understand:

> It's many times been remarked that the disciples in St Mark are conspicuously stupid. They repeatedly miss the point; they repeatedly have to have things explained in words of one syllable; and there have been some scholars who have suggested that St Mark is deliberately trying to undermine the authority of those who consider themselves successors of the twelve apostles. But I think that this misses the point: because it is absolutely vital to Mark's story that what Jesus

says is hard to digest and to understand even by those closest to him. Even those who have most reason for understanding what he's saying are going to get it wrong: and that, of course, is a reassurance to the reader. Mark is saying, 'If you're finding this difficult or shocking, don't be surprised; those who were closest to Jesus found it difficult and shocking too. If you feel stupid and at a loss when confronted with the words and work of Jesus, don't be surprised. You're not the first and you won't be the last.' So the dimness of the apostles is not a point of polemic, an axe being ground: it's basic to the scheme. Jesus in Mark's Gospel appears as someone wrestling with the difficulty of communicating to the disciples things that there are no proper words for – communicating that they have to think again about how God works, and to prepare themselves for greater and greater shocks in understanding this. (Williams, 2014, p. 44)

A summary of this argument would be, when the disciples misunderstand Jesus, do not think about how stupid they are, think about how difficult it is to really understand this point. If I were to make a list of things about Jesus' message that the Church has struggled to really understand, then shame and honour would be at the top. What is more, we have to be careful about the different ways in which Jesus can be misunderstood. Those struggling with shame-ache can hear the call to humble service as another way of denying their basic value as a child of God. Those who do not have such a struggle often seem to stand closer to the disciples than to Jesus on this. Mark, it seems to me, wants us to grasp that Jesus' teaching on shame was shocking and so, because of this, Jesus' shame and honour must be redefined.

Only now does Mark mention that Jesus has arrived at Jericho, and we realize that he is on his final journey to Jerusalem and the cross. The story progresses to what seems to be the almost inevitable conclusion. The sense of impending doom is heightened as Jesus is dragged into conflicts with the priests and Pharisees, until at the end of chapter 14 we are told that they are looking for a way to have him arrested and killed, but they fear the crowd. At this point, the assumption appears to be that the crowd is on Jesus' side. After all, he is a popular teacher, better liked than the leaders of his own people, so we are invited to hope that the crowd might stand with him even if his own prediction of a degrading death comes true. Even that hope becomes more difficult to hold fast with the next piece of devastating news: that one of his disciples has agreed to betray him (Mark 14.10–11); we are getting the first hints now that even his honour group will not stand with him. At the final Passover meal (a celebration of being the people of God that was shared with those with whom you were closest) comes the next hint: Jesus predicts that not only will one disciple betray him, all the rest will desert him and Peter will deny him three times (Mark 14.27f.).

There is a dreadful sense of inevitability about the way in which all that has been predicted comes to pass. Judas betrays Jesus and Jesus is arrested; the other disciples abandon him and Peter denies him. Jesus is dragged up before the leaders of his own people, the very people we might expect to be best placed to recognize and honour the Christ, God's own beloved. Instead, they hear testimony in which witnesses cannot even get their story straight and this leads to one important confrontation. The High Priest asks Jesus the question that we have known the answer to from the beginning and that Jesus has consistently avoided answering: 'Are you the Messiah, the Son of the Blessed One?' (Mark 14.61). Jesus finally gives a straight answer –'I am' – and even predicts that ultimately he will be honoured before everyone, and the High Priest's reaction is to cry blasphemy. Jesus is spat on, mocked and beaten – just as he predicted.

This is the first of two trials that Jesus will experience according to Mark. It is worth pausing for a moment and considering what it means to be the accused during a trial – especially one where the final verdict is guilty. Jesus, the Son of God, stands in the place of the guilty and is accused and judged by other people. Although we are constantly assured that the accusers lied (and did quite a bad job of it since they apparently contradicted one another (Mark 14.56)), nevertheless at the end of both trials Jesus is condemned. At the heart of shame is the fear of being in exactly the same place that Jesus stood – judged, condemned and treated with contempt.

His own people then drag him off for a trial before Pilate. Pilate is presented as something of a puppet who is being manipulated by the very people who should have supported Jesus, and during this encounter even the crowd turn against him. Mark presents us with the ultimate irony, or perhaps the ultimate degradation. Pilate is the only one who appears willing to even consider the possibility of Jesus' innocence. He recognizes that jealousy lies behind the actions of the priests and scribes, but is ultimately too lazy or too fearful to stand up to their manipulation. He tries to use the crowd to avoid the problem; when they ask for the traditional release of a prisoner to mark the festival, he names Jesus as the one to be let go. Instead, it is the crowd who turn against Jesus so fully that they insist he must be handed over to the most degrading death known in their world – crucifixion. Pilate simply goes along with the demands of the crowd. Jesus is just not important enough for Pilate to take a risk, even though Pilate recognizes his innocence.

Jesus is mocked and dragged off to be crucified and Mark emphasizes that the mocking continues even as he hangs there. He is taunted by the crowd, the priests and scribes, and even by those being crucified with him. In Mark's Gospel the only words that Jesus speaks from the cross is the great cry asking God, 'why have you forsaken me?' (Mark. 15.34). He is alone in his humiliation.

At this moment, we pause and remember again Gabrielle Taylor's description of what it means for someone from a shame-honour society to face public disgrace:

> Hence if a man has lost his reputation then he has lost his value in the eyes of all the members of the group, *and this includes himself.* So there is nothing left, no inner quality or whatever, which could be judged to be of value in spite of the loss of public respect. (Taylor, 1985, p. 55)

But it seems that there is one little bit of good news amid the horror. Even as Jesus dies, one person recognizes that he is God's son, which is surely a glimmer of hope. The Roman centurion, who presumably has just overseen the execution, is the only person present to acknowledge what we as readers have known all along (Mark 15.39). So a foreigner is the first to put into words the truth about Jesus with which Mark began. Is this a sign of hope? I suggest that it is only a sign of hope if we imagine that he also immediately understood that God was working in the cross. He is responding to the way that Jesus died and the evidence before his eyes is of a broken and degraded man. Possibly, his declaration is an exclamation of utter horror and despair. Imagine that Mark 15.39 has another part to the statement, 'Truly this man was God's son *and I just helped crucify him.*' I have inflicted the most demeaning death possible on the person whom God honours above all. The centurion, in this interpretation, stands for those people who are sure that they understand honour and that they know who is to be admired and who can safely be treated with contempt. He warns us that the cross can be shocking to our most basic assumptions.

Only once Jesus is dead does Mark mention that he does have a little support from some who used to follow him. There are the women who followed him and provided for him from the beginning; they are watching from a distance. Joseph of Arimathea steps forward to take care of his body. It is almost as if Jesus has to be dead before Mark can mention that he has not been totally abandoned.

Mark's Gospel ends abruptly, with only a hint of the resurrection. In this Gospel (without the endings that were added later) we do not meet the risen Christ but instead receive the message that he has been raised, which is greeted with utter confusion. The women go to the tomb, find the stone rolled away, and meet a young man who says that Jesus has been raised and that he will meet them and the men in Galilee. They run away in terror and say nothing to anyone because they are afraid, and that is where Mark ends.

Can I invite you for a moment to stand with those women? Not in the sense that we can ever really know what it was like to turn up expecting to prepare for a funeral only to be told that your dead friend is planning to meet you back home. Rather, let us stand with them in the sense of asking what it means to listen to the message sent by the cross when the resurrection is only a hint and a hope. If we remember the argument from Radzik that bad actions send messages to which we are all susceptible, then we need to take very seriously that the crucifixion had sent a very loud message that the women and those who followed Jesus would have heard loud and clear. This man was nothing; he was contemptuous and deserved all of the shame heaped upon him. His religious leaders judged him a blasphemer and wanted him dead, so clearly everything that he had said about God and about how to live the spiritual life was wrong. The crowd preferred a bandit to him, so forget any kind of popular support. Pilate knew he was innocent, but he was not worth the political risk of standing up to the crowd, the scribes and the Pharisees. In the Roman Empire, crucifixion was what happened when the Empire stamped on you and declared you to be nothing; this is the message that the women had heard. No wonder their first response to any suggestion of hope is fear and silence.

We will come to the resurrection later – but first we are going to stay with the crucifixion and the challenge that it posed then, and poses still, to our values and even our very image of who God is.

## The Shamed Messiah and the Gospel

So imagine for a moment being the apostle Paul. He believed that he had been called by God to take the message about Jesus to all people – not only to the Jews, but also to the Gentiles – and his major task is to explain that it is *good* news. One of the biggest problems facing him therefore was that he needed to proclaim to a world obsessed with honour and status that God was at work through someone who had undergone the most degrading death possible. Then, in a world that believed that an individual's honour was dependent, at least in part, upon the groups to which she belonged, he needed to invite others to join Jesus' disciples. As he put it in his letter to the Corinthians, our message is utter foolishness and in that foolishness lies the paradox of the gospel:

> For Jews demand signs and Greeks desire wisdom, but we proclaim Christ crucified, a stumbling-block to Jews and foolishness to Gentiles, but to those who are the called, both Jews and Greeks, Christ the power of God and the wisdom of God. For God's foolishness is wiser than human wisdom, and God's weakness is stronger than human strength. (1 Cor. 1.22–25)

The word that is translated here as 'stumbling-block' is the Greek word *scandalon* from which we get our word 'scandal'. According to Paul, the message about Jesus appeared to be utter folly, but it was even worse when trying to speak to the Jews. The Gentiles at least had their stories about gods doing various strange things, but the Jews believed in one God, glorious and sovereign over all the world. No matter how much they believed in the love and mercy of God, how could they possibly believe that this God had suffered such utter degradation?

So the 'good news' about Jesus gave Paul a problem; it appeared to be laughably 'bad news' to many around him. But was that all? I suggest not. It appears to me that when we read Paul carefully, we can see that the 'bad news' about the shameful Messiah was not simply something he struggled to communicate to other people; it was also something that

Paul constantly lived with, reflected upon, and that eventually came to completely and radically change his very sense of who God is and what it means to serve God in this world. In recognizing the way in which believing in the shamed Messiah came to make such a difference to Paul, we can begin to see how we also might speak of the good news today in a way that demonstrates that it is genuinely good news for all – and particularly for those struggling with shame-ache.

In Philippians 2, Paul calls upon the Church at Philippi to show that they follow Christ in the way that they live. He asks them to have the same mind that Jesus had and this leads on to one of the great statements about Jesus that Christians have appealed to again and again. Be like Jesus:

> who, though he was in the form of God,
> did not regard equality with God
> as something to be exploited,
> but emptied himself,
> taking the form of a slave,
> being born in human likeness.
> And being found in human form,
> he humbled himself
> and became obedient to the point of death—
> even death on a cross.
> Therefore God also highly exalted him
> and gave him the name
> that is above every name,
> so that at the name of Jesus
> every knee should bend,
> in heaven and on earth and under the earth,
> and every tongue should confess
> that Jesus Christ is Lord,
> to the glory of God the Father. (Phil. 2.6–11)

Many readers today have examined this passage carefully, trying to understand if this is an outright claim that Jesus was God. However, for the reader in ancient times there was a more radical message that we also need to hear today. There is clearly a call for humility. Jesus was in a position of great glory and accepted humility and death; therefore God exalted him and obviously we should do the same. However, the English translation covers up just how radical the original was by importing into the text an idea that Paul never intended.

The English makes it appear that there is a direct contradiction between being God and accepting a position of humble service. Jesus acted humbly, even though he was divine. It is not unusual for English translations to imply this, in fact the majority of English translations seem to say the same:

- New Revised Standard Version: 'Who though he was in the form of God'.
- New American Standard Version: 'Who although he existed in the form of God'.
- New Living Translation: 'Though he was'.
- Contemporary English Version: 'Christ was truly God, but he did not try to remain equal with God'.
- Worldwide English: 'He was in every way like God, yet he did not think that being equal with God'.

This fits with our common assumptions about who God is. To be divine and to act humbly are clearly opposites of each other, but it is not what the Greek actually says. Translated literally, the Greek reads:

> Let the same mind be in you that was in Christ Jesus who being in the form of God did not regard equality with God as something to be exploited.

Not an 'although' or a 'despite' in sight. Having read so many translations that slip in an extra phrase I am sometimes tempted to supply one myself. If I were paraphrasing Paul, I would want to say something along these lines:

> Let the same mind be in you that was in Christ Jesus who precisely because he was in the form of God did not regard equality with God as something to be exploited.

In other words, humble service, putting others first, accepting even the humiliation of the cross, is not something that Jesus does despite being God; it is a demonstration of exactly who God really is. Paul here makes exactly the same point that John made in his Gospel when he told the story of Jesus washing his disciples' feet. In one of the rare examples of a Gospel telling something about Jesus' inner life and motivations, John insists that Jesus acted, 'knowing that the Father had given all things into his hands, and that he had come from God and was going to God' (John 13.3). Again, Jesus can take the role of a humble servant not *despite* being God, but because he is God.

So let us pause and ask ourselves what the gospel of the shamed Messiah has said so far, and what it has said to those struggling with shame-ache in particular. I suggest that it says the following:

- That God has stood with us in the deepest experience of shame and therefore the one who struggles with shame-ache can know that they are understood even when they do not understand themselves.
- That the cross asks us (especially those whose struggle is with arrogance and the confident assumption that they matter more than others) some hard questions about who we value and who we disregard.
- That when Jesus experienced shame and took on the role of humble service, he did so because he knew that he was loved and valued. In John's words he knew that he 'came from God and was going to God'. This means that confidence in your own self-worth should enable humility and service of others and this is very different to being forced (or forcing yourself) into humble service when you are struggling with shame-ache.
- The cross questions our most fundamental assumptions about who God is and what glory means.

But Christianity is not simply about the cross. We left the women running away with fear at the first rumours of the resurrection. The early Christians had to struggle not simply with a shamed Messiah, but also one who was raised from death. How was the resurrection to shape their understanding of one who had been so totally degraded? We are going to pick up the story a few weeks later with the first example we have of a sermon attempting to explain what happened.

## The Resurrection

Imagine the scene described for us in Acts 2. It is the day of Pentecost and the disciples have just been filled with God's Spirit in an overwhelming way. They spill out on to the streets of Jerusalem and attract the attention of a large and very confused crowd. Peter stands up to preach the first ever Christian sermon. Luke re-tells that sermon for us and includes an early interpretation of Jesus' resurrection. This is what Peter says:

> You that are Israelites, listen to what I have to say: Jesus of Nazareth, a man attested to you by God with deeds of power, wonders, and signs that God did through him among you, as you yourselves know – this man, handed over to you according to the definite plan and foreknowledge of God, you crucified and killed by the hands of those outside the law. But God raised him up, having freed him from death, because it was impossible for him to be held in its power. (Acts 2.22–24)

Later, he continues:

> Therefore let the entire house of Israel know with certainty that God has made him both Lord and Messiah, this Jesus whom you crucified. (Acts 2.36)

At first sight we are back with the problem we identified before as it seems that Peter here is blaming the Jews for Jesus' death. As before, it is important to remember that Jesus and his disciples were Jews and that the emphasis lies in the way in which Jesus was shamed. We are just as capable of misunderstanding what is going on, and therefore need to hear the way in which Peter is contrasting how Jesus was treated by those around him with how he was treated by God. Both of these actions send messages about how Jesus was valued and Peter's point here is that the message of the crucifixion and the message of the resurrection stand in sharp contrast to each other. If the crucifixion proclaimed that in the eyes of those around him Jesus was despised and rejected then the resurrection proclaims that, in the eyes of God, he is Lord and Messiah.

We can find exactly the same emphasis at the beginning of Paul's letter to the Romans. In his first summary of the gospel that opens his letter, Paul includes the following statement:

> the gospel concerning his Son, who was descended from David according to the flesh and was declared to be Son of God with power according to the spirit of holiness by resurrection from the dead, Jesus Christ our Lord, … (Rom. 1.3–4)

Paul is focused here on Jesus' human origins as against what the resurrection says about him, but the interpretation of the resurrection is the same. This verse has given many Christians in recent times quite a lot of concern and an unbelievable amount of ink has been spilled over the issue of whether Paul is saying that Jesus became the Son of God at the resurrection (which means he was not God) or whether the resurrection demonstrated what was always true (that he was God). Once again, we face the problem that we examined when we looked at Mark's opening verses: we have a very developed understanding of the term 'Son of God'. Paul probably used it in the same way that the First Testament did – to refer to anyone who was beloved of God. So his point is that the resurrection vindicates all that Jesus said and did and he can be trusted to show us who God is.

If we now go back to the passage from Philippians we can see that this makes roughly the same point. *Because* he was in the form of God, Jesus submitted to shame. *Therefore*, God highly exalted him and gave him the name above every name and stated that all should bow to him. We are not to read what happened on the cross as a message that Jesus is despicable and can be ignored because God in the resurrection sent the opposite message.

> The resurrection is not just the reappearance of a dead person. It is the mighty act of God to vindicate the One whose very right to exist was thought to have been negated by the powers that nailed him to a cross. At the same time, however, the One who is gloriously risen is the same One who suffered crucifixion. (Rutledge, 2017, p. 64)

To contemplate the death and resurrection of Christ is to stand between two very different value systems. There is a message here for those with shame-ache, but there is also a wider message for all Christians – in Jesus, God turns upside down our very understanding of what is shame and what is honour. The resurrection vindicates the way that Jesus lived and his teaching on how to live.

The final question we need to ask, therefore, is what does it mean to follow the one who was crucified and rose again, and how can following him help those with shame-ache to heal?

# 9

# Looking at Jesus, Jesus Looking at Us

If we do not transform our pain, we will most assuredly transmit it. (Richard Rohr, 2018)

I am crying, because there was a part of me that only Rachel seemed to see, and I don't want that part of me to go unseen in this world. (Nadia Bolz-Weber, 2019)

## On Doing Theology with Anna

Let's return one more time to the story of Anna. Anna is partly the real person who first helped me to understand something of the struggle of abuse survivors, but I gave her a history drawn in reality from several people, so she is also partly a representative figure. The Anna I met on that Sunday evening had a deep Christian faith, but some of what she had heard from the Church had made her battle harder. For the purposes of this section I am going to assume that her history has left Anna struggling not only with issues of forgiveness, but also with a profound shame-ache. The aim of this book has been to read the Bible and do theology while being attentive to Anna's questions and issues, and to ask how faith can enable Anna to flourish.

To read the Bible with Anna is to attempt to recover Abel and is an issue of rebalancing. I have tried to emphasize throughout this book that more traditional readings of Scripture are not wrong, so much as insufficient. They have listened to the needs of Cain more than the needs of Abel. In this final chapter I will begin by summarizing some of the themes that might help preachers, ministers and theologians to enable Anna to flourish before moving on to one more biblical story, in which the resurrected Jesus meets the shamed Peter for breakfast, and finally a single verse that sums up the life of faith for those with shame-ache.

So what themes do both those with shame-ache and those who seek to help them need to reflect upon?

1 That guilt and shame are easy to distinguish in theory, but in real- life experience are so close together that they are often confused. This means that it is easy to hear the Church's language about sin through the filter of shame-ache and find that it makes the struggle worse rather than better. Stephen Pattison notes that the Church 'talks dirty to get the attention of the shamed' (Pattison, quoted in Jewett, 2011, p. 20) but then fails to address their real needs. It is possible for a person with shame-ache to exaggerate their own guilt and find themselves trapped in a constant cycle of confession of sin without realizing why they cannot find the healing that they seek. Some Christian language about being unworthy or sinful only makes this struggle harder. At the same time, the Church does need to find ways to communicate that sin is both universal and deeper than just our individual acts. It is only human to be a vulnerable vine rather than an impervious island and therefore our fight against sin should never be reduced to a lonely, individual battle.

2 That how we portray God has a profound impact on those with shame-ache. Anna was the victim of power that was abused and used against her, yet Christianity asks her to trust in an all-powerful God. We have already explored how shame may make faith more difficult, and a related theme is the way in which the idea of an all-powerful God may both appeal to, and also damage, those with shame-ache at the same time:

> Theologically, the idea that God is an all-perfect, all powerful, and all seeing 'King' can heighten their [the shamed] sense of insignificance and being seen as unworthy ... This idealized God can be powerfully attractive to the shamed who want to be healed, identified with power, and included within the loving parental gaze. But their encounter with this deity and the ideas and practices surrounding God in theology and worship can all too often reinforce the sense of powerlessness, defilement, unworthiness, and alienation. (Pattison, in Jewett, 2011, p.21)

The Christian Church has always claimed that we should understand God, and therefore God's power, through Jesus Christ. The question we need to face is how thoroughly we have really allowed Jesus, the shamed Messiah, to shape how we think and speak about God. God has experienced being in the place of the injured with all of the trauma and shame that this brings. If shame is the self judging the self and fearing the censure of others, then the various trials that Jesus endured assure us that God has stood even in the place of the condemned. Our speech about God's power must be balanced and shaped by talking also of God's solidarity with us in the experience of shame.

3 That God forgiving sin is not the same as God condoning sin. The cross of Christ takes seriously the utter wickedness of which human beings are capable. Through a mixture of ignorance and pride, political manoeuvring and outright lies, cowardice and jealousy, human beings conspired to crucify the Son of God, and in the crucifixion God stood with the shamed and the injured. All Christian understandings of forgiveness need to start with the cross and it is the crucified Messiah who demands that we never downplay the reality of the evil that we inflict on one another or mistake forgiving for condoning in any way. In Christ's death and resurrection God forgives the offender *and* identifies with the injured, absorbing the cost of sin into his very life and being. The risen Christ still bore the scars that sin inflicted, showing that God does not forget the injury but transforms it. The gospel promise is that we live in God and God lives in us, so while Anna will carry the cost of sin herself, she will not do so alone; rather, she will join Christ in the journey through the cross to resurrection and new life.

4 That while guilt may be dealt with instantly in the promise of forgiveness, shame is more likely to need a lifelong exodus which will have its own twists and turns. Like the Israelites, Anna may keep realizing the different ways in which she has been bound by the sin of others and internalized shame. There is no one experience of shame and being healed from shame, so the experience of Exodus is also likely to be individual. The message of Exodus must itself be balanced by the reminder of Exile; we continue to live in a sinful world and to be vulnerable to all of the ways in which this may mark us. It is biblical to lament and complain and rage, and Anna may need the assurance that God hears her and loves her when she does.

## When Jesus Looks at You

It is an unknown time after the resurrection when, presumably, the disciples should have been on top of the world and getting on with the task of telling others what has happened. Except they are not. John's Gospel finishes with a story that does not quite seem to fit where it has been placed. At the end of the story of Jesus' ministry, death and resurrection some of the disciples have, well, gone back to where they started. Just like several other Gospel stories, Peter is a major player and is suggesting to the others what they should do, but I want to suggest that this is a different Peter to the one we met earlier. Peter is normally the disciple who speaks the most and often appears to be confident, even over-confident; in this story we meet Peter struggling with shame-ache, which leads me to wonder if shame has driven Peter all along.

We have looked at the many fig leaves that we create to deal with the painful void that shame can drag us into, but there is a further one to which we need to give more attention – perfectionism. Perfectionism is the belief that we can protect ourselves from shame by doing everything perfectly, but it leads us into another cycle of shame and blame since we set ourselves unattainable goals and then blame ourselves for failing to achieve them. Peter, I suspect, was a perfectionist. He was the disciple who was volubly sure that he would do better than anyone else. When Jesus predicted that all of his disciples would desert him in the face of the shame of the crucifixion, Peter was the one who insisted that he would be the exception. Shame feeds perfectionism and perfectionism feeds shame; could it be that Peter needed to prove to himself that he was better than the others to avoid the ache inside?

To be fair, Peter did follow longer than most of the other men; he and one other unnamed disciple made it to the courtyard of the High Priest when Jesus was being tried before disaster struck (John 18.15f.). But it seems that the women stayed with Jesus longer, and were there when he was crucified and to see his place of burial. I wonder how that felt to Peter, who had been brought up in a chauvinistic society and presumably was constantly told that the role of men was to be stronger and braver and to protect the women. Is it too much to suggest that, for Peter, his own denial of Christ was a humiliating collapse of his perfectionist image of who he thought he should be? After years of projecting and trying to live up to an impressive image, he has failed. He is left with the other Peter, the ordinary, fallible Peter, perhaps the Peter he is not too keen on.

If that part of the story were not bad enough, then things took another turn. In John 20 we have the story of Mary Magdalene discovering that the tomb was empty; she runs back to the others, and Peter and one other man run to the tomb. Peter is outrun and arrives second (just one more small blow in a week that has brought so many) but he is the first to enter the tomb and discover that the body has indeed gone. We are told that the other disciples immediately believed but we are not told how Peter reacted.

The two male disciples then leave, meaning that according to John they miss the first resurrection appearance. The first time that Peter hears that this is a whole lot bigger than just the disappearance of the body comes when Mary Magdalene tells the other disciples. It is worth remembering again that Peter has been brought up in a society with very fixed gender roles and is likely to believe that his value lies, at least in part, in his ability to conform to those stereotypes. In Peter's world, men are supposed to be brave and lead, and they are supposed to protect women. In addition, Peter has been encouraged to see himself as the lead disciple, surely therefore the one who might be first to meet the risen Christ. So imagine for a moment, having already denied Jesus in public, then run away and later heard that the women stayed with him until the end; now you hear that you were there where Jesus appeared after the resurrection, but he waited until after you had left to arrive. What might that do to Peter's already battered image of himself?

Only after all of this has happened does Jesus appear to the men in John 20.19–23, so it is understandable that Peter seems to be unable to cope emotionally. In John's Gospel, the resurrection did not automatically put everything right or convince Peter to instantly obey Jesus' command to 'go and make disciples of all nations' (Matt. 28.19). He met Jesus and was shown Jesus' hand and side, and what does he do? He goes back to his old job.

In John 21, Peter is back with some of the other disciples at the familiar task of fishing. Many biblical scholars find it strange that the story appears here in John's Gospel, especially since the previous chapter ended with what reads like the closing words of the Gospel. However, I want to argue that reading the story here makes emotional sense for a man who is on an exodus out of shame-ache and perfectionism. Perhaps Peter is caught between joy at Jesus' resurrection and shame when he looks back on his own actions. Could there even be a part of him that really struggled with having to meet Jesus again after his boasting and then his collapse into doing the one thing he said he would not do? If faith is a relationship, then we need to be realistic about the way in which shame distorts relationships, even the one with God. If you are just beginning to realize that this man whom you loved and followed for three years, and then let down so disastrously, may possibly be more than just a man, how are you supposed to look him in the eye ever again? 'It is not that I don't want to see you,' said Cicero to his brother, 'it is that I don't want to be seen by you.' Peter, I suspect, would understand that statement.

So what does Peter do? He goes back to his old life. It seems to me that what he needed at that point more than anything else was to return to doing something where he knew he could do a good job. Forget fishing for people – at the moment Peter can barely cope with his own problems, let alone anyone else's. He is a failure at being a disciple, he is pretty sure that the others must be mad at him for what he did, and he is not too excited about meeting Jesus. Peter understands fishing and nets and boats, and that is the world that he wants right now. A world in which he might actually do that most comforting of things – achieve something worthwhile.

So he goes fishing, only to find that the only way to catch anything was to follow the directions of the stranger on the shore who turned out to be Jesus. Could this get any worse? Now he can't even fish without Jesus' help. There follows the strangely illogical story of eating fish for breakfast. Jesus helps the fishermen to make a catch (John 21.6) but has already started a fire with some fish on it (John 21.9). Nevertheless, he tells Peter to bring some of the catch (John 21.10) and then provides breakfast and appears to do so immediately, which implies they actually ate the fish that he had already cooked (John 21.12–13). In one sense, this story has some strange twists, but again I want to argue that seen through Peter's eyes it makes emotional sense. Why did Peter need to bring some fish when there was fish already? Could it have something to do with the need to contribute when you feel you have got everything wrong? Could this be the first step in Jesus enabling Peter to find some self-worth and begin to overcome his shame?

The fish are not the only slightly strange part of the story. Peter also becomes the only person I have ever heard of who deliberately puts his clothes on before jumping into the water (John 21.7). Apparently, he fished naked but could not face Jesus without some kind of covering. This may or may not be a reference back to the Genesis story of nakedness and shame and it could be that wearing clothes is simply a mark of respect for Jesus. I suspect, though, that Peter did not want to approach Jesus feeling even more exposed and vulnerable. He is clinging hard to any fig leaves he can find in a situation where he feels unwanted and vulnerable.

So what does Jesus do? Peter must have expected that Jesus would be angry and that he might be demoted from his leadership role and replaced by a disciple with a slightly smaller mouth. What Jesus actually does is invite Peter and the others to breakfast. Once again, we are reminded of the God who wants people to feel at home and who cares for basic needs such as hunger and a sense of being valued as much as she does for those needs that we think are more spiritual. Jesus himself serves the disciples food (John 21.13) before there is any discussion of what happened on the night of his arrest.

After breakfast there was a discussion, but probably not the one that Peter anticipated. Thousands of sermons have been preached on the conversation that happened next and particularly on the word play that is apparent in the Greek but not the English. For some this will be familiar ground, but it is worth going over it for those for whom it is new. John 21.15–17 uses two different ways of talking about love in Greek. *Agape* is the word that is used to describe love at its deepest. In secular Greek it was used for the love of spouse and family, and in religious Greek it came to refer to the committed love that God shows to us. *Agape*, we might say, is the love that Peter aspired to have and even believed he needed to have in order to be accepted; perfect love that is constant, determined and faithful. *Philia* has a meaning closer to affection and, if you are a perfectionist, it may feel like a lesser love. Perhaps, however, if you are battered and bruised it is a more realistic love; it is the love a human can offer without trying to match the love that God shows us.

In Greek, the conversation goes something like this:

Jesus: Simon, son of John, do you *agapas* me more than these?
Peter: Yes, Lord, you know that I *philō* you.
Jesus: Feed my lambs.
Jesus: Simon, son of John, do you *agapas* me?

Peter: Yes, Lord, you know that I *philō* you.
Jesus: Tend my sheep.
Jesus: Simon, son of John, do you *philō* me?
Peter: Lord, you know everything; you know that I *philō* you.
Jesus: Feed my sheep.

In other words, at each stage of the conversation, Jesus' question to Peter is less demanding than the stage before. First, he asks, 'Do you *agape* me more than these?' The Greek is as ambiguous as the English, so Jesus could have been asking 'Is your love for me greater than their love for me?' or he could have been asking 'Is your love for me greater than your love for them?' I suspect we should read it the first way, which puts the demand high and includes a comparison; perfectionists often persistently compare themselves to others and worry that others are more accomplished than they are. Perfectionists can make even love a competition. Peter replies simply that he *philios* Jesus. The second question removes the comparison but still asks if Peter *agapes*. Only the third time does Jesus use the same word as Peter and ask for *philios*.

What is more, Jesus who renamed Peter at the beginning of the Gospel (John 1.42) now reverts to Peter's old name, 'Simon, son of John'. According to John, when Andrew brought Simon to Jesus, the first words that Jesus spoke were, '"You are Simon, son of John. You are to be called Cephas" (which is translated Peter)' (John 1.42). Cephas comes from *kepha*, the Aramaic word for rock, and Peter from *petra*, the Greek word for rock. In Matthew 16 we are even told that the Church will be built on Peter, this rock. A rock is meant to be solid and reliable and a strong foundation, all of which must have seemed a bitter irony to Peter just at this moment. Here, Jesus reverts to his old name, which might seem like something of a demotion (back to being the old version of who Simon was), except after each question Simon Peter is entrusted with a tremendously important task. Feed my lambs, tend my sheep, feed my sheep. Jesus uses the old name to give Peter a new task.

We tend to celebrate when people in Scripture are given new names; we take it as a sign of their new identity as people of faith. Abram becomes Abraham (Gen. 17.5), Sarai becomes Sarah (Gen. 17.15) because they have found faith and a new role as the ancestors of the Jews. We forget that for those with shame-ache who cannot believe that the person they really are could ever be accepted, a new name might be the biggest trap of all. Rather than saying that the gift of faith is a new start and the chance to grow and heal on the foundation of being loved, it can send the message that for you to be accepted you must make yourself a new person (and never fall back into old habits). Simon has striven to be Peter the rock as he imagines Jesus wants him to be, and has conclusively failed. Perhaps it is time for Simon to discover that being Peter is the gift that Jesus wants to give him, if he could just trust that he is wanted and valued even when he is less than perfect.

It is when Simon stops striving to be better than others (rather than just doing the best he can), and when he stops setting himself impossible standards, that Jesus demonstrates the greatest trust in him. Only the newly humble and more realistic Simon is ready to be the Peter who will feed Christ's flock. Naturally, the newly humble and more realistic Peter is less than perfect (there is plenty of evidence that he did not get on too well with Paul, for example) but only when he accepted that Jesus loved him as he is, flawed and imperfect, could he flourish sufficiently to be able to help others. Christ did not shame the already embarrassed Peter, but shared a meal with him and helped him to have the dignity of bringing something to the table. More than that, when Peter was at his lowest and could barely look Jesus in the eye, Jesus continued to insist that Peter had a job to do. Sometimes we need more than words to help us find a sense of being valued; sometimes we find it in discovering that others trust us enough to ask us to do something important.

What is going on here is key in the battle against shame-ache. There are many ways in which shame distorts our vision and here we need to remember that, above all, it distorts our vision of ourselves. Guilt becomes shame when our bad actions and our weaknesses are all that we can see about ourselves. We want to hide from others because we judge ourselves by the worst that we have done and expect that others will do the same. The issue in this story is not simply how Peter sees himself, but how he imagines that Jesus sees him. What Jesus demonstrates in this story is that when he looks at Peter, he can see more than the man who boasted and then denied him. He can still see the Peter who is trustworthy enough to be the foundation stone of his new community and who will lead others.

This point is important enough that we need to expand it. The Christian tradition has long maintained that a realistic view of sin means insisting not just that we do bad things, but that the issue is deeper.

Some versions of the Christian tradition insist on emphasizing Paul's words in Romans 7.18, 'For I know that nothing good dwells within me.' We are sinners through and through and there is nothing we can do to save ourselves. The problem, of course, is that magnifying only our faults is a classic response of shame, and therefore some understandings of Christianity can be positively damaging for those with shame-ache. Scripture itself is more nuanced and insists that there are several truths about us that need to be held in balance. I believe that the best way of expressing this for a modern audience is to speak of God's triple vision. If, as we struggle with shame, we see only the worst parts of ourselves, we need to counter this with the knowledge that at all times and in all places God's vision of us is broader and more accurate than our self-image can ever be.

## God's Triple Vision

> O LORD, do not rebuke me in your anger,
> or discipline me in your wrath.
> For your arrows have sunk into me,
> and your hand has come down on me.
>
> There is no soundness in my flesh
> because of your indignation;
> there is no health in my bones
> because of my sin.
> For my iniquities have gone over my head;
> they weigh like a burden too heavy for me.
>
> My wounds grow foul and fester
> because of my foolishness;
> I am utterly bowed down and prostrate;
> all day long I go around mourning.
> For my loins are filled with burning,
> and there is no soundness in my flesh.
> I am utterly spent and crushed;
> I groan because of the tumult of my heart. (Ps. 38.1–8)

Psalm 38 describes someone struggling with the overpowering sense of having sinned. It is quite clear that at this moment in time this is all that he can see of his life; he has shame-ache and is blind to anything that he may have done well or to anything about him that is good, true or beautiful. I suspect that on that beach Peter would have found it pretty easy to pray this psalm.

This is, therefore, an important expression of an important truth in life. It is easy for someone who does not live with shame-ache to dismiss this psalm as morbid and too preoccupied with guilt. Having psalms in the Bible's prayer book that describe shame-ache encourages us to be honest with God without fearing that the reality of our experience will be dismissed. Sometimes the struggle with shame-ache can be made worse by being made to believe that we should not feel this way, and yet we cannot just shrug off our feelings. God never dismisses our feelings even when they do not accurately reflect who we are. As with all our 'unacceptable' emotions, the best thing we can do is pray about them and perhaps even use this psalm to help us give our shame expression. This needs to be combined with talking with good friends and trusted counsellors, quite possibly trained professionals, whose empathy can offer a way through shame.

Equally, someone with shame-ache needs to know that this experience is the truth, but not the whole truth about them or about the person who originally wrote the psalm. Some parts of the Christian tradition have used this and other such versions to argue not just that this is what we *do* experience, but also that this is what we *should* experience. We are sinners whose 'iniquities have gone over our heads' and all of us without exception should constantly call this to mind. There has been little reflection in the tradition on the possibility that different people have different struggles. Those struggling with hubris and arrogance may need to reflect on the reality of their past sins and their current vulnerability to sin's distortion of human flourishing; those struggling with shame-ache need a different message: that even in those times when all we can see of ourselves is our weakness and flaws, God sees something very different:

> For it was you who formed my inward parts;
> you knit me together in my mother's womb.
> I praise you, for I am fearfully and wonderfully made.
> Wonderful are your works;

that I know very well.
My frame was not hidden from you,
when I was being made in secret,
intricately woven in the depths of the earth.
Your eyes beheld my unformed substance.
In your book were written
all the days that were formed for me,
when none of them as yet existed. (Ps. 139.13–16)

Here the psalmist celebrates himself as a wonderful creation of God. We are reminded once more that when God created humankind, she looked and saw that all she had created was very good. If Peter stood on that beach and feared being seen by Jesus, then he needed to know that Jesus' vision of him was deeper and broader and truer than his own. Shame could have trapped Peter for ever in what he imagined Jesus saw of him; part of his exodus from shame-ache came when Jesus showed in both word and action that he saw a different Peter, and that he loved and trusted Peter though Peter could not trust himself.

Human beings can have a very narrow vision, particularly when we look at ourselves. Some of us seem to slip easily into focusing entirely on our good points or entirely on the bad. When we see only our strengths we easily slip into hubris and entitlement; the Davids among us need a strong and thoughtful understanding of sin that demands we recognize the impact of our actions on other people. When we see only our weaknesses and faults we easily slip into shame-ache, which in turn can lead us to distort language about sin into the assumption that we are somehow worthless. The Abels among us also need a strong and thoughtful understanding of sin which helps us to understand that we are vulnerable islands, just like everyone else, and that God loves us as we are. Equally, whoever we most identify with, we all need to know that at the moment we live in an exiled world that continues to shape us and one aspect of sin might be that our fig leaves end up damaging both us and those around us. God can see not only our current strengths and weaknesses, but also something more:

And I heard a loud voice from the throne saying,
'See, the home of God is among mortals.
He will dwell with them;

they will be his peoples,
and God himself will be with them;
he will wipe every tear from their eyes.
Death will be no more;
mourning and crying and pain will be no more,
for the first things have passed away.'

And the one who was seated on the throne said, 'See, I am making all things new.' Also he said, 'Write this, for these words are trustworthy and true' (Rev. 21.3–5).

Scripture holds out before us God's vision of a future in which he lives among us and is able therefore to heal all our aches (including shame-ache). The final end of the exodus from shame-ache is not the lonely struggle to make ourselves perfect so that we do not need to feel the agony of shame again, but the healing that is offered when God lives in us and we live in him and he wipes our tears away and makes all things new. Since we are vulnerable vines our healing is intimately connected with the healing of those around us and of the world we live in. The dream of the future in which God dwells with us should never be distorted by the perfectionist quest to live up to an unattainable ideal in a world still in exile.

God has triple vision. It is only an image, but I believe it to be a helpful way to counteract both hubris and shame's distortion of our vision of ourselves, which we then project on to God. Where we can often see only one aspect of our lives, God is quite capable of always and everywhere seeing three aspects at once:

- That we are fearfully and wonderfully made and are valued and loved.
- That we are vulnerable vines, liable to be weighed down by our own sins and the sins of others. We share this weakness with all other human beings and need to avoid believing that this is our own personal issue while also taking responsibility for our actions (even those that are a response to our fig leaves).
- Our future as children of God when all things will be made new and we will be free of the burdens we carry now.

God is quite capable of seeing all of this at the same time; we could even say that only God is capable of seeing all of this at the same time. God loves and forgives us in spite of our actions but not in spite of who we are. God is utterly realistic about both our weakness and our value in a way we can rarely manage.

God has triple vision all the time. In other words, God sees our sins and weaknesses and fully understands the way in which shame distorts our vision of ourselves, but also sees and delights in us as valued, loved children of God who will one day be set free. We are reminded of what psychologists frequently point out: that while hubris and entitlement are dangerous and liable to make us blind to the injury we do to others, we need a sense of being loved and wanted in order to both face where we have been wrong and behave differently in the future. Theologically the same idea is expressed by the priority of grace. We do not repent and then receive grace; rather, as God's grace touches and shapes us, we are enabled to truly repent.

John's Gospel ends very strangely. Not only did it seem to end at chapter 20, only to then continue on to the breakfast on the beach, but we are never told Peter's response to Jesus' new commission. In fact, Peter continues with the comparisons that have already caused such problems. He sees another disciple and wants to know 'Lord, what about him?' (John 21.21). Jesus makes one more attempt to focus Peter on his own discipleship without the comparisons, but we hear nothing about what happens next. This encounter with Jesus did not bring Peter instant healing; we are left with an open-ended story that hints at an exodus out of shame-ache still to come. Perhaps there is something to be learned from a story that is not rounded off and the invitation to wonder about what happened next. It is quite possible to be perfectionist about escaping perfectionism; Peter had some way to go, but still Jesus loved him, valued him and called him to be a disciple.

## When You Look at Jesus

When shame washes over us it can feel as if it has taken over our ability to think or even be aware of anything else. In such times it can be helpful to have a single verse to hold on to. I've spent most of this book sweeping through vast tracts of Scripture and trying to get an overall view on what it says. However, I want to close with a look at two verses that seem to me profoundly helpful for those who are caught in the battle with shame-ache.

Hebrews 12.1–2 come just after a list of biblical characters who struggled and suffered. The NRSV translates these verses as follows:

> Therefore, since we are surrounded by so great a cloud of witnesses, let us also lay aside every weight and the sin that clings so closely, and let us run with perseverance the race that is set before us, looking to Jesus the pioneer and perfecter of our faith, who for the sake of the joy that was set before him endured the cross, disregarding its shame, and has taken his seat at the right hand of the throne of God. (Heb.12.1–2)

As ever, it is difficult for the English translation to express all that is said by the Greek.

Let's start with the idea of sin that clings so closely. The Greek carries the meaning of something that holds us back and prevents us from running the race that we want to run. Hebrews 12.1 underlines again that we need a biblical, nuanced understanding of sin that makes sense today. The label of sinner is unlikely to help anyone with shame-ache who already regards themselves as flawed and useless. A much more helpful image is to regard yourself as being in a race (or even an exodus) and that sin is a power that tries to hold you back from reaching your goal. Being a vulnerable vine is part of being human (which is shared with everyone else), but you have a race to run. If your fig leaves are allowed to dominate your life, and if you give in to hubris, anger, perfectionism or whatever is your ultimate struggle, you will become entangled and encumbered and will be carried away from your ultimate goal. God is concerned about the way in which sin tries to shape you, not because you are unworthy or unwanted but because he longs for you to gain that prize.

Second (Heb. 12.2), there is the image of keeping our eyes on (the human) Jesus. The Greek word translated 'pioneer', is made up of the word for 'first' and the verb 'to lead'. 'Pioneer' is not a bad translation – provided we remember that a pioneer is the first to do something with the aim that others are then enabled to do the same. F. F. Bruce suggests that we translate the word as 'trailblazer' (Bruce, 1988, p. 80). Since I am not a very good translator, I want to use an entire phrase to get the point across: the writer of the letter to the Hebrews is inviting us to contemplate Jesus as the first to live out our life of faith. Keep your eyes on the Jesus who is your trailblazer because he lived out faith with all its struggles (including the struggle with shame) and has enabled you to do the same.

And what about the word translated 'perfecter' (Heb.12.2)? The Greek word comes from the word for purpose, and the point is not that Jesus will somehow make your faith perfect but that he can be trusted to bring it to its final goal, no matter how weak it may feel now.

This is the Jesus that the letter to the Hebrews invites us to contemplate. Life burdens us and sin clings to us so that there are times when faith seems an impossible struggle in which we have let everyone (including God) down. In those moments shame will tempt us to keep our eyes firmly on our own failings and the seeming impossibility of change. With Adam and Eve, we want to hide, from others, from God, and even from ourselves. What we are being asked to do is turn our gaze instead to Jesus, remembering that he lived this human life before us and knows our struggles and temptations from the perspective of an insider. Fix your gaze on him and let him shape your understanding of who God is.

John Calvin used to urge Christians to 'embrace Christ as the servant of the Father, that he may show himself to you as the Prince of Life' (Calvin, Commentary on John 6.55). This is a key principle for those struggling with shame-ache. Fix your eyes on the human Christ; direct your heart, mind and soul to the hospitable Messiah who experienced the depth of shame for himself, and allow him to draw you to the gracious, all-powerful God who created the universe. He will show you that he is that God incarnate and re-shape your understanding of that God.

The letter to the Hebrews then goes further, for we are told that Christ not only experienced shame, but that he thought it of little importance. The NRSV says that he 'disregard[ed]' shame (Heb.12.2) and it is too easy for someone with shame-ache to read this as if he easily rose above shame in comparison to the way we have been overpowered by it. It matters to remember that when he contemplated the shame of his death, Jesus became distressed and agitated and even sweated blood (Luke. 22.44). There is a challenge in this verse not just for those with shame-ache: that none of us should ever allow the threat of shame to hold us back from following Christ. At the same time, we must also emphasize that we are not saying that Christians should somehow seek shame out; Jesus understood his mission was to be faithful to God and was willing to endure the shame that this brought him. The resurrection was God's ultimate vindication of that willingness to endure shame. The letter to the Hebrews says that Jesus endured the shame of the cross 'for the sake of the joy that was set before him' (Heb. 12.2), not that he sought out shame for shame's sake. Those with shame-ache need to read this verse as saying, 'This is how important Christ's mission was to him, he regarded shame as unimportant in comparison', rather than reading it as, 'Christ disregarded shame, why can't you?'

Hebrews 12.2 includes one other virtue that is helpful for those attempting an exodus from shame – endurance. We are to run with endurance as Jesus endured the cross. The Greek word came to mean 'to bear trials with fortitude'. Sometimes, this is what the struggle with shame-ache can feel like. We endure, we persist, even though it may feel like progress is slow or non-existent; and while doing so we look to Jesus our pioneer, who knows what it is to endure trials for our sake and for the sake of a joy to come.

So who wants to talk about shame? That miserable, word-stealing, brain-freezing, soul-shrinking wash of emotion that makes us want to run and hide. Who wants to talk about that? Perhaps we should turn the question around. The Bible talks about shame from the earliest story of forbidden fruit and fig leaves through to the cross and resurrection of Christ and beyond. The Bible offers both hope to those whose lives seem dominated by shame-ache and challenges all Christians to think seriously about the way in which the fear of shame and desire for honour might distort our discipleship. Each of us needs to work out what it means to follow the shamed Messiah, without seeking out shame for shame's sake, in a world that sets such a high value on self-esteem. If that is the case, why aren't we talking about shame?

# References and Bibliography

## *Primary Documents*

Aristotle, *The History of Animals*, trans. D'Arcy Wentworth Thompson, http://classics.mit.edu/Aristotle/history_anim.7.vii.html (accessed 23.11.19).

Calvin, John, 1961, *The Gospel According to St. John*, trans. T. H. L. Parker, Grand Rapids, MI: Eerdmans.

Cicero, M. Tullius, *Letters*, trans. Evelyn S. Shuckburgh, Perseus 4.0, www.perseus.tufts.edu/hopper/text?doc=Perseus%3Atext%3A1999.02.0022%3Ayear%3D58 (accessed 15.3.18).

Donne, John, 'Meditation 17 from Devotions upon Emergent Occasions', 1624, www.luminarium.org/sevenlit/donne/meditation17.php (accessed 17.4.13).

Lambdin, Thomas O., trans., 'The Gospel of Thomas Collection', The Gnostic Society Library, http://gnosis.org/naghamm/nhl_thomas.htm (accessed 1.8.19).

Pliny, n.d., *Natural History*.

## *Bibliography*

Alison, James, 2003, *On Being Liked*, New York: Crossroad Publishing.

Anderson, Gary, 2009, *Sin: A History*, New Haven, CT: Yale University Press.

Atkins, Anne, 2006, 'Brave, but She Can't Forgive the Bombers', *Telegraph*, 7 March 2006, www.telegraph.co.uk/comment/personal-view/3623512/Brave-but-she-cant-forgive-the-bombers.html (accessed 17.1.18).

Barton, Carlin, 2001, *Roman Honor: The Fire in the Bones*, Berkeley, CA: University of California Press.

Baumeister, Roy F. and Brad J. Bushman, 2008, *Social Psychology and Human Nature: Brief Version*, Belmont, CA: Thomson Wadsworth.

Benedict, Ruth, 2005, *The Chrysanthemum and the Sword: Patterns of Japanese Culture*, Boston, MA: Houghton Mifflin.

Birch, Bruce, Walter Brueggemann, Terence Fretheim and David Petersen, 2005, *A Theological Introduction to the Old Testament*, 2nd edn, Nashville, TN: Abingdon Press.

Bolz-Weber, Nadia, 2019, 'While It Was Still Dark: A Requiem for Rachel Held Evans', Red Letter Christians, www.redletterchristians.org/while-it-was-still-dark-a-requiem-for-rachel-held-evans/ (accessed 12.9.19).

Bonhoeffer, Dietrich, 1993, *Christ the Center*, San Francisco, CA: HarperSanFrancisco.

Boulton, Matthew, 2002, 'Forsaking God: A Theological Argument for Christian Lamentation', *Scottish Journal of Theology* 55(1): 58–78.

Bradshaw, J., 1988, *Healing the Shame that Binds You*, Boca Raton, FL: HCI Books (e-book).

Brown, Brené, 2010. *The Gifts of Imperfection: Let Go of Who You Think You're Supposed to Be and Embrace Who You Are*, Philadelphia, PA: Hazelden Publishing (e-book).

——, 2015. *Daring Greatly: How the Courage to Be Vulnerable Transforms the Way We Live, Love, Parent, and Lead*, London: Penguin Books (e-book).

Brownson, James V., 2013, *Bible, Gender, Sexuality: Reframing the Church's Debate on Same-Sex Relationships*, Grand Rapids, MI: Eerdmans (e-book).

Bruce, F. F., 1988, *The Epistle to the Hebrews: The English Text with Introduction, Exposition and Notes*, Grand Rapids, MI: Eerdmans.

Brueggemann, Walter, 1982, *Genesis*, Atlanta, GA: John Knox Press.

——, 1986, 'The Costly Loss of Lament', *Journal for the Study of the Old Testament* 11(36): 57–71.

——, 1997, *Cadences of Home: Preaching among Exiles*, 1st edn, Louisville, KY: Westminster John Knox Press.

——, 2002, *David's Truth in Israel's Imagination and Memory*, Minneapolis, MN: Fortress Press.

Burke, Trevor, 2006, *Adopted into God's Family: Exploring a Pauline Metaphor*, Nottingham: IVP (Apollos imprint).

Clines, David, 1989, *Job*, Dallas, TX: Word Books.

Collicutt, Joanna, 2015, *The Psychology of Christian Character Formation*, London: SCM Press.

Crook, Zeba, 2009, 'Honor, Shame, and Social Status Revisited', *Journal of Biblical Literature* 128(3): 591.

Firth, David G., 2008, 'David and Uriah (with an Occasional Appearance by Uriah's Wife) – Reading and Re-Reading 2 Samuel 11', *Old Testament Essays*, 21(2): 310–28.

——, 2009, *1 & 2 Samuel*, Nottingham: IVP (Apollos imprint).

Ford, David F., 2007, *Christian Wisdom: Desiring God and Learning in Love*, Cambridge/New York: Cambridge University Press.

Gilligan, James, 1996, *Violence: Reflections on a National Epidemic*, New York: G. P. Putnam.

——, 2003, 'Shame, Guilt, and Violence', *Social Research* 70(4): 1149–80.

Gunn, David M., 1996, 'Bathsheba Goes Bathing in Hollywood: Words, Images, and Social Locations', *Semeia* 74: 75–101.

Gutiérrez, Gustavo, 1985, *We Drink from Our Own Wells: The Spiritual Journey of a People*, London: SCM Press.

——, 2001, *A Theology of Liberation: History, Politics, and Salvation*, rev. edn, London: SCM Press.

Hartley, John E., 1988, *The Book of Job*, Grand Rapids, MI: Eerdmans.

Hengel, M., 1977, *Crucifixion* [S.l.], London: SCM Press.

Hieronymi, Pamela, 2001, 'Articulating an Uncompromising Forgiveness', *Philosophy and Phenomenological Research*, 62(3): 529–55.

Higton, Mike, 2008, *Christian Doctrine*, London: SCM Press.

Jacquet, Jennifer, 2016, *Is Shame Necessary?*, London: Penguin Books.

Janzen, J. Gerald, 1985, *Job*, Atlanta, GA: John Knox Press.

Jewett, Robert, 1999, *Saint Paul Returns to the Movies: Triumph over Shame*, Grand Rapids, MI: Eerdmans.

——, 2007, *Romans: A Commentary*, Minneapolis, MN: Fortress Press.

——, 2011, *The Shame Factor: How Shame Shapes Society*, Eugene, OR: Cascade Books.

Jones, L. Gregory, 1995, *Embodying Forgiveness: A Theological Analysis*, Grand Rapids, MI: Eerdmans.

Lendon, J. E., 2005, *Empire of Honour: The Art of Government in the Roman World*, new edn, Oxford: Oxford University Press.

Lindsay, Hugh, 1998, 'Adoption and Succession in Roman Law', *Newcastle Law Review* 3: 57.

——, 2009, *Adoption in the Roman World*, Cambridge/New York: Cambridge University Press.

Mantel, Hilary, 2016, 'Blot, Erase, Delete: How the Author Found Her Voice and Why All Writers Should Resist the Urge to Change Their Past Words', Index on Censorship, 45.3: 64–8, https://doi.org/10.1177/0306422016670349a (accessed 20.6.19).

McFadyen, Alistair, 2000, *Bound to Sin: Abuse, Holocaust and the Christian Doctrine of Sin*, Cambridge: Cambridge University Press.

McFadyen, Alistair, and Marcel Sarot, 2001, *Forgiveness and Truth*, Edinburgh: T&T Clark.

Methodist, Church, n.d., 'His Presence Makes the Feast', www.methodist.org.uk/downloads/conf-holy-communion-in-methodist-church-2003.pdf (accessed 11.7.16).

Meyers, Carol L., 2014, 'Was Ancient Israel a Patriarchal Society?', *Journal of Biblical Literature* 133(1): 8–27.

Murphy, Jeffrie, and Jean Hampton, 1994, *Forgiveness and Mercy*, reprint, Cambridge: Cambridge University Press.

Neyrey, Jerome, ed., 1991, *The Social World of Luke–Acts: Models for Interpretation*, Peabody, MA: Hendrickson Publishers.

Park, Andrew Sung, and Susan L. Nelson, 2001, *The Other Side of Sin: Woundedness from the Perspective of the Sinned-Against*, Albany, NY: State University of New York Press.

Parkinson, Hannah Jane, 2019, 'Lives Are Ruined by Shame and Stigma. LGBT Lessons in Schools Are Vital', *Guardian*, www.theguardian.com/commentisfree/2019/mar/20/lives-shame-lgbt-lessons-schools-parent-protests (accessed 12 April 2019).

Pattison, Stephen, 2000, *Shame: Theory, Therapy, Theology*, Cambridge/New York: Cambridge University Press.

Patton, John, 1985, *Is Human Forgiveness Possible? A Pastoral Care Perspective*, Nashville, TN: Abingdon Press.

Pembroke, Neil, 2010, *Pastoral Care in Worship: Liturgy and Psychology in Dialogue*, London/New York: T&T Clark.

Potter, David S., and David J. Mattingley, 1999, *Life, Death, and Entertainment in the Roman Empire*, Ann Arbor, MI: University of Michigan Press.

Radzik, Linda, 2009, *Making Amends: Atonement in Morality, Law, and Politics*, Oxford/New York: Oxford University Press.

Rohr, Richard, 1996, *Job and the Mystery of Suffering: Spritual Reflections*, Gracewing, Fowler Right Books.

——, 2016, 'Transforming Our Pain', Centre for Action and Contemplation, https://cac.org/transforming-our-pain-2016-02-26/ (accessed 22.3.19).

Ronson, Jon, 2016, *So You've Been Publicly Shamed*, New York: Riverhead Books (e-book).

Rutledge, Fleming, 2017, *Crucifixion: Understanding the Death of Jesus Christ*, Grand Rapids, MI: Eerdmans.

Saiving Goldstein, Valerie, 1960, 'The Human Situation: A Feminine View'. *Journal of Religion* 40(2): 100.

Sampley, J., ed. 2003, *Paul in the Greco-Roman World: A Handbook*, Harrisburg, PA: Trinity Press International.

Smedes, Lewis, B., 1984, *Forgive and Forget: Healing the Hurts We Don't Deserve*, San Francisco, CA: Harper & Row.

Smith-Christopher, Daniel, 2002, *A Biblical Theology of Exile*, Minneapolis, MN: Fortress Press.

Tangney, June, and Ronda L. Dearing, 2004, *Shame and Guilt*, New York: Guilford Press.

Taylor, Gabrielle, 1985, *Pride, Shame, and Guilt*, Oxford: Oxford University Press.

Tombs, David, 1999, 'Crucifixion, State Terror, and Sexual Abuse,' *Union Seminary Quarterly Review* 53(1–2): 89–109.

Trible, Phyllis, 1978, *God and the Rhetoric of Sexuality*, Minneapolis, MN: Fortress Press.

Volf, Miroslav, 1996, *Exclusion and Embrace: A Theological Exploration of Identity, Otherness, and Reconciliation*, Nashville, TN: Abingdon Press.

——, 2005, *Free of Charge: Giving and Forgiving in a Culture Stripped of Grace*, Grand Rapids, MI: Zondervan.

——, 2006, *The End of Memory: Remembering Rightly in a Violent World*, Grand Rapids, MI: Eerdmans.

Watson, David F., 2010, *Honor among Christians: The Cultural Key to the Messianic Secret*, Minneapolis, MN: Fortress Press.

Wenham, Gordon J., 1987, *Genesis 1–15*, Dallas, TX: Word Books.

Westermann, Claus, 1980, *Isaiah 40–66, A Commentary*, London: SCM Press.

Williams, Bernard, 1994, *Shame and Necessity*, Berkeley, CA: University of California Press.

Williams, Rowan, 1995, *A Ray of Darkness: Sermons and Reflections*, Cambridge, MA: Cowley Publications.

——, 2014, *Meeting God in Mark*, London: SPCK.

Worthington, Everett, 1998, *Dimensions of Forgiveness: Psychological Research and Theological Perspectives*, Philadelphia, PA: Templeton Foundation Press.

Wright, Tom, 2011, *Simply Jesus: Who He Was, What He Did, Why It Matters*, London: SPCK.

# Index of Bible References

**First Testament**

***Genesis***
| | |
|---|---|
| 1.1–31 | 2–4 |
| 2.4–9 | 4 |
| 2.25 | 5 |
| 3 | 6–12 |
| 4.1–6 | 12–18, 45–6 |
| 38.9 | 82 |
| 39.6–20 | 78, 79 |
| 47 | 21 |

***Exodus***
| | |
|---|---|
| 1 | 22 |
| 2.24–5 | 22 |
| 4.31 | 23 |
| 5.20–23 | 23, 24 |
| 14.10f | 24 |
| 16.1–3 | 24, 25 |

***Deuteronomy***
| | |
|---|---|
| 4.9 | 156, 157 |
| 6.10–12 | 157 |
| 15.10–15 | 158 |
| 24.17–22 | 158 |

***2 Samuel***
| | |
|---|---|
| 3.6–11 | 83 |
| 8.1–18 | 80 |
| 11 | 78f |
| 12.1–24 | 89f |

***1 Kings***
| | |
|---|---|
| 1.1–2.19 | 77 |

***Job***
| | |
|---|---|
| 1.5 | 97 |
| 1.1–22 | 94, 95 |
| 4.1–14.22 | 97, 98 |
| 7.17–19 | 98 |
| 15.1–21.44 | 99 |
| 22.1–31.40 | 99, 100 |
| 27.2–6 | 101 |
| 32.1 | 97 |
| 38.1–41.34 | 106 |
| 42.5–6 | 102–6, 107 |
| 42.11 | 108 |

***Psalms***
| | |
|---|---|
| 38.1–8 | 199, 200 |
| 51.4 | 46, 47 |
| 137 | 34, 35 |
| 139.13–16 | 200, 201 |

***Isaiah***
| | |
|---|---|
| 53.1–6 | 42 |
| Servant Songs | 42–4 |

***Jeremiah***
| | |
|---|---|
| 6.13–19 | 37 |
| 6.15 | 40 |
| 28 | 28 |

*Lamentations*
1.1–4          32

*Ezekiel*
18.21–24       142
34.1–6         39

# New Testament

*Matthew*
5.23–4         61, 144
6.12           46, 53
7.1–4          63
7.12           59f
8.5–14         121
9.18–36        124–6
15.21–28       121, 122
18.21–25       148–51
19.19          59f
22.37–40       59f

*Mark*
1.1            173, 174
1.2–14         174
2.6–7          175
2.13–14        175
5.22–42        124–6
8.27–38        177
9.2–14         177–9
10.46f         122
14.10f         180, 181
15.1–15        181
15.39          182

*Luke*
8.41–56        124–6
11.4           46, 53
17.11–19       123

*John*
1.14           112–15
14.1–15.10     115–16
13.3           186
21.1–23        193

*Acts*
2              187–9

*Romans*
1.3–4          188, 189
7.18           198f
8.15–17        126, 127

*1 Corinthians*
1.22–25        184

*Galatians*
4.4–7          127, 132

*Ephesians*
1.3–6, 11–14   128

*Philippians*
2              65–6
2.6–11         185–6

*Titus*
1.12           70

*Hebrews*
12.1–2         203–5

*Revelation*
21.3–5         201

# Index of Names and Subjects

Adam and Eve  4, 5, 6–12
Adoption  126–35

Bathsheba  77
Baumeister, Roy  153
Benedict, Ruth  165, 166
Bradshaw, John  xi, 11

Cain and Abel  12–18, 45–6
Cicero,  163, 164
Creation,  2–4
Crucifixion  170–3

David  76, 77

Empathy  60, 62, 63
Exile  27–44
Exodus  21–6

Fall  6–12
Fig-leaves (as image of shame)  9, 11
Firth, David  84, 85
Forgiving  136–62

Gaze of God  3, 5, 8, 12, 13, 98, 99, 110
God and shame  1, 2, 42–4, 199–203

Group Oriented Society  64–71, 163–9

Hartley, John  96–100
Honour  64f, 68–71, 81, 85–8, *see also* Group Oriented Society
Honour Shame Society *see* Group Oriented Society

Jesus  112–15, 116–19
  experience of shame  164, 169–73, 178–83
  shame of others and  116–26, 192–9, 203–5
  knowing God through  111, 114
Job  94–108

Memory
  First Testament  156–60
  forgiving and  152–62
  uncontrollable  154–6

Perfectionism  193f
Pride  19

Radzik, Linda  18, 53–8, 183
Rage  31–5
Respect  72–3
Repentance  91, 141, 142

Resurrection 178–9, 187–9

Shame
 exodus from 26
 guide to overall argument viii–x
 good shame 60–2
 makes faith more difficult 111, 119–25, 191
 shame ache xi, 11, 13,
 sin and 9–18
 violence and 17, *see also* Empathy

Sin 14, 16, 18–20, 48–58, 73–5
 as a debt 53–8
 national 35–41
 as a power 48–52, *see also* Exodus and Exile
 situated being and 49
Sinned Against 17, 18, 23, 25, 26, 46–8, 48–58

Watson, David 173f

www.ingramcontent.com/pod-product-compliance
Lightning Source LLC
Chambersburg PA
CBHW021945290426
44108CB00012B/963